To
Tiffany and
Michael
with love
Peta

xx

GW00724672

SIMON VAN DEN BERGH
Quest for Perfection

SIMON VAN DEN BERGH
Quest for Perfection

Peta Van den Bergh-Steel

EDITED BY DENISE SEARLE

Published by P J Steel
56 Sutherland Square, London SE17 3EL
First published in Great Britain 2009
text © Peta Van den Bergh-Steel 2009

ISBN: 978-0-9564454-0-7

Text and titles typeset in Spectrum MT
originally designed by Jan van Krimpen, Utrecht, The Netherlands,
between 1941 and 1943.
Captions typest in Akzidenz Grotesk
designed by Günter Gerhard Lange for Berthold, Berlin, Germany 1896

Printed and bound in Great Britain by
Ashford Colour Press Ltd., Gosport, Hants.

Foreword
By Lord David Sainsbury of Turville

What I think is interesting, and in particular with what is going on in the world today, is that my father, a Dutch Jew, spent his life interpreting and trying to communicate what the work of an Arab philosopher meant.

Tamara Ferguson née Van den Bergh

THIS IS A BOOK about my maternal grandparents Simon Van den Bergh and his wife Sonia Pokrojski Van den Bergh. Although I knew them, I knew very little about Simon's work or their lives. When I was growing up I learnt a great deal about the Sainsbury side of my family but very little about the Van den Bergh side. This was surprising because my paternal grandmother, Mabel Miriam, was also a member of the Van den Bergh family, and when my parents got married the headline in the newspaper which reported it was 'Butter and Margarine Marry Again'. Very little was known about the Pokrojskis.

I wanted myself and my children to know more about the lives of Simon and Sonia, two remarkable people who vividly reflected the history of Europe in the 20th century, and I, therefore, asked Peta Van den Bergh-Steel to write this history of their lives. It is a fascinating story which Peta tells with great skill.

The Van den Berghs were very successful food manufacturers who felt that it was important that their children should also find success in their own chosen professions. Simon was the first in the family to become an academic. He received his doctorate for a subject which explained the work of the Arabic philosopher Averroës. His studies took him to universities in Germany, Austria, England and Ireland. He was to live many years in Paris. His wife Sonia Pokrojski was born in Suwalki, now in Poland but then part of Russia. She left her home when she was only 17 to travel to Germany to study there. Two people with totally different backgrounds and interests fell in love and married.

The wars and politics of the last 150 years were to have an effect on their lives. They were in turn to be subjected to anti-Semitism, become friends with some of the finest intellects of their days, and with their lives threatened, to become refugees.

Throughout this time Simon was working on the books which are still being used today in universities. It is a history that I hope his heirs and their families will be justly proud of.

Preface

WHEN I WAS first asked to find out and write about the lives of Simon Van den Bergh and his wife Sonia, I was told that all that was known about them was that he had been a Professor of Languages in Paris who had met his wife at Heidelberg University. And that he liked women.

Knowing little about either Simon or Sonia, and without any views on either of them, I started what became an investigation tracing records and people in The Netherlands, Germany, Russia, Poland, Austria, France, Portugal, America, Israel, Argentina and Switzerland as well as this country. Producing the information has been a very long, sometimes frustrating but mostly rewarding exercise, which has often thankfully included various coincidences that have helped with the research.

I have had to learn not to take stories at face value. European Jewish families are loathe to talk. The war is not that far away in the minds of many and is often still too painful to talk about. Memories have dimmed with age, or have been 're-written' to fit in with how the person perceived events to have happened or had wanted them to happen. In all cases I have tried to corroborate the stories where I have been able to, by cross checking the event with more than one witness. Dates and senses of time have also altered or disappeared with age and led me on several wrong tracks – which could have made Simon's life even more colourful than it actually was!

I discovered that in some countries copious records had been kept and in others they have not. Wartime meant that many had been destroyed either intentionally – as had happened in some Dutch towns such as Oss – to prevent Nazis tracking down Jews, during actions against Jews before the war or by bombing. In Germany, Freiburg Town Council was helpful in providing documents on the family of Simon's mentor Professor Reckendorf, in marked contrast to the University of Freiburg, which at first tried to deny any knowledge of Simon Van den Bergh having attended the University. They only agreed to his existence having been sent the foreword of his doctorate – obtained from Leiden University. They subsequently sent some of Simon's documents, but omitted the copy of his diploma, which he personally asked for in 1912 – but never received – and which they have still held onto! Records which could have revealed when and where Simon and Sonia actually met no longer exist.

The Late Maureen Van den Bergh, Simon's second wife, proved a font of knowledge. It was she who told me that Simon had married Sonia in Edinburgh, Scotland. I must admit to being very amused to hear that they had married in Edinburgh, which was the location of only one other Van den Bergh wedding – mine. In some ways the coincidence of having my and Simon's name in the same registers spurred me on. Obtaining that wedding certificate revealed what Sonia's maiden name had been and where she had come from. Tracking down her family seemed initially impossible. Her relatives in Poland had been wiped out by the Germans and records lost – a few records have only very recently been made available which revealed she had a twin.

After months of trawling through all the various Jewish genealogical societies I made contact with the Argentinean JGS and asked their chairman whether they knew anyone with the name of Pokrojski. Carlos Glikson mailed me back almost straight away: his grandmother Pauline Glikson had been one of Sonia's sisters. Carlos' father and mother had been close friends of Simon and Sonia's, and his mother Luba had some of the letters written to her by Simon. He had photographs of the Pokrosjki family and was able to put me in contact with Sonia's brothers' families in America. Although they had information about Pokrojskis who had left Poland, they had known little about what had actually happened to those who remained in Poland during the war.

Via Yad Vashem in Israel, I was able to track down some evidence on what had happened to Pauline, her husband, her daughter and son-in-law, and was able for the first time to put a name to her little granddaughter – Sonia's great niece Ariela – all of whom had died in the Holocaust. Without Carlos' help I would never have been able to track down Sonia's family or to find out more about her background.

I have been very lucky in that I was able to talk to those whose lives had been directly affected by those of Simon and Sonia. Their daughter Tamara Ferguson has been of great help; her humour and pride in describing her parents' relationship and putting it into the context of the times they lived proved invaluable as did her understanding of their personalities. Her friendship has meant a great deal to me. Lady Lisa Sainsbury was also very kind, sharing with me some of her photographs and memories, as did her daughter Celia Blakey.

Simon and Sonia's lives were affected not only by their backgrounds and the times in which they lived. I have tried to convey what made them the people they were. Given that they lived through two devastating world wars, I have gone into some detail to describe their Jewish antecedents, as these had so much influence on what they became and what happened to them.

Family and friends of Simon, Sonia and Maureen gave valuable help, eager to pass on reminiscences and correct wrong suppositions; Simon's academic colleagues also tried to explain what his work meant. Sadly, since the beginning of this investigation, family members Maureen Van den Bergh, Herman Marx, Rosalida Klausner née Polak and Carol Simpson née Samuel have died. Their help was invaluable and I miss them. I would like to record one more thanks and that is to my late husband Tom Steel; without his help, enthusiasm and love, this extraordinary adventure would have been impossible to undertake.

PETA VAN DEN BERGH-STEEL, *July 2009*

Contents

Chapter 1　Heritage in the making

It is a warm summer's day in Monaco in the late 1970s. The smell of yellow mimosa wafts in the light breeze. An old man sits in his wheelchair on a balcony overlooking the Mediterranean Sea. Occasionally he raises his hand to stroke his chin, as he tries to recall something he once wrote or said. He smiles perhaps, as he thinks of his youngest daughter Tamara's recent description of him as having 'mellowed with age'.

It's the sort of day that would have typically found Simon Van den Bergh enjoying the air on a walk, head down, eyes intently looking at the pavement, hands in his pockets, concentrating on talking to a companion about his favourite topic – philosophy. Age now restricts his world to a wheelchair and memories. His pleasures have been eroded: no longer can he walk among his beloved hills above Monte Carlo; deafness has robbed him of the joy of listening to music.

Members of the Van den Bergh family have been drawn to the warm climate and balmy sea air of the Mediterranean since the previous century. A family with Dutch and English roots has, time and again, been attracted to the flamboyant lifestyle of the area. Like his father before him, Simon is spending his last years among people more colourful than his own compatriots; forsaking damp and cold for warmth and vitality.

As he drifts in and out of sleep, he possibly remembers the voices of his cousins as they laughed or discussed the latest gossip; or hears the exotic eastern European accent of his first wife Sonia and remembers her with fondness – and regret. Perhaps as he listens to the soft voice of his second wife Maureen, talking quietly in the background to her cat, he also recalls the swish of a skirt, or the dainty tapping of high heels clipping over cobblestones.

So many things to remember, in such a long life. A life that witnessed so many changes.

Dairy farming and river trade depicted in a 19th-century painting of the southern Netherlands by Hermann Mevius

Simon was born in the era of the horse and cart but went on to drive fast cars around Europe and fly across the Atlantic. He was a cultured man who sought to pass on knowledge of other traditions to his students. His early years were spent in a peaceful, tolerant

The Low Countries in the 19th
century

society, yet he knew fear as a refugee and faced persecution and bigotry because of his Jewish identity.

Simon's life has been full of contradictions. Dedicated to studying, interpreting and explaining the works of the 12th-century Muslim philosopher Averroës, he had little in common with many of his ancestors and family who became famed in the food industry. He felt embarrassed and inhibited by his wealth, although it gave him access to opportunities that others could only dream of. Financial security enabled him to avoid the strain of jockeying for academic positions against other scholars who needed to earn money to survive. Yet the lack of a formal academic career led him to question whether he was taken seriously as a scholar, or merely regarded as a dilettante.

In later years he complained that his achievements had not received the academic appreciation they merited. But time has shown that his frustrations were unfounded.

In 1912, at the age of 30, Simon introduced the dissertation for his doctorate in the following manner: 'I was born in 1882. My parents Isaac Van den Bergh and Clara Van Leer were manufacturers who have now retired. I am a member of the Jewish faith.'

Those few words encapsulated Simon's cultural and social heritage, which he felt necessary to describe to the German professors of a Catholic university who would be discussing the merits of his paper. It told them he came from a privileged background that enabled him to follow the aspirations of many cultured Jews by entering the world of academia. It was a heritage he was not afraid of proclaiming to a society that only recently, and somewhat reluctantly, was admitting Jews into its presence. The professors would also have known that Simon's Semitic background shared much in common with the Arabic culture and philosophy that he had chosen to study.

Born in the town of Oss in the south of The Netherlands on 16 November 1882, Simon Van den Bergh was Isaac and Clara's only son. The Van den Berghs were a close-knit Jewish family headed by Simon's paternal grandparents Simon (after whom he had been named) and his wife Elisabeth. In fact, many of the family members' names were passed down through the generations.

Five of Simon and Elisabeth's seven sons had worked alongside their parents in founding, developing and running one of the largest food manufacturers in the country. The family had established themselves in The Netherlands through their own initiative and sheer hard work, creating a prosperity that allowed their descendants to pursue careers and lifestyles that their forefathers could only have dreamed about. Isaac and Clara's wealth gave the young Simon the chance to travel through Europe and attend some of its finest universities. They encouraged his love of learning and supported his desire to live a different, and hopefully, more rewarding life than their own.

19th-century coat of arms of the town of Oss

Simon's religious connections to Judaism were tenuous but his Semitic identity would have a profound effect upon his life and career. The history of Jews in Europe, often cruel and harsh, had forced them to find security by assimilation into the countries where they had settled. Safety and respect from the local population came by establishing themselves at the top of their professions. Intellectual achievement was highly valued and Simon grew up at a time when his fellow Jews, both men and women, began to feel a new-found confidence in their own abilities and in being able to contribute to those countries that had accepted them into citizenship. The academic opportunity offered to Simon came from the trials of his predecessors.

Windmill on the Meuse, painted by Eugene Boudin in 1884, showing the freqently flooded plain of North Brabant

Humble beginnings

Simon's ancestors had settled several generations earlier in North Brabant, an agricultural province of The Netherlands, near the borders with Belgium and Germany where the river Maas (or Meuse) leaves the Limburg ridge of hills and flows into the lowlands. Simon was born in a flat area, where peasants toiled hard to make their living in the harsh northern climate.

In 1907, Simon's Uncle Sam wrote a book to commemorate the lives of his recently deceased parents Simon and Elisabeth. He wanted their descendants to know aboout the founders of their family and what they had achieved. In the book, Sam described the bleakness of the area where they lived: 'The land is poorly endowed by nature. The soil is barren and must be tilled by the peasant "in the sweat of his brow", to give in return a meagre harvest. The population in our youth and in Father's and Mother's day were poor, a few great landed proprietors excepted ... the life of the population of that part of North Brabant must have been passed, in the "old times", in poverty and misery.'

According to Sam, the lack of Jewish family records, either in Germany or among Dutch Jewish communities, gives weight to arguments that the family might have fled from Germany in great haste. But it is not clear when this was or whether the family came from Ashkenazi or Sephardic lineage (see page 11). Simon's intellectual interests were influenced by Sephardic scholars who studied Arabic philosophies and cultures. His daughter Tamara believes the Van den Bergh background is from Southern Europe. 'I was definitely told that we had come from Portugal. It made a great deal of sense,' she said.

Sam thought differently. He believed the Van den Bergh origins were probably German, with their ancestors migrating to The Netherlands to escape persecution in the mid 18th century. However, Sam's own interest in astronomy, his brothers' in art and South American cultures, as well as Simon's attraction to Arabic philosophy, might indicate a Sephardic inheritance.

The first recorded birth of an ancestor of Simon's was that of his great grandfather,

Cover of Sam van den Bergh's book on his parents' life

Zadok, in the village of Geffen on 25 April 1769. His father was Daniel. The language used by the Van den Bergh ancestors within the family circle was a mixture of Yiddish, Dutch and German. Yiddish, a Jewish language of German grammar mingled with sundry Hebrew words, was used and understood by Simon's grandparents. By the time Simon was born it was no longer used by the family. Assimilation into Netherlands' society meant Dutch was now the language spoken at home.

The Jews of The Netherlands in the 18th century were dispersed through towns and villages, with often only one family in each location. Whereas a few families had settled in the nearby small towns of Oss and Lith, only one family was registered in Geffen and that was the family of Zadok. In his book, Simon's uncle Sam described the relationships between the Jews of the Brabant and the Dutch: 'Each village had its Jew. They were living in good harmony with the Christian population, but there was never any intimate intercourse between the dissenting parties. Generally, the Jew stood higher in morality than the common population of Brabant. He was very moderate in eating and temperate in drinking.'

Years later Simon's grandfather was to hear his father identified as, 'Geffen Zadok'. Jews in small villages were chiefly butchers and cattle dealers but Zadok's father Daniel became a general merchant when he settled in Geffen. Zadok accompanied his father, travelling through the Low Countries (present-day Belgium, Luxembourg and The Netherlands) and Germany, trading goods such as butter for other merchandise. He would eventually run his father's shop.

Zadok was successful in business and on 20 January 1807, for the sum of 2,200 Guilders, bought a house in Geffen for his growing family. He lived there until his death in 1857; Simon's father Isaac was born there in 1853. The house with its adjoining courtyard sat on the hill rising above the local common. The census for 1808 shows that a manservant and a maid were employed to look after Zadok's household. Zadok would later be described by his grandsons as being: 'A man of long and slender figure, beardless and wearing a little wig, who in his early days was dressed in a black coat, knickerbockers, black stockings and buckled shoes.'

He married Elisabeth, the daughter of Isaac van der Wielen from the nearby small town of Oss. She was born on 20 October 1774 into one of the most successful families in the locality. They owned the largest house in town and had made their fortune from tobacco trading. Marriages between cousins and close family members were common in areas with scant Jewish populations; they were a means of cementing business interests and Jewish customs. Elisabeth's uncle Abraham was to father a daughter, also named Elisabeth, who would eventually marry Zadok's youngest son Simon (the grandfather of our Simon).

Zadok and Elisabeth's house in Geffen

The first van den Bergh

As the van Den Berghs established themselves in The Netherlands, events in France would transform the lives of Europe's Jews because the French Revolution abolished the different treatment of people according to religion or origin. On 2 September 1806, following a stormy debate, the French National Assembly resolved unanimously to give Jews full civil rights. Napoleon Bonaparte abolished laws restricting Jews to ghettoes and in 1807 he made Judaism, along with Roman Catholicism and Lutheran and Calvinist Protestantism, official religions of the French Empire, which included The Netherlands.

At that time most Jews did not have fixed hereditary surnames. They were known only by their first name and a patronymic (their father's given name), for example 'Yaacov ben Shmuel', meaning 'Yaacov the son of Shmuel'. In 1808 Napoleon issued a decree requiring Jews in the French Empire to take surnames.

Zadok chose the name 'van den Bergh', which means 'comes from the hill'. This was widely believed to have been adopted in honour of the small hill in Geffen where his house stood but Zadok's grandson Sam argued in his book that the choice of name referred to an area called Bergh, just over the border in Germany. Sam suggested that 'Van der Heuvel' – 'from the little hill' – would have been the more likely name if his grandfather had wished to commemorate the site of the family's home. By 1809 some 946 Ashkenazi Jews lived in North Brabant. Thirty four Jews, including the van den Berghs, lived in and around the town of Oss.

The name 'van den Bergh' would undergo change when Zadok's two grandsons Jacob and Henry moved to England and anglicised the name by turning 'van' into 'Van'. This simple change illustrates a division between two branches of the family – the English and the Dutch – as each assimilated the customs and traditions of the country in which they lived. Simon would later follow Jacob and Henry's example. According to Simon's youngest daughter Tamara, this may have been done partly to increase the family's standing, when in 1920 they moved to Paris, a city steeped in snobbery. 'Van den Bergh with a capital "V" must have sounded superior,' she mused.

Zadok's father-in-law chose the name 'van der Wielen' and Elisabeth's mother Allegonda's family took 'van Osten', a reference to the village in East Friesland from which they had come. Zadok and Elisabeth had 13 children, of which 12 survived. The youngest, Simon, was born in Geffen on 24 October 1819. He was the first to be born with the surname 'van den Bergh' and his grandson, the subject of this book, was named after him.

Simon Senior was a bright, often naughty little boy. His mother died in 1830, when he was just 11 years old, the same year Zadok contributed 400 Guilders towards the building of a new synagogue in Oss. The youngest by some years, Simon Senior was very spoilt by his brothers and sisters and his father employed two maidservants to help look after him.

While The Netherlands lived in peace, allowing its citizens to grow in prosperity, the Napoleonic wars waged through the rest of Europe. One of the consequences was the creation of the new independent United Kingdom of The Netherlands in 1815, which included most of present-day Belgium to the south. In 1830 war came to North Brabant as the French-speaking Catholic southerners rose to claim an independent Belgium from their Protestant

Fighting in Antwerp, 1830

Dutch rulers under King William I. Hundreds of young Jewish men, including some of Simon Senior's relatives, given new rights as citizens, took the opportunity to show their loyalty to king and country by flocking to enlist in the Dutch army. Parts of North Brabant now lay behind the Belgian frontier. Dutch troops swarmed into Geffen and Oss to be quartered in the villagers' homes as they fought to quash the insurrection. Dutch Jews welcomed the soldiers, including some of their own faith, into their houses. The quiet lives of staid villagers, far enough away from the frontline not to be disturbed by canon fire, were enlivened by music and dance as soldiers sought relief from war.

Young Simon Senior, a cheeky self confident boy, was befriended by the troops and taught to beat out signals on military drums. This new 'skill' was to land him in trouble. One peaceful night the raucous beat of the alarm sounded through the village. Aroused suddenly from their dinners, soldiers ran out of the houses, benches were upturned and plates thrown on the ground as they grabbed their swords and muskets. A frantic search through the village for the enemy uncovered a little boy sitting in the main square beating his tune. Shock and alarm gave way to relief, as soldiers and villagers united in laughter at Simon's antics. His father was not so amused and applied a few suitable smacks to his bottom to ensure no repetition of this particular joke. Undaunted, Simon continued to play practical jokes well into adulthood.

Simon Senior and his wife Elisabeth would later describe to their excited grandchildren, including the young Simon, how they had watched King William I and his heir review troops on the nearby Zealand Heath. As far as the actual fighting was concerned, all Elisabeth could recall was that by putting her ear to the ground at her home in Oss, she had been able to hear the 'famous monster gun' pulverise the walls of the Antwerp citadel. Belgium was to be successful in its fight for freedom, with Leopold of Saxe-Coburg becoming King of the newly independent country in 1831.

While the Dutch were unsuccessful in their fight to keep the Belgian people subject to their rule (although Geffen and Oss remained predominantly Catholic), merchants like Zadok van den Bergh profited from the money brought into the villages by the troops. By the time the regiments left the area he had accumulated a wealth of 1,000 gold coins.

Zadok's was a religious household, strictly adhering to the customs and rules of the Jewish faith. The Sabbath was sacrosanct and the family walked several miles from Geffen to attend the little synagogue built between the village and nearby town of Oss. Zadok believed in helping Jews less fortunate than himself, offering food and lodgings to them as they travelled through the village. He passed to his children his love for his religion and its traditions and his commitment to helping those in poverty. He was to be honoured for his generosity by the Chief Rabbi of North Brabant, as was his son Simon Senior some years later.

Zadok believed it was important for his children to receive a Jewish education as well as a Dutch one. They were brought up to quote from the Talmud and to speak and read

Hebrew. He also insisted on extra lessons so they could study literature and the classics and speak German. But Simon Senior only managed to learn a few words of German. Languages were not his metier. He was sent to the public school at Geffen and in the evenings to the Jewish school on Torenstraat in Oss, which his own sons and later his grandsons, including the young Simon, also attended.

Sam wrote in his book: 'Grandfather was not only well informed in advance of his times, but he also gave his children an excellent education. It is remarkable how already in those times, the children of Zadok van den Bergh reached a high standard of culture and refinement, how conversant they were with literature and what good manners they had acquired.'

Simon Senior was left with a limp, after a poorly treated injury in childhood, but he refused to let his disability affect his love of walking and dancing. He was blessed with good looks, which the grandson named after him would inherit. He became a good horse rider, enabling him to work alongside his father. On finishing his education, Simon joined Zadok in selling haberdashery and groceries and buying butter from the peasants. The two would be away for weeks riding by horse from village to village, travelling into Germany and Belgium, and returning to sell their butter in The Netherlands and later to England.

Simon Senior's personality and charm helped increase trade. According to Sam's book: 'Father had fine dark curly hair, short round beard, but no moustache. According to Jewish law, he did not shave but cut his beard with scissors. He was rather under medium height. He always dressed simply and modestly and took greatest care of his clothes, which were always brushed and beaten by himself... He always possessed certain ways of affability and courteousness, which attracted everyone to him and he made the impression on one at first sight, as a thoroughly respectable man, who could be trusted on his "honest face". He had a childlike confidence in others, which confidence was alas often abused.'

Zadok's religious household would have treasurerd items such as a menorah, used during the festival of Hannukha

A nurturing environment

The Jewish community of the North Brabant was closely knit. The van den Bergh family in Geffen spent a great deal of time with their cousins, the van der Wielens from the town of Oss. The two families would meet at the small synagogue, travelling to one or other's homes afterwards to end the Sabbath.

During these visits Simon Senior fell in love with his pretty brown-eyed cousin Elisabeth van der Wielen. 'These visits brought our father, when a small lad, together with his cousin Betje', wrote Sam. 'We know from his own mouth that he took a fancy to her, that this feeling was returned by mother and that, though still very young, they had pledged their hearts and hands to each other. It was real fun to hear mother relate how, as little children, they played once at "father and mother", and how the little Simon was thoroughly vexed when another little boy took the part which he had reserved for himself, to play with Betje.' Sam also reported how Simon had even written Elisabeth's name in his own blood on a cloth, which he carried about with him.

Simon Senior faced competition when a German connection of the family asked for Elisabeth's hand in marriage. 'At that time', Sam explained, 'the liberty of children to dispose of their own future was very limited. Father was for hours in agony but happily it came to naught. The stranger slunk away and soon thereafter father could call Betje his bride.'

The oldest and most intelligent of Abraham van der Wielen's children, Elisabeth was also his favourite. Like Zadok, Abraham believed that education was important and held an enlightened attitude to the schooling of girls. Realising that his bright young daughter would only receive a limited education at the local school in Oss, Abraham sent her to learn French and Classics at a boarding school at St Oedenrode near Eindhoven.

Greek and Roman mythology and French fables were Elisabeth's favourite subjects. At the age of 85 she would quote extensively in French from *Les Aventures de Télémaque, fils d'Ulysse*. She also studied the Talmud, contrary to the Jewish traditions of the day, which forbade women from studying the 'holy scriptures'. These exercises were curtailed when the Rabbi found out. Sam wondered whether the Rabbi had felt challenged by Elisabeth: 'The study of Greek and of Greek philosophy was always considered dangerous to the orthodox Jewish notion. Can it be that the teachers of the Talmud had themselves not enough confidence in the strength of their system?'

On 24 October 1844 the mayor of Oss married Simon and Elisabeth in a civil ceremony. A week later, on 3 November, the religious ceremony was held at the Synagogue at Koornstraad near Oss, which they had attended as children and which had been built with contributions from both families. Elisabeth followed the requirements of her religion by cutting off her long brown hair and adopting the wig and bonnet worn by Jewish married women; from now on only her husband would see her head uncovered. Years later she told her sons how she regretted that act; she would be the last woman in the family to follow the practice.

Sam's book recalls: 'She often told us that she was considered a good looking girl with long tresses of hair. Mother's eyes were uncommonly lustrous and her whole countenance showed great intellectual activity, not even lost at her great age. She was well built, of medium stature.'

The young couple returned to live with Zadok in Geffen where, four years later, after many prayers and much anguish, their first son Jacob was born. The couple celebrated the long-waited birth by presenting their local synagogue with a Torah to honour a pledge they had made when they prayed to have a child. The prayers proved to be highly successful as they would eventually have seven sons. Jacob's arrival was followed by Maurits in 1849, Henry in 1851 and in 1853, Simon's father Isaac. The fifth son, Arnold, was born in 1857, Zadok in 1859 and Sam, the last in 1864. The two youngest were born after the family moved to Oss.

The boys had very distinct characters. Jacob was

Even in old age, Elisabeth could still quote in French from the late 17th-century novel, *Les Aventures de Télémaque, fils d'Ulysse*

Above: Simon and Elisabeth. Above right: Baby Isaac, in his cradle (an illustration from Sam van den Bergh's book)

industrious, clever at maths, with little interest in art but a natural inclination towards finance and marketing. He loved his family, sex and the first generation of fast cars. Maurits, interested in history, was curious, asking questions and observing everything around him. Henry was imaginative, artistic, studious and superb at organisation. He was also rather superior, becoming known even as a child for his 'airs and graces'.

Simon's father Isaac was quieter, less imaginative than the others and – according to his son – less intelligent. He was known within the family as a 'bringer of good luck', because during the great flood of 1854 he saved the family's lives when his cries woke Simon Senior and Elisabeth as waters from the flooding Meuse swept against his cradle. The family fled to safety higher up the little hill on which their house had been built.

The somewhat 'bumptious Arnold', as his grandson Herman Marx would later describe him, loved art and became one of The Netherlands' foremost collectors. He had grandiose ideas about building but sensible ideas when it came to planning. The two youngest sons, Zadok, a dreamer and intellectual, and the irascible, kind and generous Sam – the most intelligent of them all – were to have the greatest influence over their nephew Simon.

The older Zadok adored his youngest son and asked the growing family to continue living with him in Geffen in the hope that Simon and Elisabeth would take over his business when he died. They readily agreed but told him that eventually they would want to move to a larger town, so their sons could have a better education.

Elisabeth had high hopes for her sons and was keen to give them the opportunity to achieve their ambitions. She did not want them to stagnate in the village of Geffen, which offered few opportunities. Her children would not be forbidden, as she had been, from learning about subjects that might be contentious to their beliefs. She would send them away to be educated in other towns. Jacob, the eldest, was the first to go. He lodged with a friend while studying in Oss. Later Henry would be sent to Paris to learn French. Several of the other brothers were sent to board with their teachers in other towns. In 1868, Elisabeth sent Jacob and Henry to England to expand the business.

Simon and Elisabeth passed to their sons Zadok's belief that giving charity was part of Jewish tradition. Discussion and talk about education, religion and philosophy were an everyday part of their lives. Languages were seen as tremendously important, not only in business, but also in providing a window on different cultures and beliefs. Elisabeth learned English when she was in her seventies so she could speak in their own language to her growing London family.

Zadok died on 11 October 1857 at the age of 88. He was interred alongside family members in the burial ground he presented to the Jewish Congregation of Oss. The stone at the head of his grave stated: 'A good name is better than precious ointment'. Zadok left the family house as well as 100 Guilders to two of his sons, Simon and Isaac.

Simon and Elisabeth could now leave Geffen and move to the town of Oss, where seeds would be sown for the establishment in 1930 of the multinational company Unilever.

Mixed fortunes: early history of Jews in The Netherlands

Opposite: The Jewish celebration of Pessach (Passover) from a 15th-century Dutch illumination

This page: 18th-century Dutch Seder plate, used for symbolic foods at the Passover meal

THE JEWS IN Europe largely represent two different cultural lines: the Sephardic (Jews descended from communities in Portugal, Spain and North Africa) and the Ashkenazi (Jews descended from communities in Germany and eastern Europe). All were refugees. They shared the Jewish faith but their lives were quite unlike each other.

Sephardic Jews gravitated towards cities and towns and were thought by Europeans to be more cultured. They had lived in a liberal Islamic environment under Moorish rule. Their skills as scientists, doctors, traders, poets and scholars were generally valued by regional Christian and Muslim rulers. Sephardic Jews were accustomed to living among different cultures, assimilating some aspects, such as art, architecture, poetry, philosophy and sciences, into their way of life. Even their 'Middle Eastern' style of cuisine had more in common with that of the Mediterranean countries and Palestine, than with the central European foods associated with the Ashkenazi.

The Ashkenazi tended to live in the more peasant-based environments of central Europe. They frequently faced persecution and were mostly forced to live in designated areas, sometimes surrounded by walls, subject to raids from the ruling forces. Even those who moved to larger towns to work in tailoring and money-lending – often the only professions open to Jews – had little time to study anything other than their own religion. Despite adhering strongly to the traditions of their faith and having little to do socially with the surrounding Christian communities, the Ashkenazi's Jewish culture and language gradually took on a more middle-European aspect.

Their synagogues were also different, with the Sephardic reflecting Moorish architecture and the Ashkenazi influenced by the more solid, less decorative German style of building.

Jews in The Netherlands are thought to include both

Contrasting 16th-century views of
European Jewry (both from
Germany). Top: Persecution by
burning. Above: A sympathetic
depiction of a learned physician

Ashkenazi and Sephardic heritage. A Maastricht
magistrate's letter dated 1295 is the first to mention the
formation of a Jewish community in that town. Although
many Jewish communities had sprung up around Europe,
there are only vague references to the presence of Jews in
the area now known as The Netherlands before 1200. This
changed following the expulsion of Jews from England in
1290 and from France in 1306, and the westward movement
of Jews from large overcrowded communities in Cologne,
Worms and Mainz from the beginning of the 13th century.

Jews had been massacred and generally persecuted in
Germany from the 11th to 14th centuries, beginning with
the First Crusade and continuing with expulsions of Jews
from numerous cities and provinces. Most moved east to
Poland, Bohemia and Hungary. Those left behind eked out
a meagre living peddling their wares, travelling from one
town and village to another. They had little security, their
lives ruled by the whims of others.

Catholic Christian bigotry found Jews an easy target.
Between 1347 and 1351 the Black Death raged through
Europe and rumours abounded that it had been started by
Jews to poison Christendom. Many Jews in Brussels (then in
Southern Brabant) who survived the Black Death were
killed in 1349 after being accused of poisoning wells. Only a
handful survived: most of those were burned at the stake in
1370 and the rest expelled after being charged with

William of Orange (centre foreground) leaves Antwerp to lead the Dutch revolt against the Spanish in this 16th-century engraving

desecrating the Host by stealing wafers from the church of Sainte-Catherine. They would not be allowed to return until the 18th century.

In Spain, the Jews had enjoyed periods of wealth and tolerance, but during the 14th and 15th centuries persecution increased, including several massacres and forced conversion to Christianity. In 1492, those who refused to convert were expelled. Many fled to Portugal, but were soon forced out as the Inquisition spread its influence. Others fled to North Africa, Turkey, Northern Europe, France and Italy. The expulsions produced a new centre of Jewish thought as The Netherlands accepted the fleeing Jews. Having lived under Moorish rule, many Jewish philosophers wrote in Arabic and drew on the works of Arabic philosophers and doctors who had kept alive and introduced to the Western world the work of the ancient Greeks.

The Nazis of the 20th century with their yellow stars were not the first to physically mark out Jews as being different. The Catholic Church's Fourth Lateran Council, held in Rome in 1215, decreed that Jews were to wear special dress to distinguish them from Christians. In 1451 the Jews of Arnhem, at the instigation of the Pope's representative, were 'issued with a token that they must wear on their outer garments'. Failure to comply would lead to expulsion from the town.

Many of the restrictions placed on Jews were to last for centuries, defining how they worked and earned their living, where they lived and how they were to be identified. According to the Memorbook (the history of Dutch Jewry from the Renaissance to 1940) in the 15th century they were mainly restricted to two occupations: money-lending and medicine.

Although Jews still suffered from hatred preached by Christian Churches, some Dutch churchmen, who advocated the study of Hebrew, took a more enlightened approach. In the 15th and 16th centuries, humanists conducted their studies in Latin, Greek and Hebrew. This academic interest in languages and philosophies would continue, forming the basis for future teaching at Dutch schools and universities. Although there was little contact between Christian and Jewish scholars, Hebrew was taught in The Netherlands throughout the 16th century..

Jews showed their appreciation by giving financial support to the Protestant William of Orange (1533-1584), who led the Dutch revolt against the Spanish (who then ruled The Netherlands and the rest of the 'Low Countries') and became a champion of religious freedom. The Dutch national anthem '*Het Wilhelmus*' was sung by Jews in the Rhineland, even before they settled in The Netherlands. In 1579, the Union of Utrecht was formed, encompassing lands which today form The Netherlands and parts of

A Jewish Shopkeeper With Two Clients, an 18th-century watercolour by Jan van Grevenbroeck

Belgium. One of the first acts of the Union was to outlaw the persecution of people because of their faith.

Jews settling in The Netherlands were largely treated with tolerance, partly because the predominatly Protestant Dutch empathised with the Jews' suffering, given that fellow Protestants throughout Europe faced similar persecution. The first hundred years of Dutch independence included growing openness to the teaching of the Old Testament. Dutch Protestants did not hate Jews or blame them for the death of Jesus Christ, in contrast to the teachings of the Catholic Church at that time. Understanding the language of the Bible, its Jewish customs and traditions, and even rabbinical literature, was an essential component in the study of their own religion. The Jewish philosophy of the Mishnah and of Moses Maimonides was translated into Latin; Jewish teachers were retained to instruct university students in Hebrew.

The first Portuguese Jewish merchants escaping from persecution settled in Amsterdam in the 1590s and began one of the largest centres of Sephardic Jews in Northern Europe. In 1604, Alkmaar became the first Dutch city to officially grant Jews residency. Haarlem came next in 1605, followed by Amsterdam and then Rotterdam in 1610. In 1612, the Jewish population of Amsterdam was about 500; by 1672 the number had grown to 7,500 of whom around 2,000 were Portuguese. The remaining 5,000 or so were poor Ashkenazi Jews from Poland and Germany.

Although Jews were allowed in the cities they were not allowed to build synagogues; worship took place in their own homes. Some municipalities introduced regulations specifying which occupations Jews were allowed to enter. In 1632, Jews in Amsterdam were prohibited from most crafts and guilds and from keeping shops. They were allowed to print and sell books, and to sell meat, poultry, groceries and drugs – occupations which fell largely to the Ashkenazi.

Sephardic Jews such as Isaac de Castro and the De Pinto family made their mark in medicine and overseas trading. Baruch Spinoza, born in Amsterdam in 1632, became one of Europe's leading philosophers. Equality for Jews in The Netherlands began with the Burgerlijke Gelijkstelling (Emancipation Act) of 1796. It opened up a wider range of professions and allowed them to enter public life by becoming town councillors (Aldermen). Many Dutch Jews seized these new-found opportunities.

Jews in the Netherlands were largely
treated with tolerance, partly because
the predominantly Protestant Dutch
empathised with the Jews' suffering

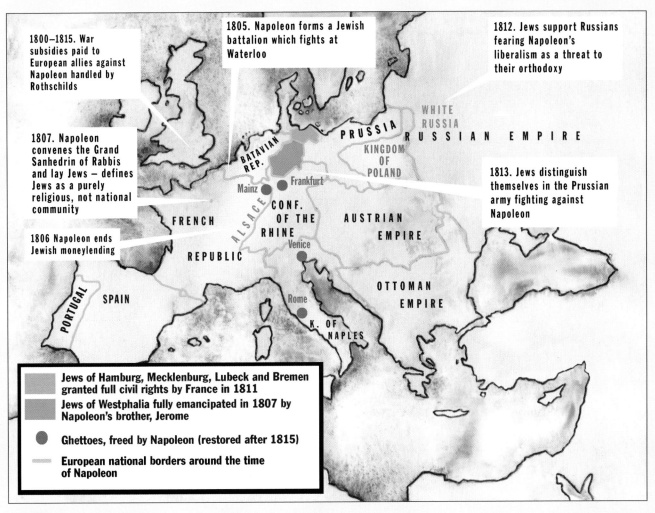

1800–1815. War subsidies paid to European allies against Napoleon handled by Rothschilds

1805. Napoleon forms a Jewish battalion which fights at Waterloo

1812. Jews support Russians fearing Napoleon's liberalism as a threat to their orthodoxy

1807. Napoleon convenes the Grand Sanhedrin of Rabbis and lay Jews – defines Jews as a purely religious, not national community

1813. Jews distinguish themselves in the Prussian army fighting against Napoleon

1806 Napoleon ends Jewish moneylending

WHITE RUSSIA

PRUSSIA

RUSSIAN EMPIRE

KINGDOM OF POLAND

BATAVIAN REP.

Frankfurt

Mainz

ALSACE

CONF. OF THE RHINE

AUSTRIAN EMPIRE

FRENCH

Venice

REPUBLIC

OTTOMAN EMPIRE

PORTUGAL   SPAIN

Rome

K. OF NAPLES

Jews of Hamburg, Mecklenburg, Lubeck and Bremen granted full civil rights by France in 1811

Jews of Westphalia fully emancipated in 1807 by Napoleon's brother, Jerome

● Ghettoes, freed by Napoleon (restored after 1815)

— European national borders around the time of Napoleon

Mixed relationships between
Napoleon Bonaparte and Europe's
Jews

Chapter 2 The Wizards of Oss

From 1850 the peasants of Oss began to switch from growing crops to keeping more cattle, as a growing population in The Netherlands and elsewhere in Europe needed more milk and butter. While wars raged through other parts of the world, The Netherlands enjoyed peace and prosperity, supplying many of the commodities needed to feed and clothe Europe's warring nations.

Oss was gradually developing into an industrial centre as new industries were attracted to the low wages and overheads. By the time Simon Senior and Elisabeth moved there in 1857, the area already hosted industries such as textiles and tobacco processing, often run by Jewish families (some of them related to the couple). The resulting new jobs had boosted the population from 3,000 in 1822 to almost 4,000.

Molenstraat, where the family now lived, reflected the growing affluence of the town and of the van den Berghs themselves. In contrast to the narrow streets elsewhere in Oss, photographs of Molenstraat at the time show a wide tree-lined, cobble-stoned street, with large neat gardens and rows of well-built grey stone terraced houses.

The wide, cobbled Molenstraat

Their home, above the shop at number 361[A], was later described by Maurits: 'It was a great square apartment, with a wooden ceiling and a floor of plain boards; on the right a glass door leading to the shop and on the left, one leading to the passage; the back part totally occupied by a wooden construction of two cupboards. Between the two was a recess with a round oven.'

The business was a substantial progression from the small, simple village shop in Geffen but life was not easy. Profits were low and the family worked long hours in their shop, which had been enlarged to sell draperies, petroleum and groceries as well as continuing their trade

Opposite: Looking to the future: *The Great Church of St. Lawrence, Rotterdam*, 1881 by William Callow

in butter. In his book on his parents' life, Sam described the demands of the citizens of Oss: 'We still recollect how the peasants going to church before six o'clock on winter mornings, rang our parents' doorbell and deposited their vessels in the shop to be filled, during their devotions, with petroleum, also their baskets, wherein they carried their miscellaneous commodities homewards. The clashing of wooden shoes over the hard-frozen causeway by those attending the church still sounds in our ears. What troublesome customers these fellows were.'

The family had to keep a constant watch for swindlers. Some of the Catholic peasants had little compunction about cheating the Jewish van den Berghs by falsifying the weight of butter or milk they would offer in barter for goods in the shop. It was not unknown for a stone or small weight to be found at the bottom of the pail. The Catholic priest on hearing the confessions of his flock, and acting on their behalf, would often visit Simon and Elisabeth to pay them back the monies owed.

By 1860, Oss had a recorded Jewish population of 160, less than 5 per cent of the population. The van den Berghs were aware of their position as a minority in the Catholic town and went out of their way to make friends with their customers. Coffee and tea, and sometimes a seat, would be offered to people queuing on market day.

The couple worked as a partnership. Elisabeth tended to the children and looked after the shop, while Simon Senior rode on horseback on his journeys, some lasting weeks, to barter goods. Her days were long as she served her customers, kept the books and oversaw the education of her children. 'How gloriously did one complement the other', wrote Sam. 'Father the somewhat gentle, placid man, had the benefit to have found in mother a strong, self-dependent, energetic wife who, in his frequent absence, educated the "boys" in strong simplicity, managed the business and attended to household matters.'

The boys' day began at sunrise, with school following breakfast. After school the children were encouraged to play outside in the surrounding fields because Elisabeth believed that fresh air and play would help her sons grow strong and think more clearly. Her daughters-in-law, following her influence, would bring up their children to enjoy fresh air as much as their studies. Years later their grandson Simon would spend many of his holidays on walking tours with his cousins. A love of walking would remain with him for the rest of his life.

Elisabeth believed that that her sons should be both dutiful and honest, which made a lasting impression on Sam: 'Mother educated us rigidly and endeavoured in the first place to encourage us in the execution of duty. She stimulated us to aspire to be at the top of the vocation which we had embraced: "Mind you are number one in your profession," she would say. "Do not rest before you are in the forefront." '

Many Dutch Jews believed their children should only be educated at Jewish schools but Elisabeth wanted her children to receive a standard Dutch education. The local school was always full in the winter but emptied in the summer when most of the boys worked on the land. Lessons at the school only covered the basics, such as reading, maths and literature. Elisabeth wanted her sons to learn more about life and arranged for them to study other subjects. They were given piano lessons and were taught about music. Later they would learn how to identify the stars and appreciate art. Above all, she taught them to ask questions and

The 'new' synagogue in Oss, which Zadok helped finance

to have an interest in science and inventions, which would have a practical application as the family firm took the initiative in developing new foods and manufacturing techniques.

The Sabbath, or 'Shabbat', was the day of rest. The shop would promptly close on Friday evening. By dusk, Elisabeth and her sons had swept and polished the house. The family would dress in their best clothes, the curtains would be lowered and the Sabbath candle lit. Simon Senior, accompanied by those sons who had received their Bar Mitzvah, would leave for the new synagogue in Oss, which his father Zadok had helped finance.

On Simon's return he would find the table set with fine linen for the Sabbath meal. He would always recite Chapter 31 from the Book of Proverbs, which praised the work of the housewife: 'Who can find a virtuous woman, for her price is above rubies...' After that he would take the silver goblet filled with red wine, chant the blessing and drink the first draught, before handing the goblet to his wife and then to his children. Each of the brothers would receive a blessing as their parents laid their hands on their sons' heads. After the meal, Simon would give the grace and then the family would join together in prayers. The rest of the evening would be spent in reading and talking over cups of tea. Not one word would be said about the business.

'The troubles of life', Sam wrote, 'were thrown off for 24 hours, cares or worries however so heavy were cast off. When the Sabbath entered our home, we felt exalted above all earthly troubles.'

Those precious Friday nights were to be celebrated for the rest of Simon and Elisabeth's lives with the family coming together as one. The sons, who would gradually reject their parents' orthodox beliefs, were to remember these holy gatherings with much nostalgia. As the sons married, the family circle increased, with more seats being squeezed around the table. Arnold and Julie, Sam and Betsy, Isaac and Clara, would take their children, including the young Simon, to join their grandparents.

The Sabbath morning was spent at services, with the family walking together to the synagogue, returning home to a specially prepared breakfast. Often poor Jews who had no money, or who lived in filthy lodging houses and had been met by Simon Senior on his travels, were invited to eat with the family. Much of the morning would be spent in praying or receiving visits from friends and relatives. They would go back to the synagogue for midday prayers before returning to their lunch, usually left-overs from the previous night's dinner. Simon and Elisabeth would then rest before, weather permitting, going out together for a stroll. It was the only time the couple had to themselves and the children knew instinctively that they should be left alone.

The rest of the day was spent with their sons in conversation, which would nearly always turn to education, philosophy and religion. There was always humour around the table.

Interior of the synagogue at Oss,
watercolour from around 1925

They had a joy of life, which they were never afraid of showing, laughing as they described the antics of their customers and their friends, or teased one another. As the sun went down, the family's lives would return to those of ordinary shopkeepers. Sabbath clothes were changed for working garb, blinds and shutters would be raised and opened, and trading would begin again.

The Sabbath remained sacrosanct to Simon Senior and would eventually lead to his early retirement from the firm, when his sons insisted that the demands of business meant they could not afford to close each week for both the 'Shabbat' and Christian Sunday.

Financial crisis

Although the shop flourished and the wholesale trade in drapery goods and groceries expanded, the butter trade on which their business was founded was less successful. The family had become established buying butter at markets around Oss and in Bergen, Schaick and Zeeland, and sometimes Germany, with peasants trading their butter for other van den Bergh goods. Using local agents, the butter would then be sold through the rest of The Netherlands and Belgium and even in Great Britain.

Bartering was a risky business. Agents acting on behalf of merchants such as Simon received a commission for handling the sale of butter in their markets, taking their cut before passing on any profits. 'The competition was large', explained Sam in his book, 'and often the price paid for the butter was more than the value of the goods given in barter. The purchase of butter in fact was a forced speculation. One never knew the price it would fetch at Amsterdam, Rotterdam and at London.'

In 1868, the van den Berghs faced financial ruin when the overseas butter markets, mishandled by their agents in London, caused them to cease trading. The agents were setting exorbitant prices to increase their cut, which meant that few customers were buying and the income received did not even cover the costs of despatching the butter to London. Simon Senior was devastated and fell into a deep depression but Elisabeth was not prepared to see the family business fail. Taking matters into her own hands, the tiny Jewish matriarch did something that was unheard of in those days, she put on her best bonnet and travelled on her own through The Netherlands. She visited each of the family's creditors and explained what the London agents had been up to. Elisabeth assured the creditors that the family would eventually pay back all they owed. Men unused to discussing business with a woman were touched by her honesty and sincerity, and agreed to give the family time to pay their debts. Elisabeth's journeys also led to an unexpected romantic by-product: two of the daughters of those creditors, Clara van Leer and Betsy Willing, married Elisabeth's sons Isaac and Sam.

Although Simon continued to work behind the scenes, it would take several years for him to come out of his depression. Simon and Elisabeth's sons were fully aware of the business catastrophe and were anxious to help. Five of them – Jacob, Henry, Arnold, Isaac and Sam – joined the business and would eventually honour all the debts.

The other van den Bergh boys were already seeking success in other professions. By 1869,

Maurits and Zadok, with the blessing and support of their parents, had embarked on studies for their chosen careers. Maurits, the second eldest, was interested in law and public service. He would eventually be one of the first Jews to become a public servant, when he was appointed Receiver of Registration for the city of Eindhoven. Zadok studied Greek and Latin under Dr Hans Roodhuijzen, one of the finest teachers of classics in The Netherlands. He went on to study at Amsterdam University and became a lawyer, practising in Amsterdam where he built up a reputation as a leader in constitutional law. Zadok never lost his love of classics, particularly Greek, which he passed to his nephew Simon. Later Dr Roodhuijzen, who became a close friend of the family, would advise Isaac and Clara on suitable academic courses for their son, Simon.

Jacob, the eldest son, was sent to London to learn about British business methods

In 1868, Jacob was sent to London to learn about British business and to find out how to prevent van den Berghs being cheated again. Henry was to follow him. The growing prosperity of Britain's middle classes had created a greater demand for butter, which had become scarce in London where the growing population had outstripped supply. This should have led to increased demand for van den Bergh goods and a rise in profits. Instead the family lost money.

Arriving at Brewers Quay in London, the centre for the distribution and sale of imported butter, Jacob and Henry realised that their supply and marketing methods would have to be completely changed. Instead of transporting their butter in hard-to-handle tubs and kegs, it was to be packed and shipped in individual paper rolls, which increased its value because the butter could be sold piecemeal without having to be packaged on arrival in London.

Packaging and merchandising techniques were important. In Oss, Belgian rather than Dutch women, looked on as being more skilful – if not cheaper – were brought in to help make up the rolls as demand for butter increased. Sixteen-year-old Isaac was pressed into service, rolling up butter in paper, as he sat in one of the workrooms, his school books propped up in front of him. Isaac was given little choice over his ultimate destiny because the loss of two brothers to other professions and sudden changes in the family fortunes meant help was urgently needed. Later his youngest brother Sam, who wanted to study law, would also be asked by his parents and brothers to join the family business, to help manufacture a new product: margarine.

Innovation and rivalry

In 1869 Napoleon III offered a prize to anyone who could make a satisfactory substitute for butter to supply the armed forces and malnourished working classes. The French chemist

Mège-Mouriès' invention,
celebrated on a 20th-century
cigarette card

Hippolyte Mège-Mouriès succeeded in combining processed, rendered cattle fat and skimmed milk to produce a butter-like substance which was a forerunner of what is now known as margarine. He was duly honoured by Napoleon III. A little later, Mège-Mouriès announced to the world that he had produced a new foodstuff, which he called oleomargarine. Margarine, with a softly pronounced 'g', was named after the flower the 'margeurite' whose colour it resembled. The new product would revolutionise the world's eating habits and with it the fortunes of the van den Berghs.

One of the leading families in Oss was headed by a Catholic, Anton Jurgens, who was interested in margarine and entered into talks with the French authorities. In 1871, he was granted one of the first manufacturing franchises, under which raw materials produced by Mège-Mouriès were sent to the Jurgens family firm to be processed into artificial butter.

One evening after working on his new product, Anton Jurgens visited his neighbour Simon van den Bergh and invited him to taste it. The two men knew each other but because of the difference in religion had never been friends. The visit was never to be forgotten by Sam: 'At the firm Jurgens, things were managed under great secrecy and we could form no idea of what was going on. One evening Mr Jurgens entered our house with a sauce of butter which he wanted father, who was considered a great connoisseur, to taste. On being asked his opinion, father replied that it had a taste of fat, when Jurgens indeed acknowledged that it was a new product, a sort of artificial butter, and that it could be not be manufactured by anyone, being patented in all countries... Scarcely had Jurgens left the house than the idea was uttered by father and all the family had the same thought: "Could we not make the same artificial butter?".'

To this day, no-one knows why Anton Jurgens visited Simon van den Bergh, why he boasted about his new product and, even more surprisingly, allowed a potential competitor – Simon – to taste it. But by doing so he was to change the van den Berghs' fortunes.

Jacob was at that time in London and came across an article in *The London Reader* about Mège-Mouriès' new 'butter'. His interest was heightened by an advertisement in a trade journal by a chandler, Daniel Hipkins from Tipton near Birmingham, who was seeking financial backing to develop a new process for producing a similar product. Jacob contacted Hipkins, who together with the van den Berghs, created a new form of oleomargarine, based on Mège-Mouriès' system but with enough subtle differences not to break any patent. The van den Berghs could now start production of their own margarine.

This placed the van den Berghs in conflict with the Jurgens, one of the most powerful Catholic families in the area. It was a bitter dispute that would last for years and lead to cases of arson, poisoning and betrayal. One long-serving van den Bergh worker was discovered spying on behalf of Jurgens. Suspicions that he had been hiding margarine under his clothing to take to their rivals were confirmed when he was invited into the van den Bergh home for coffee. His seat was placed beside the fire and within minutes the melting margarine began to drip.

The families blamed each other for various incidents, including when part of the van den Bergh factory was burnt down and Jurgens' margarine caused cases of food poisoning.

A van den Bergh building constructed to provide a new cooling system collapsed without any reason being found. The van den Berghs resorted to using code names to describe their products and techniques. Thermometers were set with false temperatures that only members of the family and a few workers could read correctly.

Promotion of the product became the byword and the brothers' predisposition to practical jokes metamorphosed into practicality as van den Bergh and Jurgens waged their 'margarine war'. Jacob pioneered the family's marketing flare when he bought the Dutch national postal frank for the day that Jurgens launched a promotional drive for a new margarine. Each card advertising Jurgens' margarine went out with the slogan 'Van den Bergh margarine is better for you' stamped on it. Many of the advertising and promotional techniques pioneered by Jacob and his brothers would later be adopted by other companies, including Unilever.

Isaac, now in his very early twenties, was found to have a talent for technical matters, which Simon Senior and Elisabeth put to good use by making him responsible for building their new factory. Arnold, still in his late teens, was in charge of management. Henry and Jacob, based in London, were given the mission of expanding margarine distribution and buying raw materials. The lives of the brothers were now bound inexorably with their parents in building the family business.

Isaac and Arnold, whose teenage years coincided with the threat to the family livelihood, lost their chances of going to university. However, their own sons would be given every opportunity for education and to enjoy the freedom of early adulthood.

Paying tribute to his brothers' work Sam wrote: 'All had experienced the misery of catastrophe and had learned the seriousness of life in the years that other boys passed in child's play. Their youth was submerged in the cares for daily bread. How sad in itself, it served to harden "the boys" in the struggle for life and their later successes may be attributed to a considerable extent to the bitter experience of their "lost youth".'

A time of prosperity

In 1871 Jacob married an Englishwoman, Lydia Isaacson, the daughter of a supplier of cartons to the family. In 1873 he took British citizenship. He was never fully fluent in English and his strong Dutch accent and grammatical faults caused great amusement among his disrespectful offspring and their children. The tall, aristocratic Henry lived for a time in France, where he acquired a taste for fine art and conversation. He travelled throughout Europe, finally settling in London in 1879. Eight years later, he would bring his wife, the equally tall and aristocratic Henriette Spanjaard, back to England where the first of their children was born in 1888. These two families became the British side of the Van den Berghs and their children were born and brought up in England.

The margarine manufacturing company, Simon van den Bergh, was established in The Netherlands in 1872. The following year Jacob and Henry set up partnership in London, trading under the name of Van den Bergh Brothers. Between 1868 and 1885, the two family firms were financed with investment from family capital and commercial credit, as they estab-

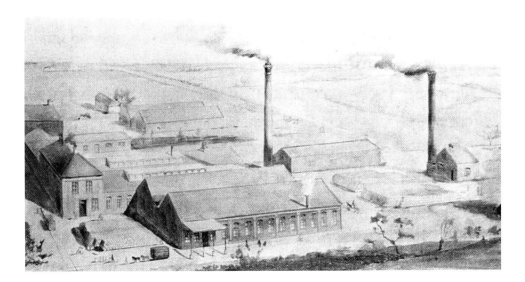

The van den Bergh factory on the outskirts of Oss

lished a trading network that enabled them to both source and buy raw materials for their margarine and to distribute it. Jacob took charge of distribution and sales, and Henry looked for raw materials. In Oss, Simon Senior worked with Isaac and Arnold, who were in charge of technical affairs and production respectively.

Van den Bergh production of margarine grew. By 1876 they were able to settle all their debts. As fortunes improved so did the social lives of the family with each of the brothers taking a wife, often a cousin or the daughter of a family that was in some way involved with the van den Bergh business. In 1885 Simon took his four oldest Oss-based sons into partnership in the 'Simon van den Bergh' business. The youngest, Sam, was yet to become a partner. Simon Senior stayed on as a sleeping partner and the sons shared equally in the profits, which were invested in building new plants, such as those in Cleve in Germany and later in Rotterdam, to increase overall margarine production.

Sam began working with the family in 1882 and would bring in managers and specialists to run the business, create new foods and find new methods of production. He forged close ties with his young nephews and nieces, including Isaac's son Simon, who would spend a great deal of time with Sam and his family, accompanying them on holiday. Sam introduced Simon and both his sons, George and Sidney, to his love of astronomy and encouraged them to ask scientific questions about the Universe. That interest continued through one of Sam's grandsons, Sidney Van den Bergh, who became Professor of Astrophysics in Vancouver, Canada and one of the pioneers of the United States' space programme in the 1960s. George and his cousin Simon would both, with their fathers' blessing, seek an academic future: George in law and Simon in philosophy. The two cousins would remain firm friends for the rest of their lives.

Simon Senior's seven sons took responsibility for each other and the interests of their children and grandchildren. In 1887 Isaac was to act as a 'matchmaker' to 23-year-old Sam, who had fallen in love with Betsy Willing, the daughter of one of Simon and Elisabeth's former creditors. The young couple approached her mother Mevrouw Willing to ask for permission to marry. The astute old lady told them she would only give it if Sam were to be made a partner in the family firm. Isaac immediately went to London to discuss the matter with Jacob and Henry. Sam and Betsy were married later that year and in 1888 Sam became a partner.

Earlier, Sam had lived with Jacob and his new wife Lydia in London while studying English. Later, Jacob's sons, daughters and grandchildren would stay with Sam and Betsy at their house in the South of France. Sam and his wife Betsy would protect Isaac and Zadok in their old age when threatened by the Germans during the Second World War. The house would also provide the backdrop to family romances including that between Isaac's granddaughter Lisa and Jacob's grandson Robert Sainsbury.

In 1878, Arnold married his cousin Julie Nathan; a year later on 1 July 1879, Isaac married Clara Van Leer. She was the eldest daughter of one of their suppliers and original creditors, Samson Barend Van Leer, a successful merchant from Gouda, and his wife Jette Visser.

Clara, also known as Claartje, was born in Gouda on 19 March 1857. She was the third of Samson and Jette's nine children. Her grandfather, Barend Mozes Van Leer, had been born in Germany and settled in Gouda in 1807, when he married Klaartje Mozes Sanders. He had become a general merchant, finally passing on his business to his son. Jette Visser was born in Amersfoot in 1830 into one of the most successful and prominent Jewish families in The Netherlands. Her nephew, Lodewijk Ernst Visser, was to become one of the country's most prominent Judges and a close friend of the van den Bergh family.

The marriage was celebrated in Gouda, with members of both families attending. Two of Isaac's brothers, Maurits and Arnold, as well as his father Simon, were all witnesses to the marriage contract. The deed was drawn up by Willem Jacobus-Droogleever Fortuijn, who was related to the Van Leer family. Other signatories included a cousin from Isaac's mother Elisabeth's family, as well as Clara's father and her brother Willem.

The Oss census of 1879 indicates the changes in the lives of the family living on Molenstraat. Although only the occupations of Simon as 'Manufacturer' and Maurits as 'Recorder of Registration', are given, the locations of the others are noted, with Jacob in London, Henry in Paris, Sam at school in Arnhem and Isaac at his new home in Vondelstraat, where he and Clara lived for the first year of their marriage.

In 1880 Isaac and Clara moved into their new house at 370 Kruisstraat, a short walk from the margarine factory. Photographs of the house show how the fortunes of the family had improved. A large, well-endowed building, surrounded by iron railings, set slightly back from the rest of the street, it was a comfortable home, filled with wood panelling, highly polished by two servant girls. Thick carpets from the Far East covered the floors and, following Dutch tradition, were also laid on top of the tables. The servant girls would beat those carpets, hanging on lines outside the house, while feather bolsters hung outside the windows to air.

It was in that house on 12 February 1881 that Isaac and Clara's first child, Elisabeth Jette (Liesje), was born after a long and difficult labour. Named after her grandmother and her aunt Jette, Liesje came into the world with one leg shorter than the other, making her lame. She also had learning difficulties and was to suffer from ill health and depression her whole life.

Simon followed on 16 November 1882 and was named after his grandfather. The family were delighted at the birth of a son, but Clara concentrated on looking after her disabled daughter so had little time to spend with him. Clara's own health had been damaged by her difficult pregnancies and she was warned by doctors not to have any more children.

The naming of Elisabeth Jette and Simon was highly significant because orthodox Jewish custom meant children could only be named after relatives once they had died. In accordance with this practice, Simon and Elisabeth Senior had only used the name Zadok for their sixth son after the death of his grandfather. The fact that Simon and Elisabeth were named after their grandparents, the first of the grandchildren to be so, illustrates the family's increasingly secular attitudes.

A teenager, Leonie Wesley, was employed to help look after Liesje and the young Simon. She would eventually become Simon's nanny and governess, and would have a great impact on his life. Despite being born in Maastricht on 8 October 1864, she was a British national. Leonie took the place of Simon's mother in raising and nurturing him. Not only would she provide him with the love and support missing from his parents, but she also spoilt him, with the result that he was incapable of doing mundane tasks for himself.

Simon's second wife Maureen talked about the problems this caused. 'He had no idea of how to get ready. I would put on his socks for him and tie up his laces,' she explained. 'He was terribly untidy, leaving his clothes all over the floor. If I complained he would tell me how Miss Wesley had done everything for him, choosing his clothes and putting them away.'

Maureen believed he was much closer to Miss Wesley than to his own mother. 'She would get him up in the morning, have all his clothes waiting for him and would dress him, even tying his shoelaces up for him. And I think she made him more helpless than he was. He couldn't do anything at all; he didn't even know how to pack clothes.'

Simon's failure to deal with the more mundane tasks of life never changed, as his granddaughter Celia Blakey later discovered: 'I noticed that his shoelaces had become untied. I pointed this out to him. He put his foot out so that I could tie them for him.'

Years later Simon talked about his love and respect for 'his Miss Wesley'. She was largely responsible for his passion for learning languages. By the time Simon was 12 years old, he could speak German, Dutch, English and French, and could read and write in Latin and Greek. Isaac and Clara unwittingly started a trend: Sam and Betsy later also employed a British nanny, Miss Cordingley, to look after their three children and Simon himself brought in British nannies and governesses for his daughters, Lisa and Tamara.

Family life was based around Simon and Elisabeth Senior, with wives and children popping in and out of each other's houses. Every day the grandparents would receive visits from their sons, daughters-in-law and grandchildren. Bigger houses were bought by the parents and brothers. Sam and Betsy moved into Arnold's old house when he built himself a larger one, which is now home to the Museum Jan Cunen.

Growing pains

By the late 1880s, Oss was becoming an affluent town, with the wealth of the van den Berghs and their bitter rivals the Jurgens contributing to its success. New roads had been built and

Top: Arnold's new house in Oss, seen in the 1800s. Above: The house today, as home to the Museum Jan Cunen.

an improved railway system had opened up new routes to Germany, Belgium and the rest of Europe. The town's population rose to over 7,500 as people moved in to take up new jobs.

Although the van den Berghs' professional and personal lives were successful, they were still not treated as full members of society. Anti-semitism meant Jews were unable to take up any position in public service and tensions grew between the local authorities and the van den Berghs when family members were not allowed to participate in the affairs of the Catholic-dominated town council.

Those tensions turned in to conflict in 1889 when the town council, supported by the Jurgens family who had members on the council, voted down plans for developing a new canal. Designed by Arnold, it would have enabled the family to send their goods directly to Rotterdam for export. Although Germany was a major market, with van den Berghs building a factory in Cleve to avoid paying newly introduced import tariffs, Great Britain had by now become the largest buyer of van den Bergh margarine. But it was expensive and time-consuming to export margarine there. The council vote against the canal, which would have speeded up transport of goods to Rotterdam for shipment to England, was seen as a deliberate slight to the van den Berghs' livelihoods.

Sam's wife Betsy, in a book about her husband's life, wrote that van den Berghs would not give up: 'They said, "if the water doesn't come to the factory, then we will bring the factory to the water." '

Isaac, Arnold and Sam met their brothers and Arnold surprised them all by coming up with plans to transfer the whole factory from Oss to Rotterdam. 'It was a magnificent concept,' wrote Sam in his book. 'Once at Rotterdam, all the expenses of transport to and from the interior were done away with. There we were 24 hours nearer England, our principal sphere of sales, where more than 90 per cent of our produce was disposed of.' The brothers agreed to Arnold's plans. Rotterdam was a thriving port that would bring them in closer contact with Jacob and Henry in England and with Zadok, who was now living in Amsterdam.

By 1889 Simon and Elisabeth Senior's three sons still living in Oss all had families of their own. Arnold and Julie had three daughters: Annie Eliza born in 1880, Bertha in 1881 and Constance in 1887; their son Leo was born in 1882. Another daughter Lydia, known as Beebs, would be born in 1892. Sam's eldest daughter Elisabeth was only a year old and Betsy was pregnant with their son George, who would be born in 1890. She would have one more son, Sidney, born in 1898. Along with Isaac and Clara's son Simon, the cousins would forge close friendships that would last for the rest of their lives.

However, as was common in those times, not all the grandchildren reached adulthood. Arnold's daughter Elisabeth died at birth and his son Siegfried died young from croup; later Maurits lost his son Simon, at the age of 15; also Jacob in London lost two young children, Therese and Clarissa, when they were less than a year old.

The modern city of Rotterdam offered a wide range of opportunities in the late 1800s

In general, family life was happy for Simon and Elisabeth Senior and one of the first grand festivals was the celebration, in Arnold's newly built villa, of their 45th wedding anniversary in 1889. All their sons with their spouses and a number of grandchildren attended. This would be the last family celebration in Oss.

Yet the van den Bergh sons and their wives wanted a better education for their children than could be provided in the small provincial town. Simon had recently joined his cousins at the elementary school, which all the parents felt was sub-standard. Lessons were based on educating the Catholic majority and largely neglected the Jewish children. Tensions arose because Jewish boys by the age of five or six were often more advanced in reading and writing than their peers. They had been given an early advantage of schooling in Hebrew and religious studies at the synagogue, starting as young as three years old.

The nearest school that welcomed Jewish children and could provide an adequate education was some 20 miles away. The brothers and their wives also wanted their daughters to receive as high a standard of education as their sons, in contrast to other residents of Oss who attached little importance to educating girls, whose lives were expected to be spent looking after their husbands or doing menial jobs. Remembering how Elisabeth's interest in studying the Talmud had been stilted by her Rabbi, the daughters-in-law, in particular Betsy who was to play an active role in the fight for equal rights for women, doubted whether their sons and daughters would receive an enlightened education in local towns.

Elisabeth and Simon Senior were in their seventies. No move could take place without them. They were now living in a large house, Kinderzorg, especially built for them, separated from the factory by the house of the baker, an old friend. Sam explained in his book: 'They were connected with Oss by many ties of relationship and by cherished remembrances, respected and loved by everyone and who, better than the younger generation, were

Simon and Elizabeth's 45th wedding anniversary celebrations, held in Arnold's newly built villa. Back row (standing, from left): Isaac, Arnold, Zadok, Line, Maurits, Betsy, Sam, Jacob. Front row (seated): Clara, Henry, Julie, Henriette, Elisabeth, Etty, Simon, Lydia

accustomed to the manners and habits of the villagers. Not only did we refrain from broaching to our parents the subject of our departure, we felt still more difficulty in proposing as well their departure from there and their removal to Rotterdam.'

Yet, knowing that the old couple would share their wishes for better lives for all their family and how much importance Elisabeth attached to education, the brothers and their wives decided to ask them if they would agree to a move. Sam recalled: 'At last after long consideration, it was resolved to lay before the old people the question "Would you be inclined, for the benefit of the business and of the future of the grandchildren, to remove to Rotterdam", adding in one breath, "if you do not feel so disposed, we will all stay here".'

Simon and Elisabeth agreed.

Chapter 3 New horizons

The move to Rotterdam was the greatest upheaval for the van den Bergh family since first settling in The Netherlands. In his book, Sam wrote: 'The departure for Rotterdam opens a new phase in our family history. The gigantic expansion from that time could not have been possible at Oss. A new horizon opened for all of us.'

Rotterdam, the once sleepy little fishing village built where the river Rotte meets an arm of the Maas delta, had become the first seaport of The Netherlands. Connected by canal with the River Schie, providing direct links with the important cloth-making towns of Delft and Leiden, Rotterdam had become the main port of entry for English wool. Wool was among many commodities — including tobacco and spices — which would be shipped via Rotterdam into The Netherlands and from there to other countries in Europe. In return, goods such as china and cloth from Europe were exported via Rotterdam to Great Britain and the Americas. Eventually people would be among the exports as they left poverty and persecution in Europe for the safety and opportunity of the New World.

In 1863, work began on constructing a ship canal, the Nieuwe Waterweg, to allow large ocean-growing vessels to enter the port. At the same time the first modern dock installation was constructed to enable cargo to be discharged straight from the ships onto railway trucks or stored immediately in purpose-built warehouses. Until then, goods had been conveyed by horse-drawn carts to warehouses in town.

The distribution of van den Bergh products was revolutionised by these new installations. The construction of the van den Bergh factory on the newly built Nassaukade (Nassau Quay) meant that instead of having to transport goods to and from Oss, raw materials could be brought directly by boat, rail or wagon to the factory, to be processed into margarine and other commodities. These could then be dispatched by ship to London and later to the United States, and by ship, canal and rail to the rest of Europe.

Isaac and Clara, with their children Liesje and Simon, were the first to move to Rotterdam in the spring of 1890. Isaac, who had been entrusted with building the factories in Oss,

The van den Bergh factory in
Rotterdam, opened on
Monday 2 May 1891

Photograph from Sam's book, showing a view of the new factory from the canal

was now to oversee construction of the new factory in Rotterdam. On Saturday 30 April 1891 the factory at Oss was closed and two days later, on Monday 2 May 1891, the new one at Rotterdam was opened. Concerned that their parents might be upset on seeing the closure of their first factory, the brothers arranged for Simon and Elisabeth to join their son Zadok in Amsterdam for an extended holiday.

'Still it was hard for the old ones', recounted Sam. 'Mother kept all right, but father was much agitated on leaving the village. We had kept secret the day and hour of departure, so that only few people came to the station to bid farewell to them.'

The families moved into homes on the newly built, fashionable Koningin Emmaplein (Queen Emma Square) in the centre of Rotterdam. Simon and Elisabeth arrived in the city to find all their possessions installed in their new house; bunting had been hung and flowers were presented to the old lady. Their children and grandchildren waited to greet them.

The old couple would be living nearer to their children and their families than in Oss. 'They found the new dwelling on the Emmaplein ready from top to bottom. Nothing was wanting,' wrote Sam. 'All the children were there, the old personnel was present as far as possible, the old furniture and objects to which they were attached, in the old position, under the new surroundings... Isaac and Clara had lived in the square since the previous year, only four or five houses distance away from them, and soon they found themselves surrounded by three of their children in the same square. That was a great boon.'

The square consisted of a terrace of 15 elegant houses inhabited by the elite of the business community. The house at one end of the terrace, owned by Isaac and Clara, was a five-storey, typical Dutch gabled house. The houses were more comfortable and ostentatious than the family's previous homes, reflecting the rise in wealth and status. The van den Bergh residences in The Netherlands and England would expand as families increased in size, and as new interests and tastes were adopted.

Rotterdam was a vibrant, growing, modern, industrial city, with a history of tolerance, having given sanctuary over centuries to people persecuted because of their faith. Since the 18th century, Rotterdam had three churches – Presbyterian, Episcopal and Church of Scotland – where services were held in English. It also had a Walloon Church and a flourishing Lutheran Congregation, founded by South Netherlanders fleeing persecution from Catholics in Antwerp. The Protestant congregations of these churches understood how the Jews had suffered and welcomed them into their city.

The Jewish community shared in Rotterdam's prosperity. In 1725 a magnificent synagogue – the only one with a clock tower – was built on the riverside at Boompjes. Simon and Elisabeth Senior were warmly welcomed, becoming great friends with the Chief Rabbi, Dr Bernard Ritter. They became leading figures in the Boompjes synagogue, where several van den Bergh weddings would take place and where their grandsons would receive reli-

Koningin Emmaplein. ROTTERDAM.

Postcard of Rotterdam's
fashionable Koningin Emmaplein

gious instruction and be Bar Mitzvahed. The synagogue would be destroyed in 1940, during
the German bombing of Rotterdam.

In 1893, Isaac's son Simon celebrated his Bar Mitzvah at the Boompjes synagogue. Uncles
and male cousins crowded around him at the service. His mother, aunt and female cousins
looked on expectantly from the gallery, as accompanied by his father, he was summoned
before them all to read from the Torah. His grandparents, Simon and Elisabeth, would have
been among the first to celebrate, looking on in pride, as their grandson, having reached the
age of 13, accepted the responsibilities of fulfilling the commandments of their faith. That
evening a party was held at The Loge, one of Rotterdam's finest restaurants, the scene of
many family celebrations. Simon, the guest of honour, made a speech in which he paid tribute to his family and talked about his aspirations for the future and possibly attempted to
make a joke or two, in the warmth of love from his parents, grandparents and beloved Miss
Wesley.

Simon, like many of his cousins, would not be a frequent visitor to the synagogue.
In 1968 he wrote to his first wife's niece Luba Glikson in Argentina, to tell her that it
had been so many years since he visited a synagogue, that he thought that God had probably 'forgotten' him.

'Thanks to God our parents soon got accustomed to the new surroundings,' wrote Sam.
'The Jewish community appreciated highly the great acquisition of our family. Father and
Mother, for whom the religious life was so important, were charmed with the cordiality with
which the Israelites of Rotterdam opened their circle to them. Soon Mr and Mrs van den
Bergh belonged to the esteemed members of the Jewish community. So lived our Parents,
in the evening of their lives, calmly and happily at Rotterdam, surrounded by three of their
sons and their families; often visited by their children and grandchildren from England.'

One of these was Jacob Van den Bergh's second eldest daughter Mabel, who was a frequent visitor to Rotterdam. She took her younger brother Henry with her to meet his Dutch cousins and in particular his cousin Simon. Both had been born in 1882 and Henry joined Simon at his Bar Mitzvah celebrations. In 1937, Mabel's youngest son Robert would marry Simon's eldest daughter Lisa. In 1893, Jacob's eldest daughter Dolly presented Simon and Elisabeth with their first great grandchild, Dorothy Lydia. Within weeks of her arrival she was bundled up in warm clothes and taken across the North Sea to visit them.

A thriving modern city: Rotterdam's Het Witte Huis (The White House), was built in the French 'chateau style' in 1898 for a pair of Rotterdam businessmen. At 147-feet it was the tallest building in Europe.

Pillars of the community

As the lives of Jews in Western Europe improved, those of their brethren in Eastern Europe deteriorated as they faced persecution during the Russian anti-Jewish massacres and riots (knows as pogroms) of the late 19th century. Simon Senior, now retired from business, became chairman of the Montefiore Society, set up to help needy Jews fleeing persecution pass through Rotterdam on their way to America or Canada. Refugees from Russia, Galicia (part of present-day Ukraine) and Romania also received help from other van den Berghs who found them places to stay and provided food. It was not unknown for female members of the family to empty their wardrobes to give the ragged refugees clothes in which to cross the hostile Atlantic. At Simon's request, the Rotterdam Jewish community donated a house to the Montefiore society to use as a refuge.

'Father's soft heart was filled with sincere pity in seeing these unfortunate co-religionists wander through the town with their wives and children,' wrote Sam. 'He felt attracted to those in need, and it was pleasure for him to be able to do something for them. Father was a frequent visitor to the refuge, and till his last days, to regulate the affairs of his poor brethren, to meet their travelling expenses to America, which money he received from the funds of the Baron de Hirsch Institution in Paris, and to assist them from his own pocket and advise and assist them in general.

'Some of the refugees would never forget the help from the man they called "Herr Baron", he soon was an extra-popular personality with these emigrants, and often there came letters from America full of thanks for the man who had provided so well for them, when they came, after the long journey from their native country to Rotterdam.'

Rotterdam provided an enlightened and liberal environment. The grandchildren learned how to play the piano, appreciate art and dance the waltz. The young Simon was to thrive, accumulating the beginnings of the thirst for knowledge that would lead him to become a sophisticated man of literature, music and art. He, in turn, would pass on a love of culture to his own family.

'Now we began to see what we had missed of life at Oss,' Sam recalled. 'We lived now amidst the liberal population of one of the largest commercial towns of the world, where there was life and energy, where we were received by the municipality and the inhabitants in general with open arms, and where they tried to promote the new industry to the utmost limit... There reigned a grand, free conception of matters, in contradiction to the narrowness and illiberality of Brabant. There we could give our children a proper education and personally take part in public life, where from we were totally excluded in Brabant.'

Instead of being banned from public service as they had been in Oss, Jews were welcomed into the public arena. A member of the Liberal Party, Sam van den Bergh was later elected member of the Municipal Council of Rotterdam. His brother Zadok would be elected a Conservative member of the Municipal Council of Amsterdam. The Netherlands was the first European country to allow Jews to be elected to Parliament, an opportunity seized upon by Sam and Zadok who in 1889 became Senators in the National Assembly, the first brothers to be elected at the same time and among the first Jews.

Sam gave valuable support to his wife Betsy in her work for women's right to vote – known by the Dutch as the 'Moaning Minnies'. He accompanied her to overseas conferences, paid towards the movement's costs and generally encouraged their work. Sam and Betsy's houses in The Netherlands and the South of France acted as venues for various meetings and fundraising parties. Universal suffrage was finally introduced in The Netherlands for men and women over the age of 25 in 1917.

Betsy's 'votes for women' activities created an embarrassing moment for Simon, who had a habit of forgetting which nights of the week he had arranged to have dinner with his uncles and aunts. His younger cousin George couldn't resist telling Simon's second wife Maureen about one particular occasion when Simon was about 16 years old and turned up to have tea at Sam and Betsy's a day early. 'Unfortunately for him, Betsy was entertaining some of her suffragette friends,' recalled Maureen. 'They insisted he stayed and spent two hours lecturing him about how important it was that women should be allowed to vote.

'Sam had taken the rest of the family to see one of their other cousins so Simon was on his own with "the ladies". George said the family had howled with laughter at Betsy's description of young Simon blushing as he helped her with the tea. But he quickly made himself at home with them and asked them all sorts of questions. Simon always claimed he had known they were going to be there!'

In 1931, Sam van den Bergh came sixth in a poll by readers of the Dutch Jewish Newspaper *Nieuw Israelietisch Weekblad* to choose the 10 most prominent Jews in the country. No longer considering himself to be at all religious, he had publicly gone on record stating that he looked on himself as being 'a Dutchman first, a Liberal second and only then thirdly a Jew'. Zadok, a successful lawyer and constitutional expert, had been recommended to South African President Paul Kruger by the Dutch Government as a suitable candidate to be the new nation's first Secretary of State. The offer was withdrawn when Kruger discovered that he was Jewish.

An illustration from Sam's family history, depicting the visit of Queen Wilhelmina and Queen Emma to the van den Bergh factory

Public recognition of the van den Berghs reached a peak on 25 September 1899, when the family were summoned to the Rotterdam factory to receive a visit from Queen Wilhelmina of The Netherlands and her mother Queen Emma. Escorted by mounted cavalry, the two Queens swept into the factory.

Sam reported the event in his book: 'The reception was brilliant, the decorations were beautiful. At the entrance a pavilion was arranged covered with valuable carpets, where the royal ladies were received by Father and his sons Isaac, Arnold and Sam. The two Queens and their suite looked at every detail, showed a great interest in the preparing of the margarine, condensed milk and soap, and seemed unaffectedly pleased with all they had seen.' Members of the family, including the teenage Simon, were presented to the two Queens, both of whom had a further conversation with his grandfather, complimenting him on his family's achievement in founding what had become a 'world concern'.

The Netherlands' monarchs played active roles in helping their Jewish subjects to assimilate. Throughout her reign, Queen Wilhelmina visited Jewish hospitals, orphanages and old peoples' homes. Prominent Jews such as Sam would be invited by her to act as advisers and to serve on various committees. In the 1920s, Sam and Henry Van den Bergh were knighted.

Both had played significant roles not only in helping the Jewish communities of The Netherlands, but also in founding one of the most successful Dutch industrial concerns and enriching the lives of the Dutch people artistically and socially. Sam's wife Betsy, who was also honoured by her Queen, would subsequently refer to herself as the 'Little Knight' and Sam has her 'Commander'. Sam was also to receive the Crown Order from the Italian Government for his work in establishing a factory in that country.

The success of the business was reflected in the lives of all the brothers. Maids and servants were employed; the latest appliances were installed in their homes. Electricity took over from gas lighting and they were among the first to have telephones. There were theatres, libraries, art galleries and parks. Rotterdam had its own daily and evening newspapers. Remembering the importance that Elisabeth had attached to the physical wellbeing of her children, the van den Berghs in the early 1920s built the city its first municipal swimming pool.

Wealth did not exclude family feelings. Across a cold North Sea, family warmth would continue to bind them together. The grandparents remained at the core, as all enjoyed the many celebrations for the arrivals of new grandchildren, birthdays and weddings. The youngest grandchildren (and later great grandchildren) from England and The Netherlands, joined together to stage elaborate theatrical extravaganzas.

One of these productions was for Simon and Elisabeth's Golden wedding anniversary in 1894, for which there were three days of celebrations. A Louis XV-style screen depicting a portrait of the couple, surrounded by all their grandchildren and great grandchildren, was presented to them. After the death of his parents, the screen was given, by consent of all brothers, to Jacob to be handed down in turn to his eldest son, Albert. The screen was destroyed during bombing in the Second World War.

A specially commissioned play *The Bruiloft van Kloris en Roosje* (*The Marriage of Kloris and Rose*) was staged at the Grand Theatre in Rotterdam, which was taken over for the occasion. The prologue was given by Frits Tartaud, one of The Netherlands' leading actors. The rest of the cast consisted of family members, including 11-year-old Simon.

The parts played by the children were described by Sam: '*The Marriage of Kloris and Rose*, in which the various cousins took the leading parts, was the "pièce de résistance" of the evening. The various allusions made to the jubilants, their sons and other family members, caused great applause. The grandchildren represented part of the wedding train of Kloris and Roosje. They were all dressed in the well-known peasant costume with wooden shoes. The smallest in front – five-year-old Sies, Zadok's youngest son; and four-year-old George, Sam's son – suffered so much from stage fright at their acting debut that both had a little accident.'

Simon laughed at George's accident and years later, according to his second wife Maureen, could not resist teasing him: 'He and George would often joke about the old days and what had happened to them. Whenever George mentioned one of Simon's embarrassing moments, Simon would point out that at least he hadn't had an accident on stage in front of hundreds of people!'

Home and away

Life in Isaac's house was quieter than in the homes of his brothers. His daughter Liesje's illness had dominated the family; by the 1890s, his wife Clara was diagnosed with heart problems. She was often tired and ill, devoting any remaining energy to her daughter. Isaac, concerned for her health and involved with expanding the business, had little time to spare for his son, who was given anything he wanted to make up for the lack of parental attention. The young Simon received little discipline and was largely left to his own devices. Often solitary, he was far from sad; to the contrary, he was a happy boy who was petted by his aunts and made much of by the maids. Simon had a talent for music and could play the piano by ear, which ensured his popularity among friends and companions, especially when it came to parties.

The van den Bergh brothers took a close interest in their many nephews and nieces. Both Arnold and Sam welcomed politicians, academics and artists to their homes and encouraged the young Simon to listen to their conversations, ask questions and take part in debates. Sam's houses, always full of books, acted as a magnet to Simon as he sat for hours on the floor, or perched on a stool, firstly nibbling apples or, when older, smoking a cigarette as he worked his way through the volumes of philosophy, literature and science.

The small, good looking, dark-haired boy, who looked very like his grandfather when he was young, may have appeared delicate but he was very tough. Outgoing with a good sense of humour, Simon wanted to discover new ideas and loved travelling. Trips and outings with his uncles and cousins were preferable to staying at home with his parents.

Simon spent much time with his Uncle Sam, whose wife Betsy described in her book one trip Simon took with her husband: 'Sam travelled with George, Simon and a couple of the others by car to Limburg on a certain date to look at the eclipse of the sun. When they arrived at South Limburg there were already a lot of cars in front of an Inn. Sam and his companions went there too...

'The simple woman innkeeper said to them: "I am glad that the eclipse of the sun can be seen exactly from here." The good woman thought that it was the only place it could be seen from and didn't understand that empty stomachs had brought all the guests to the place. The eclipse was over and Sam and the others came home excitedly.'

Simon spent several holidays climbing and walking among the hills and mountains of Switzerland with his good-looking cousin Jacobus, the son of Maurits. Jacobus was a brilliant but eccentric young man, with whom Simon would argue for hours about philosophy. Years later, Simon's second wife Maureen recounted how Simon complained that he found Jacobus challenging. 'He was a genius, very handsome, but he didn't like anyone other than Simon. He knew everything. He was very strange,' she said. 'Simon said it was very difficult to feel at ease with him. But as Simon was one of the few people who could talk on the same level as him, his parents were delighted when they formed such a bond. He pushed Simon intellectually so that was good for Simon, too. Simon said he made him examine all his fundamental ideas; they would talk for hours and Simon said he was always exhausted afterwards.'

Simon also spent holidays in England with Jacob and his family, playing by the seaside at the genteel Essex 'teetotal' town of Frinton, at Margate in Kent or in other 'warmer towns' on the South Coast. Jacob always welcomed his Dutch nephews and nieces, delighting in speaking his own native language.

Herman Marx, the son of Simon's cousin Bertha, remembered one holiday at Jacob's house in Margate: 'Jacob was terribly kind. I arrived at Harwich to find him in a Rolls waiting to meet me. He told me that he had been determined to collect me himself as he could

The beach at Frinton around 1900

talk to me in Dutch – his sons and daughters would complain when he did. He thought he spoke English with only a little accent, but his sons and daughters always said it was a terrible one.

'He was laughing about Simon who was visiting for a few days. [Jacob's son] Albert, who claimed to speak French perfectly, was having problems as Simon proved he wasn't able to.'

The youngsters and their parents found these English seaside holidays boring and constricting. Certain houses were rented and allotted to each of the families – the older and more important members of the family near the sea, the younger ones further away. Later, following Jacob's death in 1934, they would spend more time in the South of France with its fine food, cafes and casinos.

Simon's other holidays included trips with Sam, Betsy and their family, travelling through The Netherlands, looking at beauty spots and learning more about the history of his own country. His interest in art was encouraged by uncle Arnold, a collector of Dutch Masters, who spent hours talking to the youngster about the history of his paintings. Simon would pass on his own love and knowledge of art to the sons and daughters of his cousins. Simon's grandmother Elisabeth also spent time with him, talking about her love of classics and philosophy.

Simon and his cousin Leo (one of Arnold's sons) were both born in 1882 and entered the local elementary school together. When he was 12 years old, Simon began his studies at the Erasmus Gymnasium, where he was followed a few years later by his cousin George. The Erasmus Gymnasium, established in the 16th century, was one of the finest schools in The Netherlands. It had a reputation for high standards in teaching Greek and classics and introduced Simon to the subjects that would have a profound influence on his life.

Simon's governess and nanny Miss Wesley had moved to Rotterdam with the family, devoting all her time to looking after and spoiling him. Old habits didn't change and he relied on her just as much as when he was a small boy. Unfortunately for Simon, his relationship with Leonore (known to all as Leonie) Wesley began to cause problems with his

The Stedelijk Gymnasium in Haarlem where Simon reluctantly started his academc career

school studies. According to Maureen, Simon had been allowed to do much as he wanted, which tended not to be his school work. 'This meant his class grades slumped, so Miss Wesley did his homework when he couldn't manage it, so he could do other things,' she explained.

Unfortunately for Simon, the family discovered what was happening. Disturbed that their son was becoming distracted and not applying himself to his studies, Isaac and Clara decided to send 14-year-old Simon away to school at the Gymnasium in Haarlem. Simon refused to admit he had been doing anything wrong. He couldn't understand why he was being sent away, while his Dutch cousins, with the exception of Leo who was being taught at a 'superior' boarding school, were being educated at schools in Rotterdam.

On one trip with Maureen to The Netherlands in the 1950s, Simon asked Sam's eldest son George if he had known why he had been sent away. 'George burst out laughing at Simon, who was being very serious,' recalled Maureen. 'George said it was because he didn't do his studies and that Miss Wesley had done them instead. The whole family knew about it, although Simon would never admit that was what had happened. George and the others had all been made to go to school and get on with their work.'

In July 1897 Simon took the entrance examination which would allow him to enter the third class of the Stedelijk Gymnasium in Haarlem. The school had six classes, which covered six years. School records show that his parents were right to be worried about his education.

Wilhelminastraat, Harlem, at the turn of the twentieth century

He failed the examination to get into the third class but did pass the exam for the second class, a year lower than the designated one for his age. There was little to indicate that Simon would one day become a respected academic.

On 1 September 1897 Simon, under protest, began his first term at the school, which would cost his parents 50 Guilders per half year. Haarlem was prized as a centre of culture and education. The home of the 17th century artist Frans Hals, the town had many art galleries and schools producing some of the finest Dutch scholars. Yet the young Simon hated being sent away and the change to his lifestyle, particularly the strict regime at school. Bigotry might also have been responsible for this unhappiness, according to his daughter Tamara, who recalled Simon saying he had experienced anti-Semitism at school.

He and two other young boarders stayed with the school's headmaster and rector, Doctor Bernhard Wilhelm Hoffman, at 64 Wilhelminastraat, where he could be strictly supervised and given extra studies to help him catch up with the work he had missed. On 6 September 1901 he moved to live at 33 Oranjekade, the home of Doctor Herman Albertus Jacobus Valkema Blow, a teacher at the school.

Only four of the brothers, (from left) Henry, Arnold, Jacob and Sam, would be directors of the new public company, Van den Berghs Margarine Limited

The School Register lists the exams Simon took during one day: 9.30 Dutch; 9.45 Dutch History; 10.00 Latin; 10.30 German Language; 10.45 History (World); 11.00 Greek; 11.30 Natural History; 11.45 Geography; 12.00 Maths; and finally, at 12.15 French.

Miss Wesley stayed with the family helping to look after Liesje. Simon would remain close to Miss Wesley for the rest of her life and she was considered one of the family, with Clara leaving her money in her will.

Simon left the school in 1902, before taking his final matriculation exams. He had become increasingly interested in languages and the classics. It was now common for members of his generation to study or work abroad, so they could learn new languages. Jacob's eldest son Albert learned French at the family's Marseilles factory and his youngest, Henry, spent several years at Le Rosey school in Switzerland. Simon was drawn towards philosophy, which meant languages would be needed if he wanted to explore philosophies from different cultures. There would be no problem in paying for his studies because the family were financially secure.

New perspectives

In 1895, in response to the lack of funding for Dutch firms on the Amsterdam Stock Market, the family floated the British and Dutch sides of the company as Van den Bergh's Margarine Limited on the British Stock Market. This raised new capital and allowed the family to settle all outstanding bank loans, which had been taken out to expand the business as they brought in chemists and scientists to produce new techniques for manufacturing margarine and develop new types of margarine

The legal structure of the firm changed. The two old partnerships of Simon van den Bergh and Van den Bergh Brothers were bought out by the new company which paid £900,000. Isaac, Jacob, Henry, Arnold and Sam received £450,000 in cash between them plus 90,000 £3 ordinary shares. The wives and daughters of Jacob and Henry, along with several other members of the family, between them bought £50,000 ordinary shares. The change from private partnership to a public company not only created shareholders, but shareholders who were not members of the family.

Although the family retained management control, Jacob Van den Bergh worried that nepotism might have a negative effect on the company. So he laid down a ruling that only two members of each side of the family would be allowed to take up positions on the Board

Advertisement for La Réserve, one
of the many attractions of Nice

of Directors: he and Henry represented the British side; Arnold and Sam, the Dutch. Later one son from each of their families would take up positions with Van den Berghs and subsequently with Unilever.

Isaac remained a member of the Dutch management team but, in line with Jacob's policy, did not join the Board of Directors. His area of responsibility had been the technical side of the business but as qualified architects and technicians were employed, his involvement lessened, particularly as Clara's health declined. In fact changes at home might also have prompted the decision to allow Simon to leave school before passing his final exams. Hoping to find a kinder climate for Clara's health, the couple began to spend more time away from The Netherlands, on long holidays in the South of France where they joined the increasing numbers of travellers from Great Britain, Germany and The Netherlands who visited the French Riviera. This meant Simon was also free to travel.

Nice, with a temperature that rarely dropped below freezing and an average of just 60 days rain a year, had a reputation as a convalescent centre for diseases such as tuberculosis. The American novelist Kay Boyle, ill when she visited the French Riviera, summed up the effect the area had on her health: 'If I was going to die of tuberculosis, it would be easy to die in the white blaze of plaster and stone of the walls that line the precipitous road outside, and in the white and blue blaze of the houses, with the drifting curtains of wisteria hanging at the doors.'

Nice had long attracted the British. The writer Tobias Smollett in 1766 introduced the area to the British public in a series of letters published as *Travels Through France and Italy*, in which he described how the weather affected his spirits: 'There is less rain and wind at Nice than in any other part of the world that I know, and such is the serenity of the air, that you see nothing above your head for several months together, but a charming blue expanse, without cloud or speck. I never saw before such sudden and happy effects from the change of air. I must also acknowledge, that ever since my arrival at Nice, I have breathed more freely than I have done for some years and my spirits have been more alert.'

Smollett's book caught the imagination of its British readers and later those in Ireland and Germany when it was reprinted. Queen Victoria became a frequent visitor, staying at the Hôtel Excelsior Regina. The people of Nice showed their appreciation by naming the grand new walkway bordering the beach the Promenade des Anglais. It became one of the city's main tourist attractions as visitors sat in the cafes watching the daily perambulations of the Nicoise. The first train service from Paris to Nice, taking some 24 hours, was introduced in 1864; by1907 the journey had been cut to 13 hours, making it more accessible to the Dutch. As tourism grew, palm trees were planted along the Promenade, parks landscaped and restaurants, cafes and new hotels built, extending along the front and up into the hills behind. Wealthier long-term visitors – which later included Sam and Betsy – would

View from the eastern hills onto Nice's Port de Limpia and the Rocher du Chateau, from around 1900

build houses in the area known as Rocher du Chateau (Chateau Hill).

Isaac and Clara stayed in smart hotels such as the Royal Riviera. Taking gentle walks along the front, they would listen to bands play in the park or rest in the warm winter sunshine, sitting in wicker chairs surrounded by orange trees and mimosa, breathing the fresh Mediterranean air and exotic fragrances of plants used to make perfumes. Years later their son Simon would move to nearby Monaco and take many of the same walks.

In 1902 Simon was sent to school in Brussels, where he spent a year studying French and German. This was the beginning of an era that would find him wandering around the major universities of Europe, paying to attend classes and launching a life-long love of philosophy. He eventually became the first member of the van den Berghs to earn a Doctorate.

The following year Simon moved to England, where he attended classes at University College, London. He remained there until 1904, staying with his Uncle Jacob and Aunt Lydia who had moved into a large house in Ferndale Road, Hampstead. He also spent time with his Uncle Henry and Aunt Henriette's sons James and Seymour, who were living in lodgings nearby while their parents travelled and began work on renovating their new home in Kensington.

Later, in that large house, 8 Kensington Palace Gardens, Simon first ran into snobbery. Trying to assimilate into English life, Henry and Henrietta were hesitant about entertaining

Medizin, from a series of paintings in the ballroom of the University of Vienna, by the Viennese artist, Gustav Klimt, a key figure in the vibrant cultural and intellectual life of the city when Simon studied there.

their small, 'unfashionable', rather 'exotic'-looking nephew. Their own tall fair sons had been educated at the best English public schools and attended Oxford and Cambridge Universities. Maureen recounted Simon's description of what happened: 'Simon came over as a student and of course he had black curly hair and some suit made by a Dutch tailor, which wasn't up to Savile Row. Aunt Henrietta invited him round to their house in Kensington Palace Gardens, no other visitors were there. Her first greeting to him was, "You must change your name." "Why?" "It's a Jewish name." That didn't make him like them any better. They were terrible snobs, Henrietta and Henry. After a while he was invited to something at their house and somebody said to Aunt Henrietta, "Who is that young man?" She said, "that's my nephew" and the guest replied, "Oh, he looks like an artist". So then Simon was allowed to pass as an unkempt young man.'

Henry and Henriette's attitude to their nephew was typical of English attitudes towards the Dutch. Travel writer George Wharton Edwards in his book *Holland of Today*, published in 1909, tried to convince the English that the Dutch were as cultured as they were: 'The visitor to The Netherlands must not be misled as to the character of the upper classes or judge them in any way by those whom he meets in hotels or conveyances. The Dutch gentleman and lady are far removed from these. They are highly educated and their manners are those of the upper classes of the English. The young men are always sent to the university, and the young girls are most highly accomplished with a knowledge of art and music and generally speaking French, Italian and English.'

In the winter of 1904 Simon moved to the University of Vienna, the oldest university in the German-speaking world. It was founded on 12 March 1365 by Duke Rudolph IV. The university had a liberal attitude to its students' backgrounds and a high academic reputation, after the revolution of 1848 granted 'freedom of research and research-based education'. The Faculty of Philosophy became particularly highly regarded and in 1897 was the first faculty to admit women. This was where Simon spent one term attending lectures, in a city alive with ground-breaking artists such as Gustav Klimt, and thinkers such as Sigmund Freud.

In July 1904 he returned to The Netherlands to take his final matriculation exams at the University of Utrecht. This would enable him to formally enter university and begin his studies in earnest. In the introduction to his Doctorate, later to be submitted to the University of Freiburg, Simon refers to having attended Utrecht University to take his 'Reifezeugnis', the entrance exam to German Universities. Further reference to Utrecht is

Gruss aus Berlin

Serie: Berliner Momentaufnahmen.

A 1903 postcard from Berlin, one of Germany's prosperous and fashionable cities, where Simon moved to continue his studies

dropped in his printed Dissertation. It was not unusual for students to take their final exams at a different university from the one where they started their studies.

Simon did not want to study at a Dutch University, where he would be writing in a little-used language. The most important schools in philosophy, and oriental philosophy in particular, had recently been established at German universities. Since its unification in 1871, Germany had prospered. In *The Proud Tower* Barbara Tuchman, the American self-trained historian and author, described the vigour in which Germany had embraced its new found wealth: 'Energies were let loose on the development of physical resources. Germany in the nineties was enjoying the first half of a 25-year period in which her national income doubled, population increased by 50 per cent, railroad-track mileage by 50 per cent, cities sprang up, colonies were acquired, giant industries took shape, wealth accumulated from their enterprises and the rise in employment kept pace. German universities and technical schools were the most admired, German methods the most thorough, German philosophers dominant.'

In 1905 Simon moved to Munich to continue his studies in philosophy under Professors Hans Cornelius and Theodor Lipps. Cornelius was born in Munich in 1863 and had recently been promoted to Professor of Philosophy. In 1910 he moved to the Academy for Social Sciences, which would become a department in the new University of Frankfurt. Lipps had become Professor of Philosophy in 1894 and was highly influential.

From Munich, Simon transferred to Berlin, where he spent a year studying philosophy under Professor Carl Stumpf, another influential German academic. Born in 1848 in Wiesentheid, Bavaria, Stumpf was Professor of Philosophy at Berlin University from 1894 to 1921. Before that he had been Professor at the Universities of Wurzburg, Prague, Halle and Munich. From 1907 to 1908 he was Rector of Berlin University. The fact that Simon was admitted to lectures by Professor Stumpf signifies that he was determined to study a wide spectrum of philosophical movements and the Professor recognised that Simon had the ability to understand new theories.

But in 1907 Simon's travels and studies were interrupted when the family lost both its patriarch and matriarch in the space of three days.

Chapter 4   The end of an era

 Done of the last great family gatherings was organised in October 1904 to celebrate Simon and Elisabeth's Diamond wedding anniversary. Worried that the old couple might get tired, the family decided to limit the numbers to just one or two grandchildren from each of the seven families. Simon, who was attending lectures at University College, London, travelled to The Netherlands with his Uncle Jacob and Aunt Lydia, and their eldest son Albert, with whom he was staying. Uncle Henry, his wife Henriette and their eldest son Donald also made the journey.

A family dinner was held at a table decorated with flowers. Dressed in their finest clothes, Simon and Elisabeth sat side by side at the head of the table. Sam described the celebrations in his book: 'The good old folks sat in finest feast array with their children at a festive dinner. They were still active and brisk. A look at the photograph taken of them and their seven sons and daughters-in-law on that day shows clearly that in the course of the ten years that had elapsed since they had all been photographed last, the old people had changed the least of all.'

That morning, the staff at the factory presented them with a 'memorial window', depicting Simon and Elisabeth surrounded by the attributes of 'Labour', 'Prosperity' and 'Abundance'. After dinner the staff surprised the old couple by holding a concert outside the house. Simon and Elisabeth, dressed in their warmest clothes, were escorted onto their balcony to be serenaded by some 1,200 employees who paraded past the house escorted by mounted police and a band consisting of workers from one of Arnold van den Bergh's factories.

In an article in the liberal daily newspaper, *Nieuwe Rotterdamsche Courant* on 3 November 1904, the sixtieth anniversary of the couple's religious wedding ceremony, a journalist provided an insight into Simon and Elisabeth's later years: 'On entering the marble vestibule to visit them, you are generally referred by the veteran servant to the little, quiet backroom with an outlook on very beautiful gardens. By preference the old people sit together in this

The stained glass window presented to Simon and Elisabeth by factory staff

Opposite: Simon and Elisabeth in 1904

Parents, brothers and their wives at Simon and Elizabeth's Diamond wedding anniversary. Back row (from left): Isaac, Henriette, Arnold, Sam, Betsy, Zadok, Maurits, Jacob. Front row: Clara, Henry, Julie, Line, Elisabeth, Etty, Simon, Lydia

little room, where they feel themselves safe from the noises of the busy commercial town. The old lady, generally calmly resting in a low armchair, placed early in the morning at the window to have a view of the white doves returning to the shading trees after their morning flight. She wears a black lace cap over the white bandeau, resting in wide plaits along her wrinkled face over her ears. The gentle dark brown eyes glow quite brightly in her lively face, calmed by age.'

In his report, the journalist went on to describe the role Simon played among the Jewish community: 'The old gentleman is more alert and brisk, full of courtly attentions to his wife, to whom walking begins to be troublesome. He is always dressed neatly in black frock-coat and black smoking cap, and his finely-cut, spirited features are adorned with a well-groomed nice little beard.

'Weather allowing, the Father takes his morning walk generally towards the institution (Montefiore) where, for his banished co-religionists, a friendly home is provided, till their departure to far-off lands of their own. He usually finds advice and always a good word of consolation arising from his sensitive heart. If no material help can be applied, if one of the family of an emigrant is rejected and refused in sight of the golden gates of his ideals, in order to return lonely to the misery of the cruel race-hatred, then the old man is so disturbed that he cannot sleep for nights, and sits for days to think dejectedly over the poor wretches.'

Elisabeth, ageing more rapidly than her husband, began to feel ill before the end of 1906. Diagnosed with cancer of the stomach, she was operated on in February 1907. She recovered from the operation, but her health continued to decline and she became an invalid needing constant nursing. In his book, a distressed Sam wrote: 'When we saw that little shrivelled old woman lying in bed complaining of pains in her arms, legs and also internally, who had to be moved every few minutes, and who so easily could be carried in the arms from the bed to the couch, our thoughts went sometimes back over the 60 years that the same woman had braved the storms of life, not disheartened by the heaviest misfortunes, who had been to her husband and children a prop and a stay in the struggle for existence.'

Simon refused to leave his wife's bedside. In March, he began to complain of a terrible pain in his mouth. Isaac and Clara were on holiday in the South of France when they heard that he had also been diagnosed with cancer. On the night of Sunday 31 March 1907, a tumour was removed from inside Simon's mouth. Reassured by Jacob and Sam that Simon was recovering well, Isaac and Clara decided to continue their holiday. But on 2 April, hearing that his condition had deteriorated, they rushed back home. At 5pm on 6 April, at the age of 87, Simon, with his seven sons by his side, died.

Two days later, following Jewish practice, the whole family, including his grandson Simon, gathered in Rotterdam for the funeral of the head of the family and the founder of the van den Bergh business. A funeral procession of some 30 carriages followed the hearse as it made its way slowly to the Israelite Cemetery at Oud-Kralingen on the outskirts of Rotterdam. The cortege passed the Boompjes synagogue, where before his death Simon had requested it should halt. The Chief Rabbi, Dr Ritter, and members of the synagogue's governing council waited at the open doors of the synagogue; inside candles burned in the dark. The whole of the congregation fell in line behind them and followed Simon's coffin to the cemetery.

An enormous crowd of mourners, Jews and non-Jews, waited at the graveyard. Representatives of the many charities Simon supported and from all branches and subsidiaries of the company had come to pay homage to the man who founded an enterprise that had made its mark on the world. Prayers said, his body was lowered into the grave. His sons and grandsons scattered earth on the coffin. The only speech came from his son Zadok, who expressed the family's deep gratitude to those who had come from so far away: 'You have made his funeral, a beautiful funeral, befitting his beautiful, well-spent life.'

The brothers returned to their parents' house. Their wives and daughters had remained at home with Elisabeth who, because of her illness, had not been told of her husband's death. The day before she had suddenly and surprisingly rallied, holding court in her bedroom, talking of the old days, even asking about the business. But Elisabeth's condition was so delicate, the family had not wanted to endanger it further by telling her Simon had died.

Sam described the scene: 'When the first two carriages of the procession, in which the seven brothers and the Chief Rabbi were seated, reached the house of the deceased, there did not reign the stillness customary after such ceremonies. Terror lay on the faces of all. The sons were to mount immediately to their Mother's bedroom, where they found her dying...'

Her sons, joined by three of her eldest grandsons, Albert, Leo and Simon, as requested by Elisabeth, stood around her bed as she died. Neither Simon nor Elisabeth had wished to outlive the other. Their mutual devotion had caught the attention of the reporter from the *Nieuwe Rotterdamsche Courant*, whose article noted: 'The old people keep inseparably together, for the course of their long lives has woven them into one, through all of their works, all of their cares, their sincere love, their mutual unselfishness and their prosperity. They have lived one life together and live it out together.' They had told the reporter: 'When it shall be the will of the Lord to call one of us two to him, may the other follow soon'. This was

Simon and Elisabeth's joint grave in the Jewish cemetary in Rotterdam

their last ideal, their fervent prayer.

A heartbroken Sam wrote: 'Thus the wish of both of them had been fulfilled. How often had they told us that, when the time would come, they only prayed that they did not long outlive one another. That providence would even save them the bitterness of separation, that they would remain altogether unaware of each other's departure, not even they themselves could have hoped.' For the second time the sons gathered at the cemetery. Sam poignantly remarked that 'the brothers had lost their parental home for good'.

Simon and Elisabeth had met as children. They married young and spent the early years of their marriage in the little village of Geffen. They had brought up and educated their sons in the town of Oss; and had grown old in Rotterdam. Their honeymoon had been spent in a wagon travelling from Oss to Geffen; those of their sons had been spent in Paris and London. Their first years of marriage had been spent in a cottage, their last years in an elegant terraced townhouse. Their sons lived in grand houses in England and The Netherlands. Simon had travelled miles on horseback or in a wagon bartering goods for butter; his sons now travelled in carriages driven by coachmen, or in cars or trains.

Simon and Elisabeth had worked with five of their sons to set up van den Berghs, a small family-run concern, which became one of the largest producers of margarine in Europe. All their sons had been successful. They had married and had children; now they in turn had become grandparents. Jacob had started his own dynasty of nine children, seven of whom had married into other Jewish families who were either linked to van den Berghs by business or who ran successful companies of their own. Alliances through marriage had been made with the Godfrey Phillips Tobacco Company, the van Zwanenbergs (one of the biggest firms of butchers who also originated from Oss) and with the family solicitors, the Coopmans, into whose family Jacob's youngest daughter Kathleen had married.

In their will, Simon and Elisabeth expressed their fervent wish that their sons 'should let' their daughters marry Jewish men. The Jewish religion is passed down through the mother of a family so the words 'should let' would have been interpreted to mean that the daughters would be expected to marry Jews, thus continuing the faith.

Few of the family abided by the strict confines of Judaism. Few kept kosher homes, some only paid lip service to being members of the Jewish community. Assimilation into British and Dutch society entailed a loosening of ties to Simon and Elisabeth's orthodox Jewish roots. Increased wealth and changes in managing the company meant that many of the sons' interests had changed.

Elisabeth's wishes were followed by some, but not all, of the sons. Simon and Elisabeth

Jacob's daughter Mabel and John Benjamin Sainsbury photographed after their engagement

were alive when Jacob's daughter Mabel married a non-Jew, John Benjamin Sainsbury, in 1896. Mabel and John's sons and grandchildren would be brought up in the Church of England and know little about their Jewish heritage. Jacob demonstrated his support for his daughter by giving her a dowry which granted the Sainsbury family a licence to sell Van den Bergh margarine and bacon directly, without going through agents. He also helped Sainsburys organise their distribution service. In 1908, Jacob would again show his tolerance and love for his family by agreeing to act as witness to his youngest son Henry when he left the Jewish faith to marry the Scottish Presbyterian Enid Macdonald Brown, in a register office. In 1930, Jacob's brother Henry would, however, disinherit his daughter Elisabeth when she married out of the faith.

The brothers found it difficult to honour Elisabeth's other request that they should always meet at the couple's graveside on the anniversary of their deaths. The brothers' affection for each other continued but the ties would gradually weaken as geography and war made it physically impossible for them to meet.

Isaac, Arnold and Sam had remained close to their parents in Rotterdam. Now they no longer needed to live near the factory. Just as they had outgrown the town of Oss, the brothers had now outgrown the brash noisy industrial life of Rotterdam. They wanted quieter lives in a more sophisticated city where they could enjoy some of the luxuries and comforts they had earned.

Comfort and modernity

The three brothers moved out of Rotterdam, into large houses near The Hague. Considered by many the most cosmopolitan of all Dutch cities, The Hague had for centuries been the favourite residence of the Dutch royal family and the seat of government. The English novelist William Thackeray, writing in the mid-1800s in his *Notes of a Week's Holiday*, published in Punch magazine, praised the city as being: 'the prettiest little brick city, with the pleasantest park to ride in, the neatest, comfortable people walking about, canals not unsweet, and busy and picturesque with old-world life.'

By 1909 the population of The Hague, and its affluent seaside suburb of Scheveningen, was recorded as being 250,000 – some 70,000 less than Rotterdam. Built among woodland, with palaces and large houses clustered around a lake, The

Delegates at the First International Peace Conference in Queen Wilhelmina's Palace at The Hague

The affluent seaside suburb of Scheveningen, The Hague, at the beginning of the 20th century

Hague attracted the wealthy, diplomats and lovers of fine art, gaiety and life. Queen Wilhelmina raised the profile of the city when she allowed representatives of the countries involved in the First International Peace Conference in 1899 to hold their meetings in the Orange room of her palace. Since then The Hague has been synonymous with international organisations and meetings aimed at furthering peace, human rights and international justice.

Sam van den Bergh and his wife Betsy had bought a weekend house outside Rotterdam but it could no longer accommodate their growing family, so they moved into a house at the seaside suburb of Wassenaar. The large house, surrounded by extensive gardens, would become a centre for discussion and be used to hold conferences on women's suffrage and world peace.

Arnold, infamous in the family for his love of large houses, built a new one, topped by a strangely designed domed roof which gave it the nickname 'the butter dish'. The house was large enough to contain an art gallery, which enabled Arnold to continue to build his collection of paintings, including Canalletos, Vermeers and Rembrandts. Successive generations of van den Berghs would become major collectors and patrons of the arts.

In 1907, Isaac, Clara and their disabled daughter Liesje moved to 15A Van Stockweg in Scheveningen. The house had been built in 1892 and named Villa Hermina after its original owners' daughter. Isaac renamed it the Villa Lisa after his own. It cost him 68,000 Guilders, now worth some £296,500. The square, red-bricked house contained a 'built in' apartment in which Liesje lived with Catharina Siebenga, a private nurse employed to look after her. Born in Middelburg in 1877, Catharina moved from Utrecht to join the family's household on 26 July 1906. She was to live with the family until 20 July, 1911. Over the course of some 10 years, 40 servants were recorded as working for Isaac and Clara.

In the census of 1908, Isaac, Clara, Liesje and 26-year-old Simon are all recorded as living in the house. The entry notes that Simon was away from home at that time. In fact, he was to spend little time there.

Clara's health was gradually deteriorating, with an increase in heart problems. Anxious about what would happen after they died, Isaac and Clara had already decided to make her a ward of court, which had been confirmed on 23 October 1905 by the District Court of Rotterdam, when Liesje was 24. Financial arrangements were put in place to make sure she would be taken care of. Wills made by both Isaac and Clara in 1909 included details of the trusts set up for their heirs. On her death, residue from Liesje's trust was to pass to Simon.

Equipped with all the latest electrical equipment, the house at Scheveningen personified the new modernism. Clara was particularly proud of the electric crystal chandeliers in the halls and reception rooms and listed all of them in her will. Telephones were installed and a new gramophone, brought as a present from London by Sam, played quietly in the drawing room, or was moved into Clara's morning room.

The van den Berghs settled into the lifestyle of the newly rich sophisticated Dutch, with trips to fashionable shops, which vied with those in Paris, and visits to The Mauritshuis art gallery and the Gevangenpoort, an ancient tower and historic prison, or to the municipal museum, regarded as one of the finest in The Netherlands.

The daily life of the Dutch 'bourgeoisie', was described in a 1909 guidebook to The Netherlands: 'Breakfast is generally ready at eight o'clock. A mahogany bucket lined with metal and containing peat embers, in which a brass kettle is kept singing, is always placed beside every Dutch breakfast table; it appears too at five o'clock tea as well as after dinner in the drawing room. At breakfast one eats lightly as a rule, bread and butter with a thin slice of gingerbread making a sandwich. There are tea and coffee, and eggs are boiled, generally in an old-fashioned net on a ring, which is dipped into the kettle. After breakfast women gather in the garden to cull the roses. After lunch there is much driving, and afternoon calls are general.

'In the evening at the club the gentlemen congregate for an hour or so before dinner, at which the 'Borreltje' or gin and bitters is in evidence. As a rule, dinner is served at any time between six and half-past seven, and this is a formal potato purée or bouillon flavoured with chervil, and containing balls of veal force meat, and there will be water bass from the canal which are served up in a deep dish in the water in which they are boiled, and parsley flavoured. This is served with thin sandwiches of rye bread. Next comes, generally, roast or stewed veal. The vegetables are potatoes with butter, boiled endives and breadcrumbed cabbage.

'Then there will be partridge or some other game. The dessert is mostly French sweets or tarts, but sometimes English jam is served. Dessert over, both ladies and gentlemen return together to the drawing-room for coffee, which is served in the smallest and most precious of blue china, which is generally kept behind cabinet doors. Then come liqueurs, cognac and aniseed, this latter being the favourite. During the evening callers are entertained, after which tea is served, the mahogany peat bucket and its kettle having been placed by the footman as usual beside the table.'

Isaac and Clara enjoyed their lifestyle but Simon found it tedious. In the winter term of 1907-08 he left home to begin studies for his Doctorate in Germany. Dutch and German

A fanciful 14th-century Italian pen and ink drawing of the Arabic scholar Averroës (1126-98) in conversation with the Ancient Greek philosopher, Porphyry (circa 232-305)

Jews, especially wealthy ones, now had more opportunities to travel and study. German universities were finally opening their doors to Jewish students, whose fees were very welcome.

The seeker of knowledge

Simon set about accumulating the knowledge that would give him a rounded understanding of philosophy and languages. He had spent several years travelling around Europe, as a visiting student at major universities in Germany, Austria and Great Britain. He also journeyed to Ireland, spending time at Dublin's Trinity College library, with its extensive collection of oriental and Arabic papers. The green Wicklow Mountains provided him with the walks he loved and the Dublin bars with stimulating conversation and music. He would become a frequent visitor to the country, eventually becoming one of the first to sponsor events at the Wexford Music Festival.

Ancient Greek was a very important part of his studies and interests. He gradually expanded his research into Arabic Philosophy, which had acted as a conduit in keeping alive and introducing Ancient Greek to Western culture, and which in turn had many associations with Judaism. Until 1873 only three universities in Europe taught Islamic (or Oriental) philosophy. These were Paris, Oxford and Zurich. One of the first schools of Arabic language and philosophy was set up at the Sorbonne in Paris during the Middle Ages. By the time Simon began to study the works of Averroës (see page 61), other European Universities were taking tentative steps to set up their own departments.

As Simon commenced his studies, Germany's universities were undergoing one of their golden periods. The German authorities, in their quest for world cultural leadership, supported experimentation with new ideas – by Jews and non-Jews alike. German Jews felt there was a strong link between the Jewish rationalising spirit and the liberalising aims of modern Germany in attempting to devise and apply rational solutions to social, economic and philosophical problems. From the early 1830s onwards, Jews began entering universities as students and more slowly as professors. They responded to this new intellectual stimulus by helping to establish world-class schools of medicine, science and philosophy.

The interest in Orientalism, as it became known in Germany, began in 1874-75. It was introduced as a subject by Professor Friedrich Delitzsch, who was a co-founder of the German Oriental Society and founded a dedicated school at Berlin University. He established the first chair in what became known as Assyrian Studies, to which Professor Eberhard Schrader, previously Lecturer in the Old Testament at Vienna University, was appointed. Schrader was responsible for connecting the Assyrian alphabet and script with the Old Testament. Simon realised that he needed to learn all the nuances of the different Arabic grammatical structures if he was going to understand Arabic philosophy and study the works of Averroës. Professor Hermann Reckendorf wrote and taught Arabic syntax at

The main entrance to Freiburg University today, flanked by statues of Homer (left) and Aristotle (right)

Freiburg University, so Simon decided to study under him.

Albert-Ludwig University in Freiburg, one of the oldest universities in Germany, was founded by Archduke Albrecht IV of Austria in 1457. Built on the western edge of the Black Forest, a conservative area dominated by the Catholic Church, the University's first faculties were theology, law, medicine and philosophy. They were established by Archduke Albrecht to provide legal staff for the administration of his province, as well as recruits for the Catholic Church. The University's reputation as a bastion of the Catholic faith was established in 1620, when Jesuits joined the teaching staff and were put in charge of many university departments. This adherence to the church was still very much in evidence when Simon began his studies.

New branches of scholarship were opened up by the university reforms of Empress Maria Theresa (1717-80) which lessened the power of the church in higher education. In 1820, Grand Duke Ludwig of Baden arranged an endowment for the university to safeguard its financial future. In return he was celebrated as a second founder and to this day the Albert-Ludwig University of Freiburg honours both Albert (the Latinised spelling of Albrecht) and Ludwig in its name. The university earned a reputation for being secular and tolerant. Modern languages, dancing and fencing were added to the curriculum as the university sought to entice the scions of the German landed class to its establishment.

The university expanded with the foundation of the German Empire in 1871 and students from northern Germany enrolled in new courses. Departments differentiated themselves from each other and became more specialised. Clinics and institutes for scientific sciences – which ranged from biology and chemistry to pharmacy and mathematics – were founded on their own campus in North Freiburg. In 1870, 200 students enrolled at the university; 15 years later this figure had grown to 1,000. In 1904, three years before Simon arrived, there were 2,000 students.

Freiburg was typical of German universities, with various fraternities set up to reflect the traditions and aspirations of young German gentlemen. Scars on faces from duels were still looked on as proof of manhood. Noisy students drinking in beer gardens, singing raucous nationalist songs, were common. Germany was feeling wealthy and success was reflected among its young men, many of them sons of old Prussian army stock. At the same time, a generation of young idealists interested in new ideas and new cultures were beginning to make their mark, as they argued about politics and philosophy. To a student from the peaceful Netherlands, the atmosphere was exhilarating, as well as chilling.

Simon followed the practice, accepted in Germany, of beginning work on a doctorate without obtaining a first degree. Students wishing to pursue a particular topic would attend classes by a junior member of the faculty for one or two years in the hopes of raising enough interest from a professor, who would then support his application to take a doctorate. A Privatdozent (assistant professor) would encourage students to join his classes because their posts were usually unsalaried and their income depended upon the number of students they could attract. Simon would later hold a similar unpaid position in Paris.

Simon's years of studying in London, Vienna and Berlin had brought him to the attention of Professor Reckendorf. A Jew, born in Heidelberg in 1863, Reckendorf had been educated in Berlin and Heidelberg, taking his degree in Leipzig. In 1898, he became Privatdozent at Freiburg. He was appointed Professor at Freiburg in 1908, a role he was to hold until his death in 1924. His major book *Die Syntaktischen Verhaltnisse Des Arabischen: Nachdruck Der Erstausgab* was published by Brill in Leiden in 1898. It is still used as a textbook in universities.

Reckendorf took Simon under his wing and planned his syllabus. A 'Certificate of Attendance' drawn up in 1909 by the University of Freiburg lists which subjects Simon had studied over the previous two years. These ranged from the English poetry of Percy Bysshe Shelley, John Keats and Geoffrey Chaucer to Babylonian culture; and from the romantic poets to Dante. In 1909, as part of his studies, Simon was sent back to the University of Berlin (now Humbolt University) to study Orientalism under Professors Barth, Freidrich Delitzsch, Adolf Erman, Hartmann, Eugen Mittwoch and Eduard Sachau. Each specialised in different aspects of orientalism, which would augment those he studied at Freiburg. They would furnish him with the knowledge of subjects such as religion, oriental philosophy and languages that he would need to begin to understand the work of Averroës.

A postcard from liberal Berlin at the turn of the 20th-century

Simon studied religious philosophy under Professor Barth. Born in 1851 in Flechingen/Baden, Barth studied the bible and religious philosophy at a Rabbinical Seminary in Berlin. In 1876 he took his degree at Berlin and became assistant Professor. Simon's understanding of ancient Egyptian text and languages would come from Professor Adolf Erman. A Catholic born on 31 October 1854 in Berlin, Erman had begun his studies in Leipzig, before moving back to Berlin, where he became a professor at the university, establishing a school of Egyptian grammar. A member of the German Reform Church, he was also a Director of the Egyptian Department of the Berlin Museum. Erman was an honorary member of the Munich, Vienna, Budapest, Göttingen, Copenhagen, Stockholm and British Academies. He died in 1937.

Eugen Mittwoch, born on 4 December 1876, taught Simon Arabic language and Hebrew philosophy, in which he was a renowned expert. Simon was particularly close to Mittwoch and the men would keep in contact until Mittwoch's death. Privatdozent, lecturer and, from 1905 to 1917, Assistant Professor at Berlin University, in 1917, Mittwoch moved to Greifswald University where he remained Professor until 1919. He returned to Berlin University in 1920 when he became Professor and Director at the Centre for Oriental Studies.

Mittwoch remained at Berlin until 1933, when as a Jew he was sacked from his job. He is

'I'm ready!': Kaiser Wilheim II
sharpening his sword in a caricature
from *L'Assiette au Beurre*,1908

featured in the *Notgemeinschaft Deutscher Wissenschaftler im Ausland* (*Displaced Scholars*, Bogo Press, 1993), originally published in 1936, which listed academics still living in Germany who had been dismissed from their positions. In 1938 he escaped to France, where he taught alongside Simon at the École des hautes études. On the outbreak of the Second World War, Mittwoch moved to England and worked for the BBC and MI5. He died in 1942.

Professor Freidrich Delitzsch supervised Simon's studies in Assyriology. Delitzsch was born in 1850 in Leipzig. Helping Simon understand the philosophy behind translating and the Arabic language was Professor Eduard Sachau. Born in Neumunster in 1845, Sachau had earned his reputation by translating Arabic science, philosophy and geography.

Simon's time at the University of Berlin was one of the most influential in his life, when he would experience the tensions between the new militarism and old traditions of liberalism, and between Berlin and the rest of the country. Berlin was beginning to establish itself as a vibrant centre for art and culture. From the mid-19th century onwards, the population had grown rapidly from 400,000 in 1849 to 2,040,148 in 1905. Berlin had flourished as the Prussian Government subsidised extensive building projects. New cities breed new ideas and Berlin rebelled against Kaiser Wilhelm II's nationalistic agenda with its conservative cultural tastes, becoming a model for 20th-century cultural modernism.

In her book *The Proud Tower* Barbara Tuchman wrote: 'The Germany of intellect and sentiment, the Liberal Germany had withdrawn from the arena, content to despise militarism and materialism and sulk in a tent of superior spiritual values. Its representatives were a caste of professors, clergy, doctors and lawyers who regarded themselves as the Geist-aristokratie (aristocracy of the mind) superior to the vulgar rich, the vulgar nobility and the vulgar masses.'

Tuchman described how one professor of philosophy, whose rooms overlooked Unter den Linden in the centre of Berlin, stopped his lectures at the sound of a military band playing during the changing of the guard and stood motionless to demonstrate his disgust until the noise faded away. Berliners earned themselves the fury of Kaiser Wilhelm II (1859-1941) when they reacted against the vulgarity of his aristocracy by renaming the Siegesallee (Victory Avenue), which was lined with statues of past kings, knights and generals, as the Puppenallee (Avenue of the Dummies).

Simon was in Berlin during the university's centennial celebrations in 1910 and witnessed the collision of the worlds of intellectualism and militarism. Tuchman wrote: 'The two Germanys met when the academic community found itself invaded by their fierce moustachioed monarch in the golden cuirass [armour] and golden-eagled helmet of the Garde du Corps, with the retinue in gorgeous uniform, heralded by the terrific blasts of a trombone choir.

Satisfied that the Kaiser "looked even worse than his caricatures", the audience consoled itself with the thought that such an intrusion could not trouble their halls again for another hundred years.'

Rights and recognition

The emancipation of German Jews had been a slow and gradual process, which had finally received legal endorsement with the unification of the German States in 1871. The Emancipation Law of that year applied to the whole realm and abolished all restrictions on civil and political rights derived from 'religious difference'.

German Jews could hold jobs and professions without having to compromise their religion. Writing in his *History of the Jews*, Heinrich Graetz ends his eleventh and final volume, published in 1870, on a note of triumph: 'I may conclude my history in the joyous feeling that in the civilised world the Jewish tribe has found not only justice and freedom but also recognition. It now finally has unlimited freedom to develop its talents, not due to (Gentile) mercy but as a right acquired through thousandfold suffering.'

Integration into German society had come through economic success and participation in a new German culture. Berlin's urban lifestyle, with its papers, journals, art galleries, theatres and discussion groups, offered a new stimulus for the more sophisticated assimilated Jews. They embraced a modernism that enabled them to enter a society that welcomed their support.

In Berlin, Jews like Paul Cassirer and his cousin Bruno – later friends of Simon's – owned art galleries and were publishers. Herwerth Walden promoted avant-garde art and literature in his newspaper *Der Sturm*. Jews served on the boards of museums and galleries that exhibited modern and contemporary art. Leading artists, including Max Klinger and Max Liebermann, and poets, historians and critics attended the semi-private salons set up by wealthy Jewish families such as the Bernsteins and the Cassirers. Café life flourished as poets, writers and artists argued and discussed their work. Theatre director Max Reinhardt, who was also Professor of German Theatre at Berlin University, and Ernst Lubitsch, making his name in the new art form of film, pioneered fresh ideas. All this was seized upon by young men and women excited about how Germany was allowing Jews to influence cultural life.

In these Jewish circles Simon met and made friends who offered him intellectual stimulus and were to play a significant part in his life. One such friend was Eugen Marx, who Simon met during his earlier stay in Berlin. A young German Jewish medical student, Marx had taken his exams at Utrecht and was studying for his doctorate in Berlin. He went on to become one of The Netherlands' most eminent eye surgeons and to surprise Simon by marrying his cousin Bertha (Arnold's daughter).

Simon did not approve of the engagement, warning his friend that Bertha was not intelligent enough to provide him with intellectual companionship. Eugen ignored his friend's advice and married Bertha in 1908. According to their son Herman, Simon's fears were unfounded and the couple enjoyed a happy, successful married life. 'Simon was wrong,' said Herman, 'she may not have been as intellectual as my father but their marriage, unlike

The influential filmmaker, Ernst Lubitsch, one of many Berlin Jews who were influencing cultural life in the late 19th and early 20th century

Simon's Sunday afternoons were often spent talking with friends in Berlin's Tiergarten, pictured here in 1912

Simon's, was very good. They were very happy.'

Parks in the summer and cafés in the winter were an important part of young Jews' lives, where they could socialise with non-Jewish friends away from the inhibitions of homes and parents. Simon and his friends spent their Sunday afternoons in the Tiergarten, sitting by the bandstand, listening to the resident group of moustachioed gentlemen musicians play the overture from Rossini's *Thieving Magpie*, the favourite music for Berliners to relax to as they walked around dressed in their 'Sunday best' clothes. They would talk about current developments in philosophy and admire the 'chic' young women dressed in their flowing long gowns with fashionable hats planted on beautifully coiffured hair. Or they might watch families walking around nodding their hellos to each other; stopping to talk about the latest scandals and admire each other's babies. Years later the families would run away as thugs dressed in brown paraded through the gardens shouting Nazi slogans

It was here that Simon met and became close friends with the philosopher and science historian Professor Alexandre Koyré and his wife. Born in 1892 in the Ukraine, then part of Russia, Koyré would play a particularly significant part in Simon's life by helping him establish his professional reputation.

On 6 July 1911 Professor Reckendorf, Simon's academic supervisor, wrote formally to Freiburg University asking them to accept Simon's paper for his Doctorate. The paper was finally submitted on 11 October, with a supporting report attached from Professor Reckendorf. The application was signed in support by Simon's other professors and was accompanied by his curriculum vitae and a certificate attesting to his syllabus. The doctorate would be printed and published in 1912 by the Dutch publishers Brill in Leiden, and lodged in Freiburg, Madrid and Leiden.

In Simon's curriculum vitae, he thanked his academic benefactor Professor Reckendorf. He also wrote that in 1910 he had married Sonia Pokrojski from Russia.

Averroës: a source of inspiration

SCIENCE, MATHEMATICS, MEDICAL theory, astronomy and philosophy were subjects the Arab world introduced, or had made available, to the Western world. Arab thinkers were excited about the diversity of theoretical perspectives, particularly when connected with specific Islamic areas of enquiry such as law and theology. Medieval Jewish philosophers, including Yehuda Halevi and Moses Maimonides, had worked under Moorish rule, within the traditions of Islamic philosophy, contributing to the cultural exchange of ideas while maintaining their religious identity.

Cultures influenced each other. The Arab world had been responsible for keeping alive Ancient Greek culture and introducing it to Western Europe. Many Greek terms were translated into Arabic, with its own distinct cultural context; secular aspects of Greek culture suddenly became Arabic terms with a religious force in Islamic philosophy.

Aristotle (384-22 BC) had introduced the systematic study of logic, developing a system for describing and assessing reasoning that remained at the core of the discipline until the nineteenth century. Contemporary categorical grammar can be traced to Aristotle's interest in the functioning of words, giving him a special place in philosophical logic and linguistics. He discussed the soul, or psyche; that which makes something alive and capable of the activities characteristic of being. In claiming that the psyche is dependent upon the body, he anticipated the mind/body debate which continues to this day.

Aristotle's writings were neglected for long periods but revived in the first century BC. Scholars then studied and commented on Aristotle continuously in the ancient world. After the fall of the Roman Empire, his works – apart from a few essays translated into Latin – were lost to Europe because scholars could no longer read Ancient Greek. Aristotle's work was rediscovered by medieval Arab scholars, notably Averroës, and translated into Latin. This shaped the development of medieval thought in the arts and sciences.

Averroës was the Spanish name of Ibn Rushd, the Islamic philosopher who wrote a series of commentaries on Aristotle, which provided a guide to his texts and were influential in the Christian world from the 13th century onwards. Averroës was born in Cordoba, Spain in 1126 and was to have a greater effect upon Jews and Christians than in his own Muslim world. He considered Aristotle's works the highest achievement of philosophy and his

voluminous commentaries were important in introducing Aristotle's thought to Christian scholars. Averroës' writings became the subject of Simon Van den Bergh's lifetime work. He would write books that would not only translate Averroës' writings, but would also attempt to explain and discuss the meanings within the texts.

Averroës was a polymath and leader in: early Islamic philosophy, theology, law and jurisprudence; logic; psychology; Arabic music theory; and the sciences of medicine, astronomy, geography, mathematics and physics. He practised law and became Chief Qadi (judge) of Cordoba (a position also held by his grandfather). Later he became personal physician to the Caliph Abu Ya'qub Yusuf and his son Abu Yusuf Ya'qub. Averroës' defence of philosophy was often controversial and provoked opposition from clerics and jurists, resulting in his banishment to North Africa, although he was later rehabilitated.

During his life, Averroës wrote a number of scientific, philosophical, astrological and religious works. These included the medical encyclopedia *Kulliyat* (or *Colliget* in Latin). His major religious philosophy book was *Tahāfut al-Tahāfut* (*The Incoherence of the Incoherence*), which defends the use of Ancient Greek philosophy, particularly that of Aristotle, within Islamic thought. It was a dialogue in reply to the Persian mystic and theologian al-Ghazali's 20-chapter attack on the use of rationalism in matters of divine law in his book *Tahāfut al-Falasifah* (*The Incoherence of the Philosophers*). Al-Ghazali felt the philosophers' approach was contrary to Islamic teaching and should be restricted to discussions of sciences such as mathematics and astronomy.

Many of these philosophers had been influenced by the school of Baghdad, which was the focus of logic studies in the Arab world. Despite most members being Christians, the Muslim Abu Nasr al-Farabi (873-950) had written commentaries and logical works, which influenced later Arabic logicians. By 1050, the school of Baghdad had declined.

Averroës, working in Moorish Spain in the 12th century, revived the tradition of both the school and al-

Averroës' writings were important in introducing Aristotle to Christian scholars and became the subject of Simon Van den Bergh's lifetime work

Opposite: Aristotle, with Plato to his right in the centre of Raphael's *The School of Athens* (1510–11) in the Vatican, Rome. Averroës is in a turban at bottom left, looking over Pythagoras' shoulder.
Below: A statue of Averroës outside the cathedral at Cordoba.

Farabi by writing penetrating commentaries on Aristotle's work. Averroës developed al-Farabi's view of the relationship between philosophy and religion and argued that religious truth and philosophical truth could not be contrary to each other. He claimed that there was just one truth and that there were a number of ways in which that truth could be expressed.

Averroës' reputation was based on his own immense philosophical keenness and enormous influence on certain phases of Latin thought. Averroës' school of philosophy, known as Averroësm', exerted a strong influence on Christian philosophers such as St Thomas Aquinas and Jewish philosophers such as Levi ben Gershon (Gersonides). St Thomas reconciled the Aristotelian doctrines with those of Christian theology and they remained a key part of higher education in Europe from the 13th to the 17th centuries and beyond.

Despite negative reactions from Jewish Talmudists and the Christian clergy, Averroës' writings were taught at the University of Paris and other medieval universities. Averroism stimulated a great deal of philosophical work in Europe from the 13th to 16th century.

Many leading thinkers were to use Averroës and his extensive set of commentaries as their path to Aristotle. Averroës' views on the links between religion and reason earned him a particularly important place within some Jewish communities. Translations into Hebrew were often made of his independent writings as opposed to his commentaries on others' work, which meant that the closest representations of Averroës' real philosophical views tended to be in Hebrew.

Simon's translation of Averroës' *Tahāfut al-Tahāfut* would form the basis of the dissertation for his doctorate and for his first book.

Chapter 5   East meets West

B y his late twenties, Simon Van den Bergh had matured into a very attractive young
man who could compete with any matinée film idol. Women were drawn to him
and he was equally attracted to them. Sophisticated, sociable and much travelled, he
was able to converse fluently in many languages, quote poetry, play the piano and appreciate music and fine art. Miriam Hodges, the daughter of Professor Erwin Rosenthal, an
academic friend of Simon's, was still a teenager when she first met him in the late 1950s.
Simon was well into his seventies, but had lost little of his attraction: 'I remember this exquisite man: small, but tough, beautifully dressed and with a twinkle in his eye. He was
charming.'

Simon's future wife was unlike any woman he had met. The teenage Sonia Pokrowski,
was a tall, elegant, Jewish, red-headed, blue-green eyed, language student from the town of
Suwalki, now in the Bialystock province of north-east Poland, then in Russia. According to
Simon's family, the two met in Heidelberg while they were both studying at the university.
This is what their daughter Tamara believed: 'He got his PhD at Heidelberg University and
that was where he met my mother. They were both students at the university. My mother
had come to Heidelberg to study for a degree and she met and fell in love with my father.

'He was supposed to have been engaged and to have married the daughter of his professor but he met Sonia, went back to Holland to work out what do and then returned to
marry my mother, who was very beautiful.'

Some aspects of this story are true: Simon did meet and marry Sonia and she was very
beautiful; and he was engaged to his professor's daughter. But Simon never lived or studied
in Heidelberg; he did his doctorate at Freiburg University. In his written introduction to his
dissertation, he refers to all the universities where he had studied. No reference is made to
him having attended Heidelberg. Neither are there any records in the town or the university of either Simon or Sonia studying or living there.

Professor Hermann Reckendorf, under whose auspices Simon studied, was born in

Sophisticated and sociable: Simon
was attractive to women

Simon's doctorate from Freiburg

Heidelberg and had many close associations with the city. He moved to Freiburg in 1886 and lived there for the rest of his life. His three children, Cecile, Arnold Otto and Angelika, were all born in Freiburg: the eldest Cecile, known as Lilli, in 1888 and Arnold Otto and Angelika in the 1900s. It is highly likely that Simon lodged with Professor Reckendorf in Freiburg, a common practice at that time.

A more plausible explanation is that Simon and Sonia met in Berlin. As part of his curriculum for his doctorate, Simon spent one year from October 1909 studying at Berlin University. There are no records in Berlin to show whether or not Sonia or Simon studied or lived there. Most were destroyed during the Second World War. But as Simon was officially registered as being at Freiburg, and his courses with the Berlin professors had been arranged by Professor Reckendorf, he probably was not required to register with Berlin University. Sonia, like many other Eastern European students, would have been drawn towards Berlin because it was a more cosmopolitan city than Heidelberg and better known.

Simon's meeting and new-found love for Sonia was to cause problems. He had become engaged to Lilli, the eldest of Professor Reckendorf's two daughters. Although originally Jewish, the Reckendorf family had left the faith and now belonged to the German Lutheran Church. Simon's parents had, perhaps surprisingly, welcomed the engagement.

Reckendorf's decision to convert to Protestantism may have been due to more pragmatic reasons than those of religious belief. Jobs in the civil service, law or academic life had in the past been governed by membership of the church, with Jews only gaining entry by conversion. In 1822, the Prussian Government issued a royal decree explicitly outlawing the employment of Jews in universities and the public sector.

The poet and philosopher Heinrich Heine and his friend Eduard Gans – a star pupil of the philosopher Georg Hegel's at Berlin University and one of the first German Jews to earn a doctorate in jurisprudence – were among those who left the faith, the latter having been refused employment at Berlin. Heine, supported in his studies by his wealthy uncle, hoped conversion would allow him to seek financial independence by obtaining employment in the civil service. Heine was to swiftly regret his decision, complaining that his situation had not improved: 'On the contrary, I have had nothing but misfortune!' Gans had more success: expediency was promptly rewarded in 1826 with an associate professorship of law at Berlin. Although more recent laws tackled discrimination on religious grounds, old insecurities remained.

Although they never denied their Jewish roots, to all extent and purposes Isaac and Clara led the lives of the wealthy Dutch middle class; they no longer abided by the rules laid down by their faith nor kept a 'kosher' home. They may well have understood the reasons for Professor Reckendorf's conversion. Their son's engagement to the daughter of an eminent professor would have been regarded as a prestigious match. They did not approve of Simon breaking the engagement for his new-found love.

Sonia and Simon's backgrounds were different, both culturally and socially. Simon had been brought up in a privileged middle-class society. Although he had faced anti-Semitism at school in Oss, the move to Rotterdam had enabled him to enter a more cosmopolitan, enlightened environment where his religion was accepted. Sonia's life had been typical of

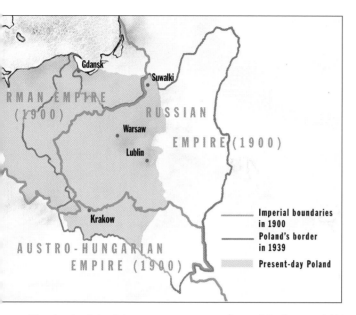

Map showing Poland's borders around the time of Sonia's birth, at the start of the Second World War and the present day

Most of Sonia's family circa 1895. Back row (from left): Rosa Raiza, Leah, Pauline, Chonel, William. Front row: Sonia, Archie, Eddie, Anna

the Middle European Jew facing a daily battle against pogroms. She had been brought up in a repressed, still largely ghettoised Jewish society.

Insecurity and hard work

Sonia's home town of Suwalki was a frontier town with a population whose fortunes fluctuated with every change of ruler. Nowadays located in the north-eastern corner of Poland, in Sonia's day it came under Tsarist Russia's harsh grip. Sonia, or Sara as she was officially named, was born on 21 November 1891 to Homel (Chonel) Berko Pokrojski, a wealthy general merchant and his wife Leah (Lise) Gollanderski. Sara – after the patron saint of gipsies, an appropriate name for a girl who would live in many different countries – was the seventh of Chonel and Leah's nine surviving children. Sonia had a twin brother, Nisel, who was born 30 minutes earlier. He died some three and a half months later.

The registration form, Document 116, written in Russian states: 'That on 30 November 1891 at 10.00 in the morning Chonel Berko Yankelevich Pokrojski, merchant aged 32 years "came" and in the presence of Mendel Tsodyk, houseowner, and Leyba Vilenski, tailor, both 60 years old living in Suwalki, introduced "us" to his baby girl, stating that she had been born in Suwalki on 21 November at 12.30 at night, by his wife Leah, née Gollanderski, aged 33. At birth this baby was given the name of Sara.' The document was read out to those present, as was the custom, and signed by Tsodyk, Chonel Pokrojski and an official of the Register Office. Vilenski was noted as having stated he was 'illiterate'.

Document 115, the form for Sonia's brother, differs in stating that he had been born at 12.00 on 21 November 1891 to Leah Davidovna Gollanderska and that he had been given the name Nisel at his circumcision. A third certificate states that on 10 March 1892 at 10.00 in the morning, Mendel Tsodyk, houseowner, and Leyba Vilenski, tailor both 61 years old and living in Suwalki, informed the Register Office that Nisel Pokrojski, the son of Chonel Berko Yankelevich and Leah née Gollanderski, had died in Suwalki at 11.00 in the morning on 9 March. The document, signed after Nisel's death, 'had been verified by sight' of the baby's body.

The dates given are according to the Gregorian calendar. From 1700 until February 1918, countries under Russian rule adhered to the Julian calendar which ran 13 days behind those of the Gregorian, which is the internationally accepted civil calendar. Sonia's family, like other Poles, adopted Gregorian dates and those are the ones given in all her official documentation including her marriage certificate.

The loss of Sonia's twin brother may have affected her deeply. Throughout her life she was often described as being of a rather 'solitary' disposition. It is common for surviving twins to report feeling as though part of them is missing. Sonia kept her deceased twin a secret from her children. 'She never mentioned it, I certainly had no idea,' said her daughter Tamara. 'Perhaps it explains why she was so worried about her health. She was always going on trips to various health centres because she was worried about her heart.'

Sonia's other brothers and sisters were: Moise, otherwise known as Max, born in 1878; Pauline in 1879; Smuel or Samson, later to be known as Sam, in 1880; Rosa Raisa in 1884; William in 1888; Anna in 1889; Jeruchim or Eddie, as he became known, in 1893; and Aaron, later Archie, in 1894. Chonel and Leah's children discarded their Jewish first names years later as they cut their ties with their homeland, taking either the English, Polish or French equivalent.

Under Napoleonic regulations, Jews of Eastern Europe for the first time – like their Dutch brethren – adopted new surnames. However, surnames had already been required for taxation purposes for those restricted to living in the 'Pale of Settlement', an area created by Catherine The Great in 1791, to include much of present-day Lithuania, Belarus, Poland, Bessarabia, Ukraine and parts of western Russia. Suwalki is located near the present-day Lithuanian town of Pakruojis, once known as Pokroy, which has a rare, surviving wooden synagogue. Members of the Pokrojski family believe their surname may be connected with the town. Carlos Glikson, the grandson of Sonia's sister Pauline, explained: 'When Jews were forced to take a surname by the Tsar they took surnames originating from places where they lived. Pokrojski was shortened to Pokroy by relatives living in France. It is likely that this is where the family came from, the 'ski' at the end of the name meant son, or "coming from".'

Jews first settled in Suwalki in 1808, with a small community of 44 people; by 1827 it had grown to 1,209. A large synagogue was built in 1821. While Jewish communities in the smaller towns either stagnated or shrank as a result of Russian restrictions, persecutions and edicts, the opposite happened in Suwalki, where the Jewish community quickly grew in both population and influence. By 1840, Jews dominated economic life throughout Suwalki and the surrounding Podlaskie province. By 1857 some 6,687 Jews lived in the town.

A recent photograph of the Suwalki synagogue

In 1863, the Poles rose against their Russian rulers. Many Jews in Suwalki, conscripted previously into the Russian army or harassed by Cossack pogroms, took an active part in the struggle against Russia. One of Sonia's uncles was recorded as having been hanged by the Russians when he tried to avoid conscription. Jews fought alongside and supplied the Polish National Guard with food, raided government banks and smuggled arms.

Suwalki grew rapidly because it stood halfway along the new road between Moscow and Minsk and became

an automatic stopping-off point on route. People of many national backgrounds lived in and around Suwalki: Lithuanians, Russians, Poles and Germans. Lithuanians, living in the northern parts of the surrounding province, were the largest group, with Poles and Germans living mainly in the less fertile south. Russian-Polish Jews were subject to restrictions about how they could live their lives and were not permitted to marry outside their own province.

Above: *Polish Insurrectionists of the 1863 Rebellion* painted on wood by Stanislaus von Chlebowski (1835-84)

Below: Sonia's maternal grandmother, Chana Guttel Gollanderski

In the ghetto

The Jews of Suwalki were wealthier than those in many other Polish towns, building up successful enterprises by trading with Germany, particularly in agricultural produce, timber and horses, and supplying the local garrison. By 1897, despite years of famine and epidemics in other provinces, the Jewish population had grown to 7,165, some 40 per cent of the population. Several Jewish hospitals and hotels had been built. In 1908, the census recorded 13,002 Jews in Suwalki.

Jewish schools and clubs were set up, newspapers were launched and charitable institutions established. Jews worked in retail trades and crafts, leather processing and in manufacturing prayer shawls. Sonia was raised in a ghetto-like society in which Jews worked among non-Jews but lived apart from them in designated areas and had little or no social contact.

Chonel, Sonia's father, was a wealthy man. He ran several shops and travelled the area trading in gold and jewellery. He and his wife worked hard to support their nine children. Sonia rarely talked about her parents but on the few occasions she did, Tamara remembered her referring to the long hours they worked: 'Both of her parents worked hard in the store with the result she hardly ever saw them. She never talked about her background other than to insinuate that she had faced anti-Semitism.'

Simon Van den Bergh's grandmother Elisabeth had fought hard for her family and played a significant role in the business. Sonia's maternal grandmother was equally formidable. Chana Guttel Gollanderski had become a leading member of the town's Jewish community, with a reputation for giving good advice. Chana was described by her fellow townspeople as being of 'exceptional intelligence', breaking down barriers between the Russian authorities and Jews. Unusually for those times as a woman and a Jewess, she became the confidant of General Nicolas Gonetzky, the Governor of Suwalki. He often visited Chana's home to take tea and talk; important local businessmen also consulted her.

Chonel, despite physically resembling some old figure from the bible, did not adhere to the highly orthodox teachings followed by other Jews in the area. Martin Gorman, the grandson of Sonia's brother Eddie, has an idea why: 'Chonel wasn't religious. He hadn't taken it seriously after discovering the local Rabbi, who ran some schul

Above: A studio portrait of Sonia and her younger brother Eddie.
Below: Rosa Raiza with her niece, Mina

[synagogue] behind his store, in a compromising position.' He never told Eddie what that compromising position might have been.

Chonel took a liberal stance towards the education of his sons and daughters, sending at least one of them to a Catholic school and others to local Polish state schools. Education was seen – as it was by the van den Berghs in The Netherlands – as a way of improving the children's lives and enabling them to escape persecution. Memories of past pogroms, in which members of their own family were murdered, would have influenced the Pokrojski parents.

Despite their prosperity, Chonel and Leah Pokrojski, like other Jewish parents, were terrified at the threats to their family and encouraged their sons to find safety in America. Sonia's five brothers had already left for the United States, wading across rivers, hiding from police, escaping over the border into Germany without official papers, so they could sail to safety. Sam Pokrojski, born in 1880, was the first to leave home. Threatened with conscription in 1895, he escaped to America. Brothers Max, Billy and Archie followed him.

As an American citizen, Sam returned to Europe in 1909 to visit his family and took his younger brother Jeruchim back to America. Jeruchim changed his name to Eddie Hollander and arrived at Ellis Island, the main point of entry for immigrants into the United States, on 14 October 1909 aged 17, on board The Deutschland, which sailed from Hamburg. The records describe him as being of Russian Hebrew origin, 5ft 6ins tall, with a fair complexion, black hair and blue eyes. In the ship's manifest he was described as being neither a 'polygamist' nor 'an anarchist'. Armed with only 25 dollars, he gave his future address as being Sam Hollander's home at 339 Central Avenue, New York.

The Austrian writer and poet, Joseph Roth, wrote in the 1920s about young Jewish emigrants: 'They want to leave the country where a war might break out from one year to the next, and from one week to the next, a pogrom. And so they leave on foot, by train, on board ship... America signifies distance. America signifies freedom. There is always some relative or other living in America. It is rare to find a Jewish family in the East that doesn't have an uncle or cousin in America. Someone emigrated 20 years ago. He fled the draft or he received his call up papers and deserted.'

Having worked for years to raise the money to send their sons to America, Chonel and Leah were concerned for their daughters if they stayed. Now they made plans for their futures.

Escape to opportunity

Sonia, the youngest of the couple's four daughters, had a driving ambition to succeed. The bright girl had a talent for languages. She wanted to learn more than German and Russian, the two languages students living in Russian-controlled areas were required by law to learn. She also spoke Polish, learnt in secret having been officially banned by Russia as part of its campaign to assimilate local people into the Russian Empire.

Chonel and Leah continued their policy of giving their children a non-Jewish education and sent Sonia to a Christian high school outside the Jewish area. In one of the few reminiscences of her life, Sonia described to her daughter Tamara how isolated she had been, explaining that she was the only girl to go to a Christian high school outside the ghetto but she never spoke to other children as she was Jewish.

Sonia's nephew Abrasha, the son of her eldest sister Pauline, told his son Carlos about the problems he had encountered when attending the local school in Suwalki. 'My father mentioned in a letter that he left school because at his school, the best in Suwalki, Jews were not accepted,' recalled Carlos. 'He said that in a town where most of the population was Jewish, his school – the state gymnasium – had five Jewish pupils out of a total of 400. He was given several serious beatings.'

Simon and Sonia Van den Bergh would later help Abrasha financially when he left Poland on his way to Argentina, where he hoped to wait for a visa enabling him to enter the United States.

Sonia was only 17 years old in 1908 when she packed her bag, put her on her best hat and took the train across Poland to Germany to study languages. Her brothers were forbidden from travelling because they could still be conscripted into the Russian army so had to travel with false passes and often by foot. In contrast, Sonia clutched her official passport and travelled freely across Europe. In Germany, unlike Poland which only allowed small quotas of Jews to study at its universities, she hoped to be able to make the most of her natural talent.

The decision to leave was to ultimately save Sonia's life. Her sisters Pauline (who later married Naftali Glikson), Anna and Rosa Raiza remained in Poland. Some 6,000 Jews were still living in Suwalki at the outbreak of the Second World War.

Sonia's eldest sister, Pauline, stayed in Suwalki

Many Eastern European Jews changed their names to avoid prejudice. Sonia was no exception. She accompanied her departure from Suwalki with a change of name, in an effort to throw off her Eastern European past and assimilate into her new homeland. Her original Jewish name of Sara was turned into the more Christian-sounding Sonia. Years later, Nazi Germany would require all Jewish women to use the same of Sara on their identity papers. Men would have to attach Israel to theirs. Sonia kept the surname Pokrojski, unlike her brothers who adopted a westernised surname on arrival in the United States by shortening their mother's name of Gollanderski to Hollander, the 'G' becoming 'H' in the change of alphabet. Other Jews who left for America from Holland also ended up as Hollanders, thanks to customs officers at Ellis Island. They were not noted for their language skills and were often responsible for giving immigrants new names, based on a derivation of their original name, or a rash guess at what the immigrants were saying, which tended to include the name of the country or port from which refugees embarked.

According to Joseph Roth, names held little significance: 'Don't be surprised at the Jews' lack of attachment to their names. They will change their names with alacrity, and the names of their fathers, even those particular sounds, which to the European sensibility are charged with emotional weight. For Jews their names have no value because they are not their names. Jews, Eastern Jews, have no names. They have compulsory aliases.'

Within weeks of her arrival in Germany, Sonia met a sophisticated intellectual man, some 10 years her senior. She was an entrancing, young and innocent 'foreigner', travelling alone, and seemingly very independent, brought up in a different environment from Simon

Van den Bergh, yet who shared his interest in languages.

Simon, fell in love with Sonia. But he was worried about the reaction of his mentor, Professor Reckendorf. He was, after all, betrothed to his daughter Lilli, and he was coming towards the end of his studies under the Professor's auspices. He went back to The Netherlands to think through his options. On his return to Freiburg he broke the engagement off, which did not seem to affect his relationship because he continued to receive Professor Reckendorf's support.

Lilli Reckendorf, the spurned wife in waiting, remained in Freiburg and became head teacher of a girls' school. Her brother Arnold Otto and sister Angelika emigrated to America in the early 1930s. In 1934 Lilli lost her job when, despite being an official practising member of the German Church, she was deemed a full Jew. In 1940 she was arrested by the Gestapo and, with other Jews from Freiburg, expelled to France from Germany. Some 7,500 German Jews, along with others from various parts of France, were rounded up with less than one hour's notice and dumped unceremoniously on the German/French demarcation line. Lilli was imprisoned in the Gurs concentration camp at the foot of the Pyrenees but avoided deportation to Auschwitz. She mysteriously appeared in Switzerland in 1943, where she remained until after the war. How she arrived there, managing to avoid deportation and the camp and border guards, was never fully explained. She returned to Freiburg where she died in 1953.

Simon's relationship with Sonia failed to receive parental approval. Isaac and Clara were furious that he had become involved with someone they looked on as a peasant. Simon told his second wife Maureen that his family were worried that: 'poor Jews from Russia might descend upon them'. Isaac and Clara van den Bergh's judgement could have been based on seeing the poorly dressed, hungry Jewish refugees from Eastern Europe passing through Rotterdam. They were orthodox Jews from Poland with flowing beards and ringlets, long black coats and fur-trimmed hats, or poorer, more dapper-dressed, coarser people holding their bundles of possessions; people of the same faith yet so different from themselves.

Sonia and Simon's marriage certificate from the General Register Office, Edinburgh

Simon ignored his family's opposition. On Friday 28 September 1910 in Edinburgh, in secret and without telling his parents, Simon and Sonia were married. Simon was by that time studying in London but Sonia was only 18, and therefore under the age of consent in England, whereas in Scotland couples could get married without parental permission. So Edinburgh provided the perfect answer. It was impossible for the couple to travel at that time to Suwalki because foreign Jews such as Simon had been forbidden by

Russia from entering the country. Simon would never meet Sonia's parents.

Although Simon ran into opposition to the marriage from his immediate family, he received support from other members, including the 'English' families he had connected with while studying in London. He often visited the homes of his two uncles, Jacob and Henry, whose sons and daughters were around Simon's age. Jacob, in particular, had shown a more liberal approach to the romances of his children, including his eldest daughter Dollie who had a long relationship with a married court wig maker and her subsequent marriage to a non-Jewish champion angler.

Jacob was sympathetic to the young couple, as was his son Henry's father-in-law Dr John Macdonald Brown, who came from Edinburgh. A former Lecturer at Edinburgh University, Dr Macdonald Brown had written several books about Robert Burns and Robert Browning and had studied many of the same subjects as Simon. Dr Macdonald Brown advised the couple how to comply with the rules and regulations governing marriage in Scotland. He remained closely in contact with them and would deliver their first daughter, Lisa Ingeborg.

Simon and Sonia's marriage certificate states that the ceremony took place at 15 Bernard Terrace, Edinburgh after 'Publication and According to the forms of the Jews'. Simon's witness, Rabbi Rabinowitz, who conducted the service, had established a small synagogue at that address, one of the first in Edinburgh. Edinburgh jeweller Louis Lucas, a former refugee from Suwalki, by then naturalised as British, was a witness along with a Simon Sherwinter. Lucas allowed the couple to give his address, 18 Waterloo Place, Edinburgh, although they were not required by law to live there. Sonia gave her name as Sara, which would only be officially recorded once more, when she had her first baby. From now on she would be known as Sonia Van den Bergh and would automatically become a Dutch citizen.

There are no photographs of the wedding and, with the exception of the certificate, no record of it having taken place. In some ways the lack of mementoes foretells the marriage, which despite the birth of two daughters, became one of great sadness. A romantic story of a beautiful girl, escaping persecution, who travelled across Europe to study in Germany, only to meet and marry an exciting, attractive, wealthy Dutchman, should have had a happy ending. Instead the relationship would descend into bitterness and frustration.

From sanctuary to persecution: Poland and its Jewish population

Opposite: Polish Jews, in a late 18th-century engraving

Below: 17th-century negative allegorical depiction of a Jewish moneylender

JEWS HAD SETTLED in Eastern Europe from the time of the original Babylonian diaspora around 2,500 years ago, although the first record of Jews living in Poland was in Krakow in the middle of the 11th-century. Ancestors of some of the early settlers were likely to have migrated to Poland via Hungary. Many were refugees from early pogroms, which took place after the First Crusade of 1096-1099. Others came from Germany and Saxon lands, again escaping persecution. Some were drawn to the country by economic opportunity.

They were Ashkenazi Jews who, by and large, were artisans, merchants, traders, and moneylenders. A few became international traders and grew wealthy. A number worked for the Polish aristocracy, running their estates. They brought Talmudic learning, books and a reverence for the written word into a land where many households were illiterate. They were welcomed by the Polish monarchy and tolerated by ordinary Poles; Jews and Christians lived alongside each other.

At a time when Western European Jews were forced to wear some form of identifying mark or to live in designated areas, the Jews of Eastern Europe were not. However, they did still feel threatened by outside sources, so they tended to live near each other for safety. Gradually, as the Jews assimilated, they lost part of their original culture. Hebrew was forgotten as Yiddish was increasingly spoken at home.

But the Roman Catholic Church took a stronger hold in Eastern Europe, curtailing the independence of problematic Polish bishops, and Jews became subject to the anti-Semitic sentiments of the church. The stereotype of the cowering, scared, swarthy and devious foreign character prepared to do anything for money, was created by folk pageants and Catholic morality plays.

The Polish peasants saw themselves as simple people wedded to nature and the land. Jews were seen as being clever, wily and transient. Engaged in commerce, trade and finance, all professions that Poles believed were beneath their dignity, Jews filled the jobs that many Poles did not want or could not undertake. At the same time, some Poles were jealous of the alliances formed between Polish nobles and Jews.

Yet Poland, regardless of the gradual rise in anti-Semitism, remained the country where Jews expelled from other countries felt they might be safe. Throughout the late

In the 1550s Jews were allowed to elect their own leaders and in 1573 the Poles enshrined religious equality in a Statute of General Tolerance

Many Eastern European Jewish traditions of clothes and culture were introduced in the late Middle Ages

Middle Ages and the Renaissance, migration continued, with Polish Kings encouraging Jews to come and participate in the commercial growth of the country. Despite prejudices, Jews at this time were treated civilly. They were left to their own devices and found a form of stability. They consolidated their own communities in which they could practise their beliefs and live their lives according to their scriptures and rules. Jews had a particular style of clothing, often derived from Polish nobility: black caftans and fur-trimmed hats for the men; black dresses for the women. Many of the traditions of clothes and culture, which were anathema to Western European Jews and were to define and identify the Eastern European Jew, were introduced in the late Middle Ages.

During the Reformation, when Western Europe was racked by decades of religious wars, Poland provided a sanctuary for refugees from persecution. The Polish 'Golden Years', from the 15th century to the mid-17th century, saw sects such as the Anabaptists and the Mennonites and communities such as Armenians, Italians and Germans settle in the country. In the 1550s Jews were allowed to elect their own leaders, and in 1573, some 20 years before Jews found acceptance in The Netherlands, the Poles enshrined religious equality in a Statute of General Tolerance.

This tolerance was not to last as Ukrainian peasants and

The Cossack chieftain, Bogdan
Chmielnicki

Napoleon Bonaparte's attempt to
encourage Jewish assimilation was
rejected by the Jews
of Eastern Europe

Crimean Tartars, led by the Cossack chieftain Bogdan
Chmielnicki, rose up in 1648 against their Polish overlords.
It is estimated that between 70,000 and 80,000 Jews, some 20
to 25 per cent of the Jewish population, were killed in the
battles and massacres that followed. Decades of wars,
famine and epidemics drove Poland towards economic
ruin. Cossack massacres were followed by war with Sweden
and an invasion that led to the devastation of many newly
rebuilt Polish towns and villages. This was followed in 1672-
76 by war with the Ottoman Empire and then by Russian
attacks on parts of Poland and Lithuania. Suwalki, the town
in which Sonia was born, lay within this troubled area.

The position of Jews living in Poland worsened during
this time. They were forced to pay increased taxes and levies
to cover the costs of the wars, while trying to raise
emergency funds to help Jewish victims of the wars and
persecution. They borrowed from Polish nobles to try to
keep up payments but fell into debt, which drew hostility.

In 1764, the Council of Four Lands, which had been the
central body of Jewish authority in Poland and Lithuania,
was dissolved by the Polish parliament because the Council
had failed to deliver the taxes it had collected. Eight years
later, Poland and Lithuania ceased to exist as political
entities, as they were swallowed up by the Russian, Austrian
and Prussian Empires, in the first of the partitions that were
to govern the lives of their people over the next century.

The lives of Jews would again be subject to pogroms and
persecution.

Suwalki was absorbed into Russian territory and came
under the Pale of Settlement. In 1807, Emperor Napoleon
Bonaparte, on his defeat of Prussia, ordered the
incorporation of the Duchy of Warsaw into his Empire. Like
their Dutch brethren, Prussia's Jews came under French
rule and Napoleon's protection. But unlike the Jews of
Western Europe who welcomed moves to help them
assimilate, the Jews of Eastern Europe rebelled against the
1807 declaration of the Grand Sanhedrin (an assembly of
Jewish notables set up by Napoleon), which defined Jews as

Poland, once the country with the highest density of Jews in Europe, would become one of the most anti-Semitic

The town hall at Suwalki, built in the mid-19th century

a religious community and not a race. In 1812, Jews of Eastern Europe supported Russians in their war against the French invaders, seeing Napoleon's liberalism as a threat to their orthodoxy.

The Austrian writer and poet Joseph Roth travelled extensively through the region in the early twentieth century. He believed his fellow Jews' success in the areas governed by Russia were defined by their past. Writing in his book *The Wandering Jews*, Roth compared the attitudes of Jews and Russians: 'The Russian peasant is a peasant first and a Russian second, the Jew is Jew first and then peasant. It's an old destiny, an old, richly experienced blood. Jews are of an intellectual cast. They are a people that has had no illiterates for nearly 2,000 years now; a people with more periodicals than newspapers; a people whose periodicals, probably uniquely in the world, have a far higher readership than its newspapers. While the other peasants around him are struggling to read and write, the Jew, behind his plough has his mind on the problems of relativity theory.'

However, the Jews' success was not welcomed by all. In 1904 some 30 pogroms were 'officially' recorded as having taken place in Russia. Protests in Poland against Russian rule, with renewed calls for autonomy, led to outbreaks of looting and the imposition of martial law. In Russian-occupied Poland, which included Suwalki, Jews were

Headstone wall at Suwalki Jewish
cemetary

blamed for causing all the hardship. The Tsarist Secret
police, the Okhrana, looking for a way of diverting public
anger away from the Government, whipped up anti-Jewish
sentiments by accusing them of plotting against Russia. On
8 November 1905 Russian peasants taking part in a horrific
pogrom in Odessa massacred over 1,000 Jews. Shops and
houses were looted and burnt; some 5,000 Jews were injured
and 6,000 families were made homeless. Gangs calling
themselves the Black Hundred were formed to hunt down
Jewish people.

Jews fled to countries in Western Europe or to America.
Many of them, often poverty-stricken, would pass through
Rotterdam on their way to New York. Jewish families saved
and sold all they had to raise money to ensure their
children could get safely away. The unpopular Russo-
Japanese War in 1904 created the additional threat of
enforced conscription of young Jewish men into the
Russian Army, which led many more to emigrate.

Poland, once the country with the highest density of
Jews in Europe, would eventually become one of the most
anti-Semitic. It was not by chance that the Nazis sited more
concentration camps in Poland than anywhere else during
the years of the Holocaust.

Chapter 6 Strained relations

The second decade of the 20th century heralded dramatic changes in the political landscape of Europe as the conflicting interests of Empires caused wars and revolution. Industrial expansion, new technologies and fresh ideas opened up opportunities for Western industrialised Europe, which grew wealthy on manufacturing and overseas investment. Meanwhile Eastern Europe endured a more turbulent time as downtrodden peasants and city dwellers found themselves pushed further under the yoke of old tyrannical orders such as the Austro-Hungarian Hapsburgs and the Romanovs of Russia. The German military, under Queen Victoria's grandson Kaiser Wilhelm II, jealous of the British Empire, made agressive noises. Students and workers demonstrated and strikes were put down by gunfire as the world slipped into the bloodiest of wars that few people at the beginning of the century could have foreseen.

There were also changes in the lives of the van den Berghs. Advances in business practices and the long-term illness of Clara were responsible for Isaac's decision in 1910 – the year Simon married Sonia – to retire from the family firm. By then the company was established as a highly successful manufacturing concern with factories in several countries. Isaac had never formally trained in industrial design, relying on natural instinct to plan the factories in Oss and Rotterdam. Van den Berghs was now a public company answerable to its shareholders and could afford to hire professionals, fully trained at universities in new techniques, to take on much of the work previously carried out by the brothers. This allowed them to concentrate on devising overall strategies for the company. Isaac's position in charge of the technical side of designing factories became less significant.

Arnold and Sam became involved in the cultural and political affairs of The Netherlands. Arnold, interested in art, accumulated a large collection of paintings. His house, the Villa Constance in Oss, had been turned into an art gallery and is now known as 'Museum Jan Cunen'. Sam, also interested in art, had become actively involved in politics and was sitting as a Senator in the Dutch Assembly. Isaac, with few outside interests and concentrating on

Serbian nationalst, Gavrilo Princip, assassinated Archduke Franz Ferdinand, heir to the Austro-Hungarian Empire, and his wife Sophie while they were on a state visit to Sarajevo, creating the spark that ignited the First World War (from the illustrated supplement to the Italian newspaper, *Corriere della Sera*)

the health of his wife and daughter, began to grow apart from his brothers. After his parents' 60th wedding anniversary there are no known photographs of Isaac at family gatherings and anniversaries.

Isaac was closer to Maurits and Zadok, neither of whom lived in The Hague. They would be witnesses and executors for both his and Clara's wills. These three van den Bergh families had drawn closer together and the young Simon forged relationships with his uncles and cousins, often staying with them.

Clara and Isaac's lives revolved around their disabled daughter Liesje and their house. Clara's deteriorating health meant it was becoming more difficult for the couple to make their customary trips to the Riviera. Later that year, on 14 December 1910, Simon's childhood companion Miss Wesley left the family to move to Maastricht. Now Simon had married Sonia, her role as governess and companion was no longer needed although there would continue to be warm contact.

Isaac shared little in common with Jacob, Henry, Arnold and Sam, the four brothers he had worked alongside, and even less with his son. Simon and Isaac did not have the close relationship that Simon's cousins George and Sidney enjoyed with their father Sam. There had been none of the walking trips nor visits to the planetarium, none of the intellectual conversations and discussions. Simon was independent. He travelled around Europe immersed in learning. He had studied under some of the finest professors in Europe and his friends were fellow students, with whom he could argue and debate. Isaac's life had been devoted to his work, his wife and his daughter. He was more interested in acquiring shares than collecting books and paintings.

Simon's daughter Tamara recalled that he didn't talk much about his father. 'He didn't think that he was very intelligent,' she explained. 'He didn't think that his father had contributed much to Van den Berghs. He didn't have much respect for him.' Isaac and Clara's refusal to support Simon's marriage, or to welcome Sonia into the family, damaged the relationship further and caused a schism that would only be healed by Clara as she was dying.

After their marriage in Edinburgh, Simon and Sonia returned to Freiburg so he could continue to work on his doctorate. He submitted it in October 1911. In 1912 his inauguration dissertation *Umriss de Muhammedanischen Wissenschaften nach Ibn Haldun* was published in The Netherlands, Paris and Germany. It was republished by the Leiden University Publishers Brill in 1924, following further research, as *Averroës (Abdul Walid Muhammed ibn Ahmed ibn Rusd) Die Epitome der Metophysik* (which roughly translates as *Averroës The Epitome of Metaphysics*).

In 1912 Simon wrote to the Dean of Faculty at Freiburg, informing him of the publication of his dissertation, which formally recognised his qualification as a Doctor of Literature. He expressed his concern that the university had not yet sent him his diploma. He was never to receive it, despite several requests. A recent request for it, during research for this book, met with the same negative response.

Sonia, with the exception of a few letters, no longer communicated with her parents but she remained in contact with her brothers and sisters. Max, Sam and Billy now lived in America. In 1911 her younger sister Anna, also known as Jenny, stayed with Sonia and Simon on her way to join her brothers. A photograph taken of the sisters shows two beautiful girls,

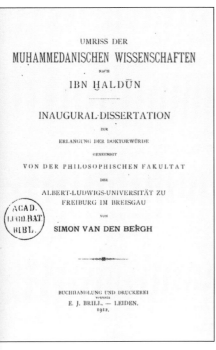

Title page of Simon's dissertation, published in 1912

Sonia (sitting) and Anna in 1911

looking happy; one recently married, the other about to embark on a new life in America. This was to be their last photograph together.

Anna spent some time in The Netherlands before going to the United States; several photographs were taken of her by a Dutch studio. She was partly deaf so could have fallen foul of the United States' tough immigration restrictions against people with disabilities. But Anna was supported by her brothers and, helped by having a trade (she was a trained milliner), was allowed entry. She remained in America until the mid 1920s, when her youngest brother Archie would take her back to Germany, from where she returned to Poland.

Births and deaths

Anna's visit to Sonia was much appreciated. By July 1911 Sonia was pregnant. Simon, unsure of the reception his wife might receive in The Netherlands and having decided where his interest in philosophy lay, returned with Sonia to England. At that time, the British were enjoying peace and prosperity. The Rolls Royce had become the car of choice for the wealthy to travel to see their new King George V open the Festival of Empire at Crystal Palace or to watch him unveil a memorial to his grandmother Queen Victoria outside Buckingham Palace. Young people danced to new music from America, as Alexander's Ragtime Band became a hit in clubs and dance halls.

But unrest was growing as strikes in 1911 paralysed the ports and other parts of the UK's economy. In the streets of London, suffragettes campaigning for votes for women caused thousands of pounds worth of damage to shop windows and property. A reminder that anti-Semitism still lay below the veneer of the supposedly civilised society came in August that year, when Jewish properties were attacked in a few south Wales towns in response to the economic crisis and reputed high rents charged by Jewish landlords.

Jacob Van den Bergh and most of his family had settled in the leafy, genteel Hampstead area of London. His brother Henry's children had earlier been boarded with friends nearby, in Prince Henry Road, as Henry and Henriette made changes to their new house in Kensington. Simon and the pregnant Sonia, seeking family support, moved into a maisonette at 3a Eton Road, Haverstock Hill, Hampstead, just a few minutes away from his uncle and cousins, and from the family doctor.

Their first daughter, Lisa Ingeborg, was born on Sunday 3 March 1912, at 6 Dennington Park Road, then a nursing home. The birth was supervised by Dr John Macdonald Brown, whose daughter Enid had married Jacob's youngest son Henry and who had advised Simon

Sonia with her and Simon's first daughter, Lisa, photographed in London, circa 1913

and Sonia to marry in Edinburgh. Macdonald Brown, a consultant with rooms in Harley Street, supervised the births of other members of the Van den Bergh family, including his own grandchildren. Simon would have been sent a bill for the delivery, given that Macdonald Brown had no hesitation in charging his son-in-law on the birth of his own grandchildren. Simon registered the birth on 9 March 1912 under the name of 'Bergh', in contrast to the British side of the family who all included 'Van' in their children's surnames.

Until now the Van den Berghs had led charmed lives. Simon and Elisabeth Senior had lived well into their eighties and the brothers, having been brought up with healthy lifestyles, must have expected to live as long as their parents. But as Isaac fought to keep Clara alive, the family were shocked by the sudden death at 53 of Maurits.

The second of Simon and Elisabeth's sons, Maurits had been the first to move out of the family business when he became Receiver of Registration at Eindhoven. His first wife Ester Colaco Osorio had died, leaving him with two young sons, Simon and Jacobus, to bring up. Young Simon had died suddenly in 1895 at the age of 15. Jacobus, a brilliant but eccentric young man, with whom Simon Van den Bergh had climbed in the Alps when they were boys, suffered mental illness and eventually had to be hospitalised. Simon continued to visit Jacobus throughout his life, making a last trip to see him just before the Second World War.

In 1908 Maurits had married Carolina van Creveld, a charming widow with a daughter from her previous marriage. The following year she gave birth to a daughter called Louise (Loutie). Carolina became a popular member of the family and was particularly close to her sisters-in-law, including Clara. Just four years into her marriage, she was left with the responsibility of bringing up her own daughters and looking after her stepson.

The birth of Lisa, her first granddaughter, delighted Clara. It ended the row between Simon and his parents as his mother, knowing she was dying, asked the family to return to stay with her in The Netherlands. Miss Wesley, Simon's former governess, rejoined the family to help look after the new baby and act as a companion and nurse to Clara. But before the family were able to move to The Netherlands, Clara died on Wednesday 5 February 1913 at around 9pm. Two of Isaac and Clara's friends, Mozes Goudsmit and Gerrit Huisman, both merchants, witnessed the death certificate. She and Isaac had been married for 34 years. Simon rarely talked about his mother but in 1921 he dedicated his first book to her.

Concerned about Isaac's welfare, Simon and Sonia decided to move to The Netherlands permanently. On 2 May 1913 Isaac bought a house for the couple on the same street as his own. Van Stolkweg 8 was a double-fronted villa made from two houses. It cost Isaac 40,700 Guilders, equivalent nowadays to £175,000. On 23 October 1913 Simon and his family returned to The Netherlands. Sonia was again pregnant. Plans for Miss Wesley to look after her beloved Simon and his family were cruelly denied when she suddenly died on 9 Novem-

The double-fronted villa on Van Stolkweg that Isaac bought for Simon and Sonia (photographed some years later)

ber 1913. Simon was crushed at the loss of the woman who had been a real 'mother' to him.

Simon's younger daughter Tamara believes the lack of maternal care was largely responsible for Simon's lifelong search for the 'right' companion. 'He was very self-centred when it came to looking for what he wanted,' she recalled. 'He constantly looked for the love and companionship that he hadn't had from his mother.'

Meanwhile, unrest was growing in Europe. Some 400,000 workers went on strike in Belgium after their parliament rejected universal suffrage. The Netherlands, in an effort to bring countries together, hosted an International Peace Conference in The Hague but it had little effect as Europe headed inexorably towards the mighty conflict of the First World War. David Lloyd George, British Chancellor of the Exchequer, warned against the 'insane' build up of arms in Europe.

War wasn't the only threat to family life. Sonia's brothers had left their homeland to seek safety, peace and better fortune in the United States. On 7 April 1914 William was shot dead in a hold-up while working in his brother's liquor store in Brooklyn, New York. He was 26 years old. The Pokrojski family were cruelly reminded that nowhere was safe.

Tamara was born at her parents' home in 's-Gravenhage on Monday 25 May 1914. Records show that four female servants worked at the house while the family lived there. Sonia, little more than a girl herself, without the support of either a mother or mother-in-law, needed help to look after two baby girls and run a house.

Conflict across Europe

The summer of 1914 was one of the hottest on record. Unrest grew in central Europe. Marching songs were sung at German universities. People returned to their homelands as forecasts of war filled the air. On Monday 15 June, The Netherlands, Denmark, Sweden and Switzerland, determined to stay neutral and stay out of any possible conflict, united together to form a formal defence league.

On Sunday 28 June the Hapsburg Archduke Franz Ferdinand of Austria was assassinated in Sarajevo. On Tuesday 28 July, Austria declared war on Serbia; four days later the German Kaiser declared war on Russia. On Sunday 2 August, without warning and to the horror of the neutral Dutch, Germany invaded Luxembourg. The Grand Duchess Marie-Adélaïde and her Prime Minister Paul Eyschen attempted to stop the German troops crossing into Luxembourg City by blocking the Adolphe Bridge with their two cars. They failed. A day later Germany declared war on France.

On Tuesday 4 August the Kaiser declared war on Belgium, disregarding British protests against the violation of the 1839 Treaty of London, which guaranteed Belgian neutrality. Britain retaliated to protect 'plucky little Belgium'. Within days Europe was at war. The First World War – 'The Great War' – was said in 1914 'to be over by Christmas' but was to last four disastrous years.

The Great War had a profound effect upon the Van den Berghs and the Pokrojskis. Simon and Sonia with their young family remained in the neutral Netherlands, while hostilities raged outside. Accustomed to travelling where he wanted to pursue his studies, Simon was frustrated. He was limited to living in what he considered a rather dull country, without any of the intellectual stimulus he needed. Simon looked on aghast as friends in Germany and Austria fought against friends and family in Britain. Reports that opposing Poles and Cossacks fighting in the Suwalki area were slaughtering Jews, driving them out of their homes, horrified the couple. Cut off from her family in the East, Sonia didn't know what had become of them. Sonia's parents' fears for the safety of their family were becoming realised.

Jews being driven out of Suwalki
during the First World War

Even the neutral Dutch side of the business felt the impact of public fear created in the run-up to war. *The Times History of War*, published in 1919, describes the uproar: 'It produced a panic which for the time being paralysed the peaceful activities of the nation. Many people, acting as if the country were already besieged, laid in large stocks of provisions...' The population of The Netherlands hoarded gold and silver. Shortage of non-paper money became so acute that on 1 August 1914 the van den Berghs were unable to pay the wages of workers at the Rotterdam factory in the customary silver. The family solved the problem by issuing printed vouchers, which were accepted in lieu of money by Rotterdam shopkeepers until new currency came back on the market. The system so impressed the Dutch Finance Minister, that he later introduced it as a means of payment in various municipalities.

Members of the family would show similar initiative in the Second World War. Jacob's grandson Robert Sainsbury, a Director of the Sainsbury Group of grocery shops, would install a system for rationing and supplying goods that was adopted by the British Government and other stores.

Shipping between The Netherlands and England was interrupted for the first few weeks of the war, which halted margarine exports to England. Sam and Arnold, in charge of the Dutch operation, got around the blockade by chartering a steamer and sending it to England filled with margarine. However, the success of the operation led to accusations in the

British Parliament that the companies had been stockpiling raw materials used for margarine and soap making – which were also vital for the production of munitions.

Van den Berghs and Jurgens had signed an agreement in 1908 to collaborate in sourcing raw materials, marketing and profit-sharing, which raised suspicions. They came under heavy criticism as the British Government tried to prevent shortages of goods forcing up prices. Particularly vicious in criticising his Dutch rivals was William Lever, head of the British soap manufacturer Lever Brothers. The two companies were accused of showing favouritism to their German factories.

A 1911 advert for Lever Brothers' Sunlight soap

Anton Jurgens and Henry Van den Bergh were summoned to appear in front of a special House of Commons committee to explain how their companies were operating during war time. The accounting firm Price Waterhouse was sent to the Van den Bergh factory in The Netherlands to investigate charges that the company had broken its neutrality by supplying Germany with margarine. Britain was at the same time being supplied with margarine by Van den Bergh's British-based company. Price Waterhouse spent some six months checking every document at the Dutch factory and the family was eventually cleared of all charges. One of the Price Waterhouse accountants remained with the company throughout the war and would eventually join the staff permanently.

Lever himself, although a competitor, was an old friend of Sam van den Bergh's. He travelled to Holland in secrecy, risking his life, to reassure Sam that his attacks were aimed at the company and not at Sam personally. After the war, Sam became the driving force behind the merger between Van den Berghs and Jurgens, and later the amalgamation with Willam Lever's Lever Brothers to form Unilever (see page 99).

At the outbreak of war, speaking in the White Hall of the Imperial Palace in Berlin, the Kaiser stated that all Germans were now equal in his eyes, irrespective of faith and ethnic origin. This heartened Jewish families and community elders, who supported their young men as they rushed to join up. Martin Buber, a young Jewish philosopher and graduate of Vienna University, where he had studied alongside his friend Simon Van den Bergh, called for Jewish history to be embraced as part of German culture.

Claiming that the war would finally unite Germans and Jews in a joint 'world historical mission to civilise the Near East', Buber celebrated the war that would rouse Europe from its 'bourgeois lethargy'. He wrote: 'Never has the concept of the Volk become such a reality to me as during these weeks. Among Jews too. The feeling is one of solemn exaltation.'

The Austrian Jewish author, Stefan Zweig, a former critic of German nationalism, was also swept away in the war fever: 'As never before, thousands and hundreds of thousands felt what they should have felt in peacetime, that they belonged together... All differences of class, rank and language were swamped at that moment by the rushing feeling of fraternity ... Each individual was no longer the isolated person of former times, he had been incorporated into the mass, he was part of the people, and his person, his hitherto unnoticed person, had been given meaning.'

Unlike other ordinary German soldiers, Jews would not be offered any form of pension or compensation for injury. Jewish soldiers and supporters of the war became demoralised when right-wing agitators stirred up anti-Semitic sentiments by claiming that Jews had 'hidden behind desks'. In October 1916, when nearly 3,000 Jews had died on the battlefield, Prussian War Minister Adolf Wild von Hohenborn ordered a census of Jews in the army to determine the actual numbers serving on the front lines as opposed to those serving at the rear. The census, showing that 80 per cent were actually fighting at the front, was never published.

Ten years later Adolf Hitler, who was a lance corporal in the 16th Bavarian Reserve Regiment on the Western Front in the First World War, was to use the lies to stir up hatred against the Jews: 'The (military) offices were filled with Jews. Nearly every clerk was a Jew and nearly every Jew was a clerk. I was amazed at this plethora of warriors of the chosen people and could not help but compare them with their rare representatives at the front.' It was a statement he was to repeat time and again in his speeches and in his book *Mein Kampf*.

In 1914, 93 German professors supported their Fatherland's aspirations with their *Manifesto of the German University and Men of Science*, which stated Germany's case for war. They declared: 'We hereby protest to the civilised world against the lies and calumnies with which our enemies are endeavouring to stain the honour of Germany in her hard struggle for existence – a struggle that has been forced upon her.'

Simon's former Berlin University professors, Friedrich Delitzsch and Adolf Erman, were among those who signed the document. Erman's eldest son John-Pierre Erman was to fall in the Battle of the Somme on 1 July 1916. Other signatories included Professor Paul Ehrlich of Frankfurt am Main, Fritz Haber, Professor of Chemistry at Berlin, Professor Adolf Harnack, General Director of the Royal Library and Max Reinhardt, Professor of German Theatre. The scientist Albert Einstein was one of the few who refused to sign.

In Eastern Europe, some 2 million Poles marched off to The Great War; 450,000 of them died. Russian troops settled into what became known as the Eastern Front, reaching from the Baltic Sea to Moscow and the Black Sea. In reply, German and Austrian forces invaded Poland. Germans translated their Emperor's rousing declaration of war into Yiddish and appealed to Polish Jews as 'middlemen' – suppliers of foods – to the Russian armies to turn on these 'anti-Semites' and support German troops. In August, the Russian army received one of its greatest defeats at Tannenberg. Three months later, Eastern European Jews, crushed by Russian pogroms, welcomed the German Army as it advanced on Konigsberg in East Prussia and on Warsaw in Poland.

Few are safe

The effects of the First World War came suddenly and harshly to Sonia's family in Suwalki. On Wednesday 15 September 1914 German Troops seized control of the town, hoping to cut the nearby Petrograd-Vilna-Warsaw railway. The people of Suwalki were enjoying the late summer days and many were away from their homes, relaxing in the surrounding forests

Austrian troops march into Lublin, Poland, on 30 July 1915

and lakelands. These included Sonia's father Chonel, his daughter Pauline and her three children – her husband Naftali having remained at home in Suwalki .

However, their relaxation was interrupted when Asher Glikson, an uncle of Pauline's husband and owner of a transport company, realised his nephew's family might be in danger, so close to the East Prussian border. He collected Chonel, Pauline and her children (Abrasha, Zygmund and Mina) in a couple of carts and evacuated them to Minsk, to the East. Pauline and her children would not be reunited with Naftali for four years. Twenty five years later, Pauline would again flee eastwards, this time to the Ukraine, to escape the German invasion of Poland.

Pauline's attempts to save her family from violence came to nothing. Her eldest son Zygmund, aged just 16, ran away to join the Russian fighters and was never seen again. The family eventually heard he had been killed in skirmishes during July 1916. In the First World War, Russian troops seized over 100,000 Eastern European Jews, despatching them to the Russian interior. German troops, with the help of the oppressed Jews, captured thousands of Poles and Lithuanians sending them to Germany as slave labour.

The Times History of War, describes German action around the Suwalki area, during 1914: 'The chief physical feature of this region is the immense forest, 30 miles long and 20 wide, on whose western edge Augustowo is situated. Intricate chains of lakes stretch on either side of the road from Suwalki to Seiny. It is not a country for rash adventures. A reserve army from Grodno, including a fresh corps from Finland and a fine Siberian corps, had been defeated with some difficulty at Lyck and again in Augusto. Suwalki, the administrative centre of the Russian frontier province, was occupied by the Germans, who set up a permanent administration, and allowed the wives of officers to join their husbands.'

The Germans wreaked devastation on Suwalki. The Pokrojski family house was taken and used as an officers' residence. All the merchandise in Chonel's stores was looted. In June

A German telephone station in
occupied Suwalki

1916 the Germans evacuated the town stealing everything that could be taken with them.
The people of Suwalki returned home to wasteland.

An American, Laura de Gozdawa Turczyniowicz, married to a Pole was living in Poland
at the time. On her return to the United States she described the scene in Suwalki: 'Curious it was that return! There were many things to seize our attention: ruined houses —
houses had been set on fire, broken-down-fences. My beautiful house was ruined. Knee-deep
it was with things strewn about the floor, every drawer, every closet emptied out. Papers,
books, clothes had lain in the accumulated dirt. Books were torn to pieces. China, glass,
linen, trodden upon; used and thrown down. Rows upon rows of jam pots, marmalade, pre-
serves, and honey glasses had been emptied of their contents, filled with filth and returned
to their shelves. Furs, travelling rugs, our food supplies, wines, all linen, most of the silver,
much jewellery had been taken. On all sides of Suwalki had been the battlefield. There were
great holes torn in the earth, trenches dug, and men buried. On one hillock we passed,
where the rain had washed off the slight covering of earth, we saw boots sticking out. The
man driving us said ten thousand were buried there. Wherever we went there were graves.'

On 1 September 1915 Marshall Joseph Pilduski launched a movement for a free Poland.
A provisional Parliament was set up in January 1917 and five months later its Council of State
demanded German and Austrian agreement on its independence. Suwalki was officially
incorporated into the newly independent Poland and the town's Jews thought they would
be safe living in a country with the largest Jewish population in Europe.

Sonia heard nothing about her family until the end of the war when she received the
sad news that her mother had died in 1918. Chonel would now be looked after by the daughters who had remained in Poland, until his death in 1932.

In Great Britain, the Van den Berghs were devastated at the death of Henry and Henriette's two sons, Seymour and James, the tall golden-haired boys, both graduates from

Fighting off the coast of Belgium:
naval warfare and blockades led to
shortages of imported raw materials

Cambridge University. James died fighting in France in 1916 and Seymour in Palestine in 1917. Henriette never recovered from her loss. Jacob's youngest son Henry was among those in charge of catering for the British army and rose to the rank of Major.

In The Netherlands, the Dutch Government, having seen Luxembourg overrun, on 31 July 1914 called up its young men to safeguard their borders and protect its neutrality. Sam and Betsy's youngest son Sidney was conscripted and stationed at Breda and Bergen op Zoom in the south. The proximity of war was brought home to the couple on one trip to see him. 'We saw people suddenly rushing very quickly to the water where a pilot was landing from one of the warplanes,' wrote Betsy. 'The pilot was interned. He told them that he had made a mistake and hadn't meant to land in Holland. Later on he was released.'

Blockades and trade embargoes imposed in 1917 by both German and British governments on The Netherlands and other neutral countries led to shortages of raw materials which spurred manufacturers to try out new methods of production. Tensions grew as both German and British navies sunk or seized Dutch merchant ships and fishing trawlers.

The Dutch van den Berghs trod a careful balancing act, trying to keep in contact with their British brothers and cousins, while remaining neutral. Sam and Betsy had bought a weekend house called Selvetta in the woods outside Rotterdam. Among the tennis courts and gardens, Sam and Betsy looked after some of the interned soldiers. Betsy wrote: 'Soldiers who, fighting in Belgium, had crossed over our border were interned. The German internment camp was at Rotterdam; and the English one at The Hague. There was also an English internment camp in Groningen where the young people had formed a comedy group called "The Timbertown Follies", which performed some very good shows. One of the internees was famous as he appeared beautifully in a woman's costume...

'Sam had received requests from his friends in trade and foreign acquaintances to do something for their interned families and acquaintances in The Netherlands and so every Saturday the Germans, and on Sundays the English – separate days so as to avoid conflict – came to Selvetta. But by accident an Englishman turned up on a Saturday – the German day – to visit us and asked if he could be admitted. They were just playing tennis. Sam sent his son-in-law Andriesse to tell him it was a German day and that it wouldn't be pleasant for him to meet them. The Englishman laconically answered "never mind we are not on the battlefield". And indeed later on they were all playing tennis in a friendly way.'

As the Dutch, cut off from their trading partners and still fearing invasion, tried to deal with the vagaries of wartime, Simon was cut off from European universities. He concentrated on working on his books and bringing up his family. But two tiny girls held little interest.

Isaac and Anna's house on
Nassaulaan

Simon's relationship with his father deteriorated, particularly when, on 2 November 1916, Isaac remarried. His bride was 52-year-old Anna Sloenhek, who was born in Den Helder. Isaac's brothers Arnold and Sam and a friend Salmon Van Embden were witnesses. Isaac's new wife was deeply unpopular with the family. 'Aunt Anna' was described by them as being 'very common'. She and Isaac were accused by Simon, and his uncles and aunts, of 'supposedly' drinking a bottle of champagne every day. They moved into a luxurious 26-room house, surrounded by servants ready to answer their every whim.

Years later Simon outlined his concerns to his second wife Maureen: 'Her one aim in life was to spend as much money as possible so there would be less for Simon,' recalled Maureen. 'Of course she couldn't get Isaac to leave everything to her. But she spent a great deal of his money. She would take a house furnish it, leave it and move onto another one.' Records show a slightly different story. Far from moving from one house to another, they remained in their main house at The Hague until 11 May 1928 when they moved to 11 Nassaulaan. On 20 January 1931 they moved to 11 Nieuwe Duinweg, where Isaac was registered as living until 1939.

The relationship between Simon and his father further deteriorated when Anna's orphaned nephew Hendrik William Sloenhek moved in with Isaac and Anna on 29 August 1918. Born in 1907, he was the son of Anna's brother Hendrik who died in 1916, his mother dying a year later. Hendrick moved out six years later on 29 August 1924.

A bitter row broke out between Isaac and Simon over the way Anna treated his mentally ill, disabled sister Liesje. Simon felt Anna put the welfare of her nephew over that of her step-daughter, particularly when she tried to persuade Isaac to put Liesje into an institution or a boarding house, where she could be confined and looked after. Simon was furious and won the argument. Liesje remained at home living with her father. But Isaac, although

Simon and Sonia's house on
Nassau Ouwerkerkstraat

Top: Sonia and the two girls at home in The Hague. Above: Tamara and Lisa in the garden

taking a more sensitive approach to his daughter's welfare, was equally furious at the aspersions made by his son about his new wife and cut off financial support to Simon and his family.

The relationship between Simon and Isaac was only restored in 1936 when Anna suddenly died. Isaac was then 83 years old. Maureen was with Simon when he heard the news of his stepmother's death: 'Simon went back to be with his father for the funeral. Isaac was lonely, he had no one else. He asked Simon to stay with him. And from then on they were close.'

On 30 April 1928 Liesje would finally move out of her father's home into a lodging house at Valkenbosplein 4, in The Hague. The house was owned by Mattias Verhoeks, a shopkeeper selling cheese and butter, who was a customer of the Van den Berghs. He was paid to help look after her and try to give her a sense of the independence she craved. Liesje committed suicide on 15 February 1930, aged 49.

Simon was not wholly dependent on Isaac's funding because he had money of his own, left to him in a trust fund by his mother, which he augmented by writing articles and reviews for Dutch newspapers. Clara had owned stocks and shares in diverse concerns such as American railways, Smithfield Meat Market in London and of course Van den Berghs. Although these had in the main been left in trust to Isaac, they were expected to go to Simon after his death. On 23 December 1918, following the distribution of his mother's estate, Simon and his family took over the ownership from Isaac of their house at Van Stolkweg 8, which they subsequently sold for 60,000 Guilders, moving on to Nassau Ouwerkerkstraat 10. They remained there until 2 May 1919, employing an English nanny to help bring up their children.

Although there was less money coming into the family's coffers, it was still a life of ease. Four female servants worked for them at Van Stolkweg and three while they lived at Ouwerkerkstraat. Some of the household goods, such as carpets, tables and lights inherited from Clara, ensured they lived in comfort and style. Photographs taken at the time show a beautifully dressed Sonia, wearing the flowing kimono-type outfits she favoured, with her two beautifully turned out little girls in their frilly short dresses and ribbons in their hair.

A new era

In 1918 at the eleventh hour on the eleventh day of the eleventh month, the First World War came to an end. German troops on the Western Front, returning home to cheering crowds, were acclaimed as heroes. The Germans were told that peace had come with an armistice and not with defeat. Revolution had already broken out in Germany, triggered by a sailors' revolt in the naval ports of Wilhelmshaven and Kiel, which spread across the country within days to the army and industry. It led to the proclamation of a republic on 9 November 1918 and shortly thereafter to the abdication of Kaiser Wilhelm II.

The Kaiser fled to sanctuary in The Netherlands, leaving Germany's newly appointed leaders to seek peace. Germany had suffered 6 million casualties, including 1.8 million dead, leaving 2 million orphans, 1 million invalids and 1 million widows. It faced starvation and ruin, as America, France, Britain and their allies met in Paris to discuss terms to be imposed by the Treaty of Versailles.

On 28 June 1919, the newly constituted Weimar Republic's provisional Federal Government of six ministers, led by the Social Democrat Friedrich Ebert and including two Jews, finally signed the Treaty, agreeing to give up its claims to territory in Poland. The population and land area of Germany was reduced by about 10 per cent, as Alsace and Lorraine were returned to France, three small areas in the northwest were given to Belgium and, after a plebiscite, Northern Schleswig was restored to Denmark.

The Treaty imposed harsh reparations on Germany, decimating its economy. As politicians fought for the survival of their new democracy, the country was riven by anger at the loss of life and sudden collapse of their industrial war machine. Revolution and disquiet affected nearly every state. Nationalistic Germans turned on their politicians in fury at the loss of territories. The Russian revolution of 1917 spilled over into Germany and old soldiers fought against workers, crushing Communist risings in Berlin. A 'Soviet Republic' was founded in Munich.

Although Germany faced financial ruin and turmoil, the founding of the Weimar Republic led to a wave of optimism throughout the country as old barriers of class, religion and ethnicity fell. Universities for the first time opened their faculties at all levels to men and women no matter their race or religion. A new party, the German Democratic Party, founded by Theodor Wolff, the editor of the *Berliner Tageblatt*, won the support of Jews such as the scientist Albert Einstein and the industrialist Walther Rathenau. Until then Jews had been unable to participate in political life. The German Democratic Party was one of the mainstays of the new Republic during its first years.

Meanwhile, another new political force, the German Labour Party, was being formed. The party had little in common with other Labour parties such as that in Great Britain. It would later change its name in 1921 to the Nationalsozialistische Deutsche Arbeiterpartei, later known as the Nazi Party. On 12 September 1919 it gained a new member, a 30-year-old former soldier called Adolf Hitler. At its first public meeting, held in Munich on 24 February 1920, Hitler newly elected as Chairman, set out a 25-point programme. Most of the demands called for the unification of Germany and the restitution of its former territories. Chillingly, Point Four defined who would qualify as German citizens: 'Only a member of the race can be a citizen. A member of the race can only be one of German blood, without consideration of creed. Consequently no Jew can be a member of the race... ' Hitler's intentions towards the Jews were set out in that programme and his notorious book *Mein Kampf*, published in 1925 and written while he was serving a jail sentence for high treason following his 1923 abortive coup in Munich. Sadly many refused to believe what they read.

Anti-Semitism, fanned by right-wing groups such as the Nazi Party, began to surface as the German people looked for someone to blame for their defeat and humiliation. Two leading Jewish politicians were to pay the penalty: the Social Democrat Prime Minister of Bavaria and Weimar Cabinet Minister, Kurt Eisner, was assassinated on 21 February 1919, followed in 1922 by Rathenau, who had become the Weimar Republic's Foreign Minister.

Tamara and Lisa, briefly settled in Switzerland

Moving on

Peace, though uneasy, meant that Simon and his young family could now travel again. The couple had moved to The Netherlands at the request of Simon's ill mother. Now there was no need to remain. His father's new marriage, coupled with the bitter row between the two men, had shattered any responsibility he felt towards him.

In 1919 Simon decided to move to Switzerland, where he could work for Dutch newspapers, writing about European culture. Simon could have settled in Germany among philosophers and academics, many of whom had become his friends, but the country's political instability and shortage of food hardly provided a secure home for a young family. Switzerland, like The Netherlands, was a neutral country, unblemished by war. Its snow-covered mountains offered Simon the walks he hankered for and the clean air appealed to Sonia, who was becoming increasingly concerned about her health. Switzerland would, they both hoped, provide a happy environment in which to bring up their daughters.

However, the family's youngest member, Tamara, was not in favour of moving. 'We had a beautiful garden. I loved it with its trees and flowers', she recalled. 'I hated the idea of moving to Switzerland I didn't want to give up my garden.'

In May 1919 the family moved to Heemskerckstraat 32, as they prepared to decamp to Switzerland. No maids were employed to help them during this time, indicating that financial worries had finally prompted some cutbacks. On 15 August 1919 the family moved to Geneva, where Simon worked as an arts correspondent for various Dutch newspapers. This move proved to be temporary, as there are no records to show that they ever officially registered as residents in the country. In fact, life in Switzerland left very little impression on Simon and Sonia's eldest daughter Lisa because they were there for 'only a very short while, hardly at all.'

Courtyard of the Paris Sorbonne, with which Simon's school, École des hautes études, was associated

In 1920 Simon and Sonia moved to Paris, where he had been offered a position as chargé de cours (lecturer) at the prestigious École des hautes études, which was associated with the Sorbonne. The couple settled into an apartment in Rue Peguy, Montparnesse. Lisa and Tamara were sent to the École Alsacienne in Rue Alsace Lorraine. Founded in 1874, the private school covered all three ages of education: nursery, primary and secondary.

Simon and Sonia had spoken in English when they lived in London, Dutch in The Netherlands and now in Paris, French became their everyday language. Tamara was only six years old when they moved to Paris. She would joke that she was the only little girl with a Dutch passport who didn't speak the language: 'Our parents spoke French at home all the time so that we would pick up the new language. They wanted to make sure that we would settle in and not have any problems.' Lisa, in particular, had happy memories of the École Alsacienne, which she felt was a very good school. She spoke French fluently and, like her sister, forgot her Dutch. On walks to school she became interested in art, having spotted a gallery en route which drew her time and again to its exhibitions.

Simon's position at the École had been found for him by his old, close friend from Berlin days, Professor Alexandre Koyré, who lectured on the Philosophy of Science. Koyré suggested that the move to Paris and an association with the Sorbonne would open up new opportunities for research. Koyré had studied at the renowned German University town of Göttingen before moving to Paris. Originally trained in the history of religion and philosophical thought, he later moved to the history and philosophy of science, including his highly-respected studies on the rise of early modern science and the change of scientists' perception of the world.

Simon was delighted to have been offered the position. He would be able to live in one of the most exciting, sophisticated cities in Europe, surrounded by beautiful galleries and

Cosmopolitan Bohemia at Cafe La Rotonde, Montparnasse, a lithograph from the early 1920s

full of libraries. According to Tamara, Simon found his teaching duties far from arduous, giving him the opportunity to use the university's facilities: 'He taught a course weekly, supervised the students' dissertations and spent most of his time in the library. It was wonderful for him, he had access to all the books and papers held in Paris and he spent hours lost among them. He was a perfectionist and wrote a limited number of articles.'

Simon's way of working remained the same throughout his life. His wrote in tiny handwriting, beautifully formed, a hand remarked on by everyone who was to receive letters from him. Cigarette in hand, Simon would spend hours wracking his mind over each word and line that he translated or wrote. Later, his second wife Maureen experienced the time he spent in his study: 'The door used to be closed. He would start working early in the morning. It would be hours; he would go over things again and again. He would write down one meaning of something and then he would go over that, put it aside and then look at another interpretation. Then he would go back to his original meaning and compare that with his new one, then he would go back over it all again, examining every nuance, every meaning that was behind the phrase.

'It took a great deal out of him; he was having to question himself intellectually on every level. He was looking at differences between Greek and Arabic meaning for each word, and then defining it, as he believed it should be into English, German or French. He was scrupulously honest about what he was doing and was determined not to make mistakes, or to redefine things to suit what he thought they should be to support his own arguments.'

Paris would be the family home for 20 years. It was here that Simon began work on his book *The Incoherence of the Incoherence*.

Enemies no more: the birth of a multinational conglomerate

Opposite: Unilever House in London, completed and opened in 1932

Below: Schicht was one of Van den Berghs' competitors in Eastern Europe, eventually becoming part of Unilever

IN 1908, VAN DEN BERGHS and their old enemies Jurgens formed an uneasy peace, with the two sides agreeing to cooperate in sourcing raw materials, setting quotas, agreeing advertising budgets and sharing profits in various areas of their respective margarine businesses.

The agreement followed years of dispute between the companies, dating from when Van den Berghs, according to Jurgens, 'had stolen their scheme for producing margarine'. The dispute gradually died down as the two companies faced an increase in margarine consumption alongside shortages of raw materials, such as the butter, fat and oil used in manufacturing, so they made a series of 'pooling agreements'. The 1908 agreement was the first, followed by two others in 1913 and 1920. Other forms of commercial cooperation were established during the First World War.

The end of the First World War brought new prospects for the companies, especially in exports to Britain, which had a highly lucrative market. Although both families had established British factories neither wanted to risk handing over all their production. By 1919 Van den Berghs were shipping some 30,000 tons a year, representing three quarters of its Dutch production, to the English Market from Rotterdam. Sales continued to rise and by 1920 Van den Bergh's sales in England reached 63,000 tons; Jurgens' had nearly doubled from 39,000 to 76,000 tons. Both companies, which continued to hold conferences on buying raw materials, had branched into other areas such as manufacturing soap, with Van den Berghs providing strong competition to the British-based Lever Brothers.

Van den Berghs and Jurgens were now exporting to Denmark, Sweden, France, Germany, Austria, Belgium and the West Indies. Both companies also refined raw materials, such as nut oil, in Africa. Factories had been built in Germany, to overcome import restrictions on goods from The Netherlands imposed because of Germany's economic problems. Yet the companies wanted to expand further and began to consider Eastern Europe and in particular Czechoslovakia.

Two Czech companies, Schicht and Centra, had dominated the scene in their country. Both companies had

'... this case is one of the biggest gambles undertaken in defiance of the Gambling Act' – Sir John Simon, Jurgens' barrister

The original Jurgens factory in Oss

difficulty sourcing raw materials and after the end of the First World War they faced the prospect of their previous Eastern European market being divided up among the Succession States – the new countries such as Poland, Yugoslavia and Hungary created or restored to self governance under the terms of the League of Nations, which broke up the old Austro-Hungarian empire and stripped Germany of some its territory.

In October 1919, Van den Berghs took a 50 per cent share in Centra, unveiling plans to build a large factory at Krischwitz on the Elbe. Georg Schicht described the move as 'Sam Van den Bergh's invasion of Czechoslovakia' which compounded the company's existing troubles and forced

him into an agreement, which took the form of two 'treaties' known as the Little Entente and the Great Entente. Negotiated between Schicht on one side and Jurgens, Van den Bergh and Centra on the other, the Little Entente signed on 22 November 1920 was the most important as it covered Schicht and Centra's principal markets in Czechoslovakia, Austria and Hungary. It specified how the companies were to operate in those countries, partly based on the pooling arrangements between Van den Berghs and Jurgens. The Great Entente, signed on 31 December 1920, covered a larger area, including Poland and the Free City of Danzig, Yugoslavia, Romania, Switzerland and Germany.

The Great Entente stipulated that none of the parties should 'come to an agreement or take an interest in, or come to an arrangement with Lever Brothers or any of their subsidiaries without all the parties agreeing'. Lever Brothers, with its American interests, was recognised as being the companies' single greatest competitor.

However, it was not all plain sailing. A series of disagreements between Van den Berghs and Jurgens over the 1920 pooling agreement (which had been broken by all parties) and the lack of profit-sharing since 1912 led to a request by Van den Berghs in 1924 for arbitration. The issues had become so convoluted, that no-one really understood how the agreements were to be interpreted.

Sir John Simon, the barrister speaking at the

Poster introducing Blueband
margarine to Germany in the early
1900s

Below: A Lever Brothers' Sunlight
Soap advertisement from 1887

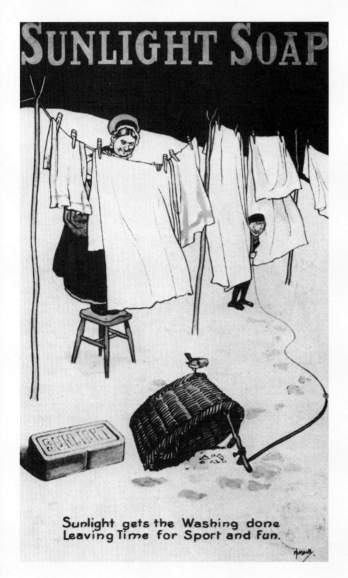

Arbitration hearing on behalf of Jurgens, summed up the problems: 'I do not know whether it is a merit or a demerit of this arbitration but I should rather infer that even the extremely distinguished accountants on either side, who seem to have spent their lives on the subject, have not the least notion as to what is the result in the end in figures of any particular contention of the hundreds of thousands of contentions which suggest themselves to ingenious minds. In that respect this case is one of the biggest gambles which has ever been undertaken in defiance of the Gambling Act.'

The extreme complexity of the arbitration case forced the two sides to look at their positions again, with Sam Van den Bergh making recommendations for a new pooling arrangement. Jurgens proposed that the two companies should combine their interests and on 24 September 1927, after months of talks, both families bowed to the inevitable and agreed to form a new company with a combined management. Other Van den Bergh family members, though unhappy at the merger with Jurgens, had taken advice from Sam who suggested that the best solution would be for them to become shareholders in the new company.

The dual organisation, Margarine Unie NV and Margarine Union Ltd, was founded in November 1927. Its structure, copied from the Van den Bergh Group, meant that although they were bound in one unit they still

Unilever, the Anglo-Dutch family business, was on its way to becoming one of the largest multinationals in the world.

A 1930s campaign promoting Blue Band's butter-like qualities

operated as separate companies, with a figure laid down for maximum production that could not be exceeded by other parts of the company. Margarine Unie/ Margarine Union inherited a combined workforce of 5,600 salesmen. In January 1929, the partnership was joined by another large Dutch manufacturing company, Hartog's. The Union, as it now became known, dominated European manufacturing of margarine. Soap was also high on their list of successful products.

The British company, Lever Brothers, manufacturers of both soap and margarine, was soon feeling an impact on its business from the power of the new Union in bidding for the common raw materials required for both soap and margarine manufacturing. In fact talks had begun between the companies in the latter part of 1928, when Margarine Unie approached Lever Brothers with a proposal to buy Levers' margarine business, Planters, which operated in Holland and other parts of continental Europe. Lever in turn made a counter proposal that it should take over Margarine Unie's soap interests in Holland and France. The talks continued through the rest of 1928 and 1929, culminating on 2 September 1929 with the agreement that Margarine Unie should merge with Lever Brothers and Schicht.

In 1930 the multinational, Unilever, was formally established. The name came from Sam Van den Bergh who,

1948 press advertisement for the
Unilever washing powder, Persil

unhappy at the larger merger, had retired in 1929. He
suggested adding 'Uni' to the front of 'Lever', so that 'Uni'
would register as the most important part of the new joint
brand name.

The dual structure of Van den Bergh's Anglo-Dutch
management was again adopted. The original 33 directors
appointed to Unilever would include four from the Van den
Bergh family, four from the Jurgens family, two from
Hartog, three from Schicht and one from Lever Brothers.
The first two Joint Chairmen were Francis D'Arcy Cooper
from Lever and the Earl of Bessborough, who had been
chairman of Margarine Unie Ltd and Margarine Unie NV.
Other independent directors included Major General S S
Long, Horatio Ballantyne and Clement Davies.

Unilever, the Anglo-Dutch family business, was on
its way to becoming one of the largest multinationals in
the world.

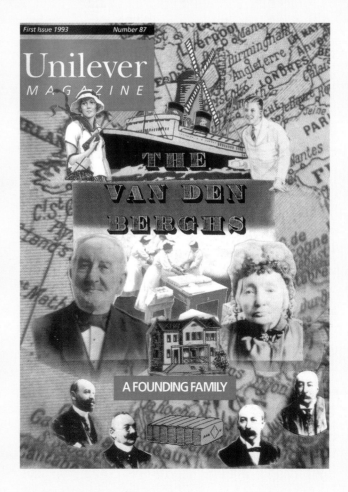

Unilever Magazine from 1993,
featuring the Van den Bergh family
history

Chapter 7   Hedonism before the Terror

If Simon had thought that the move to Paris would bring stability to his family, he was wrong. Paris was exploding with vibrancy, as France recovered from war and its people turned towards new ideas and ideals. These exciting times benefited some of the family but brought frustration and loneliness to others.

Against a background of painful post-war reconstruction, revolutions simmered throughout Europe. Communists fought Socialists; Fascists fought Communists and Socialists. The end of the Austro-Hungarian Empire and the fall of the Russian imperial order saw borders redrawn as nationalities became 'nations'. Czechs and Slovaks united in the new state of Czechoslovakia. Poland finally won its independence, establishing new borders, which included territories formerly under German and Russian rule. Suwalki returned to Poland.

Writers, poets, philosophers and artists gravitated to Paris. The narrow streets around the Left Bank (La Rive Gauche) and Montparnasse, with their little hotels and artists' studios, were packed. Restaurants and bars, such as La Coupolle, Les Deux Magots and Café de Flore, did big business as members of the 'intelligentsia' grouped around the tables deep in discussion. The American writers Ernest Hemingway and Gertrude Stein (who was also an influential art collector) joined company with the likes of the anti-fascist French writer André Malraux – winner at age 33 of the prestigious Prix Goncourt literary award – the feminist author and philosopher Simone de Beauvoir, philosophers Jean Paul Sartre and Raymond Aron, and the novellist and essayist André Gide.

The cultural environment would have included new paintings by Pablo Picasso, films by Jean Renoir and plays by Samuel Beckett and Eugene O'Neill. Paris night clubs played the latest jazz by black American musicians, who found their colour ignored and their talents welcomed, or soulful music from lost homelands as aristocratic refugees from Russia mixed with unshaven revolutionaries from Germany and the Balkans. They would in turn be joined by German Jews, Czechs and Austrians fleeing growing totalitarianism.

Cafe life in 1920s Paris

American author Scott Fitzgerald, a soldier in the First World War trying to return to normal life, epitomised the spirit of the time. Alcohol, drugs and dance filled the vacuum of war. Like other American intellectuals, he and his wife headed for France. His books *Tender in The Night* and *The Great Gatsby* appeared to sum up the era of change.

Describing life on the Left Bank, the Austrian-French novelist and essayist Manès Sperber, friend to Arthur Koestler, Malraux and Gide, wrote in his autobiography *Until My Eyes Are Closed With Shards*: 'An emigrant could feel at home on the terraces of the cafés Dôme, Rotonde, Coupole and Select, even if he had only the price of a small beer or a *café nature*. He could recognize his kind in all the people who sat there, artists who were already famous or had only recently made a name for themselves and most of whom, like the emigrant, regarded conditions and their own situation as provisional.'

Writing in *The Wandering Jews*, Joseph Roth, the Austrian novelist who moved to Paris when Hitler came to power in Germany, described how the city welcomed his fellow Jews: 'There are some quite superficial reasons why it should be easier for them in Paris. Their faces do not give them away. Their vivacity does not attract notice. Their sense of humour meets that of the French part way. Paris is a real metropolis... Crude Anti-Semitism is confined to the joyless, to the royalists, the group around the [nationalist] Action Française. In Paris there is a great tradition of practical humanity.'

Cafés and discussion, music, galleries and theatres offered an intellectual stimulus to Simon that he could have only dreamt of in The Netherlands during the war. Paris had also become one of the foremost centres for the study of Arabic languages and culture. Napoleon Bonaparte's Egyptian campaign and his fixation with ancient Egypt had encouraged French interest in its archaeology and culture. New students flocked to the Sorbonne and its schools to learn about a culture, which although older than their own, offered fresh perspectives.

Simon continued to teach at the École des hautes études and study in the library. In 1934 he wrote the preface to *Voir au Supplement Madkour (Ibrahim) L'Organon d'Aristote dans Le Monde Arab – analyses puises principalement d'un commentoire indedit d'Ibn Sinai* (Ibrahim Madkour's *The Philosophy and System of Aristotle in the Arab World – its translations, study and applications*). Published by the Bibliothèque d'histoire de la philosophie, copies are still held in the French National Library.

His closest friend in Paris, Alexandre Koyré, was a man of wide vision and many interests who shared Simon's delight in debating philosophy. The two men spent hours together wandering through the parks, sitting over the last coffee at dinner laughing and disagreeing over various points and enjoying each other's company.

Tensions at home

Although it was a rewarding time intellectually for Simon, his marriage to Sonia became increasingly unhappy. The couple shared a gift for languages – Sonia spoke Russian, German, Polish, English, Dutch and French, and would eventually learn Spanish – but they had few common interests. As Simon became more involved with the academic and cultural life of Paris, he had less time to spend with his wife. The sheer enjoyment of living in Paris should have brought happiness to the couple; instead tensions grew between them as they found

Sonia: a beautiful, solitary person, according to the couple's frequent visitor in Paris, Herman Marx

less and less to talk about.

Living in a hotel apartment in Paris, with a husband who spent most of his time in libraries or working intently on his papers, far away from her homeland and without the companionship of her sisters, Sonia grew increasingly isolated. Studies and intellectual development had been curtailed by marriage to Simon. She had given birth to two daughters by the time she was 22. Simon, like most Dutch husbands at that time, expected her to stay at home and look after her children. Very few women in The Netherlands, especially those from the wealthier classes, were expected to work after marriage. Although her parents were relatively well off and had employed help to bring up their children, Sonia had no idea of how to run the sort of sophisticated household Simon expected her to maintain. Neither could she provide the erudite conversation and companionship he sought.

According to their youngest daughter Tamara, her mother found it difficult to interact with other people. 'It would have been good if she had had some sort of profession but in those days, and in our family, women were not supposed to work if they had families,' she reasoned. 'She never had a chance to develop an interest. She very rarely talked about her own life. The only thing she really got interested in was wanting to be a dancer. She was fascinated by Russian dancing.'

Sonia was always beautifully dressed: one photograph shows her lying in the grass in Paris' Bois du Boulogne, in an exquisite flowing dress; another shows her dressed in a Spanish robe. Yet, surrounded by all that Paris had to offer by way of intellectual stimuli, she floundered, turning from one idea to another. She tried to make an impression on her husband and his friends by interjecting her latest findings into their discussions, usually to Simon's annoyance. He showed little patience towards his wife and her attempts to join in conversations with his friends. Sadly, she had very little sense of humour and often failed to understand Simon's academic jokes or banter, which made things worse. Rosalida Polak, the granddaughter of Simon's uncle, Arnold van den Bergh, noticed the tensions when she often visited the family in Paris. Sonia, she recalled, always seemed to be unhappy: 'She would sit in a corner, often crying, very sad. She was very beautiful but seemed very young and out of her depth. It was very difficult for them all, she so much wanted to be part of what was going on but didn't seem to know how to.'

Rosalida remembered Sonia as being very kind but during her visits Simon would take over. 'He was full of energy, excited about things, and she would be forgotten,' Rosalida said. 'Simon would put Sonia down in front of people. He would get angry, complaining that, "She doesn't know what she is talking about". It led to quarrels. Then she would go away to take cures at various spas and sanatoriums.'

Another frequent visitor to Paris was Herman Marx, the son of Simon's cousin Bertha and her husband, his old friend Eugen. 'Their marriage wasn't happy, that was evident,' Herman said. 'She was rather extraordinary. She sat there in a chair watching him and didn't say anything. I remember a woman of great beauty who never seemed to be part of what was going on. She was a rather solitary person who seemed distant from everyone, even her own daughters. She was always very kind and hospitable but she found it difficult to sit and talk to you, it was a little like she was scared to. I think that she must have felt very lonely. She never seemed to have any of her own friends and although she saw quite a lot of Simon's family she must have missed her own.'

Sonia's family in Poland in 1924. Back: Mina and Abrasha. Front: Pauline, Chonel, Naftali (Alter) Glikson

Although Sonia kept in touch with her brothers and sisters, Tamara cannot recall her mother corresponding with her parents in Suwalki: 'I saw various notes written in Yiddish but she never talked about these or about her parents. She never made any attempt to take us to Poland to see them. Nor, with the exception of telling us about leaving the ghetto to go to a Catholic school, would she talk about growing up in Poland.'

Sonia's brothers and her sister Jenny had visited her in The Netherlands on their way to America. In 1924, her 17-year-old nephew Abrasha, the next member of the family to leave Poland in search of a better life, stayed with the couple in Paris on his way to Argentina. Her sister Pauline's son intended to spend a year in Buenos Aires, where he hoped to obtain a visa so that he could eventually join his uncles in the USA. A change in American immigration quotas meant he was to remain in Argentina, becoming an Argentine citizen. He would later marry Luba, whose own family had also been refugees from Poland. Abrasha and Luba became close friends of Simon and Sonia.

Sonia showed little interest in her two daughters. Her eldest, Lisa, loved growing up in Paris. Like her parents, Lisa was very good looking, so she had several boyfriends, which worried Simon who was always very judgemental about both his daughters' boyfriends and made his feelings clear. Lisa called this 'a typical father's reaction', but was more puzzled by Sonia's behaviour. 'My mother was completely detached from it all,' she recalled. 'She couldn't care less what I did with my life. It wasn't sad but typical of some people. You didn't bring up your own children, you left it to other people.'

Sonia's attitude towards her daughters may have stemmed from her parents, who had put hard work before spending time with their children. Her mother-in-law Clara had died before being able to give advice and help. Without a role model, Sonia may have simply been too young to deal with the responsibility of bringing up a family, a theory supported by Tamara. The girls were often left alone as Sonia suffered breakdowns and, convinced she was in poor health, frequently left Paris to visit various spas in the Pyrenees where she felt the air and waters would improve her mental and physical condition. Sonia was becoming a hypochondriac. With few friends, she became even more withdrawn.

Family members celebrate Arnold and Julie van den Bergh's wedding anniversary in 1928.

Back row, standing from left: Joseph Van Raalte, Jacques Polak, Katie Coopman, Herman Marx, Loutie Waterman, Harry Tels*, Lucie Juliette Tels.

Middle row, standing from left: Louise (Loutie) van den Bergh*, Laura Marx, Lydia (Beebs) Van Raalte*, Constance Polak, Leo van den Bergh, Bertha Marx**, Annie Waterman, Eugen Marx**, Frtiz Van Raalte.

Front row, sitting from left: Aunt Lena, Sam, Henry and Betsy van den Bergh, Julie van den Bergh holding Martinus Tels, Arnold, Jacob, Annie and Carolina van den Bergh.

Bottom row of children seated on the ground, from left: Constance and Frans* Van Raalte, Arnold, Rosalida and Adolph Polak.

*Murdered by the Nazis

**Committed suicide under threat from the Nazis

Lisa and Tamara, looked after by nannies, lived in apartments and boarding houses. Simon's second wife Maureen explained this meant they had no home life. 'They had nowhere they could bring their friends to visit – and that was difficult in Paris before the war, which was very snobbish', she said. 'You had your home, you had your parents and grandparents in the country. You had no great standing but you had a certain rank, bourgeois manners certainly. The girls found it very difficult having such a dysfunctional background.' According to Maureen, Lisa in particular did not get on well with her mother and she found the lack of a home life especially hard to deal with as, being the older of the girls, she had to find her own way forward. She said Lisa and Sonia fought like 'cat and dog'.

Although Simon adored his daughters, some members of the family, such as Rosalida, felt he did not give them much support with their social lives or their academic studies. 'They were such bright girls but I can remember him pooh-poohing their studies,' she said. 'He was closer to Tamara. She was very much her father's daughter, delightful and warm. She stayed in Paris and saw far more of her parents than Lisa did. Lisa wasn't happy. She didn't like the fact that Simon liked other women and she had very little time for her mother.' Tamara presented a different picture. She found her father supportive but felt he was unable to help with problems he could not understand: 'He was always very generous but when you experienced something he couldn't imagine, he couldn't help you. It wasn't something that he was likely to go through.'

Simon and his family still saw a great deal of the other Van den Berghs. Simon visited his uncle Jacob during the summers at his holiday homes in Frinton and Margate, and joined him and uncle Sam on driving holidays to Baden-Baden and Marienbad. Sam and his wife Betsy had a house near Nice, which quickly became a holiday base for all Sam's brothers and their families.

Nice was now a flourishing town, as holidaymakers enjoyed the new hobby of sun-

A family get-together in Nice. Betsy
is seated at the centre of the group

bathing. Rich Americans, fleeing the oppressive American laws of prohibition, were drawn to the French Riviera. A new luxury hotel and casino, the Palais de la Méditerranée, opened in 1929 on the Promenade des Anglais. Air conditioned and with dance halls, bars and a swimming pool, the hotel soon became a major attraction for the Van den Berghs, most of whom – both Dutch and British – enjoyed gambling. Here they could wander around the gaming tables, pretending not to stare at the Shah of Persia or the Queen of Romania; or take a box in one of the theatres to watch the latest form of dance originated by the likes of the American Isadora Duncan and the Ballet Russes.

Meanwhile, younger members of the Van den Bergh family were despatched to Paris, where Simon would introduce them to the city he loved and which had become his home. Herman Marx was one of this next generation to become a friend of Simon's. 'He was a very close friend of my father and they would often see each other,' explained Herman. 'I went to Paris from school and Simon introduced me to art. He would take me around all the galleries, not just the famous ones but also the smaller, sometimes more esoteric ones. He would talk away about paintings describing the meanings behind them, telling me about the artists. I still remember him with gratitude.'

Herman felt Paris helped to keep Simon young: 'He seemed to understand what young people wanted to see and do. Paris seemed a city for the young – and that applied to everyone; they became ageless. He once said to me that Paris had made him feel alive and vital. There was so much to do; everything was there. He seemed happier living there than anywhere else.'

Women played an important part in Simon's life. Herman remembered him being involved with a beautiful Polish woman other than Sonia. According to Herman, they stayed somewhere near La Coupole restaurant. 'There is no doubt that he liked women. I think that he was always looking for the perfect companion, someone who could talk to him about all the things that he was interested in. He needed someone who was not only beautiful and charming but someone with whom he could feel really close to and hold a dialogue with... Sadly he didn't have that sort of relationship with Sonia; I can't remember them really talking together properly in real companionship. No-one really fitted the bill, and I think that's why he always seemed to be trying to find the right person.'

The perfect companion?

In the late 1920s, while on holiday in Switzerland with his family, Simon met and fell in love with Maureen Cullinane from Cork, the daughter of Jeremiah Cullinane, a Chief Petty Officer in the Royal Navy. At just 20 years old, she was only two years older than Lisa. Maureen realised that Simon was married but 'it was one of those things'. The two began a liaison that would last for over 40 years, although they would be married for only 10 of them.

Maureen was a beautiful, independent girl, who appeared older than she was. She had left home when she was 16 years old, to learn Italian as an assistant to an Italian opera singer. Her childhood was similar to Simon's in that her parents concentrated their attentions on her brother Harry, a severe asthmatic: 'I was left very much to myself, which I liked. I didn't have girlfriends. I didn't want any children. I had a cat that I adored, books and that was all I wanted. It meant that I wasn't reliant on anyone and could take care of myself.'

Maureen was just 18 when she told her mother Molly that she would not 'under any condition' marry an Irish man or live in Ireland. 'I felt that you were shut in, men went off and played golf or something, and you had children and that was your life,' she explained. 'You had a holiday, perhaps, but that was all. And that to me was a waste of a life. Irish men were very selfish and life in Cork was very quiet, nothing happened. So I had a feeling that there was so much in the world to see, there must be wonderful places, and I am not going ever to tie myself down here.'

Maureen moved to Paris to be near Simon but quickly became frustrated with the relationship. Tired of just being his mistress and getting increasingly annoyed by his failure to marry her, she left Paris and returned to her parents in Ireland. 'The point came when I decided it was hopeless,' she explained, 'I realised that I didn't know whether Sonia would divorce him or not, but he felt very attached to his two girls, and that meant he was hesitant about breaking off the marriage. I went back home. So Simon then got frantic, he asked Sonia if she would divorce him, and the answer was yes. He came at that time; he had to come by train over to Ireland to see my parents and ask them to allow me to marry him.'

Not surprisingly, Maureen's parents, living in a rigid Catholic society, were less than delighted to meet Simon. 'He was like the devil,' she recalled, 'so there was no question of being allowed to marry him or have a relationship. I was told never to have any contact again with him... He had to promise not to write. And for one year, unless it was at table and when anyone was there, my parents never addressed one word to me.'

However, Simon did send Maureen cases of books, which enabled her to read translations of Russian, German and other books not available in Ireland. 'Every single book was gone through and examined by my parents to see if there were any messages for me,' she remembered. Maureen was certain Simon was trying to contact her and discovered that her parents had missed a message in one of the books: 'By accident I found a little note written to the General Post Office in Cork. And I went there, and there was a letter. It said: "I want news of you, write to me *poste restante*." So I made contact with him. I had a passport and that was that.'

Maureen left her parents and travelled to London. Simon was waiting for her. If she had any doubts about their relationship, their time in London seems to have banished them. An interest in music brought the two closer together. Simon took Maureen to concerts, which she'd had no opportunity to experience in Ireland, as well as to galleries. 'Bit by bit I was getting more interested,' she explained. 'I think in a way there was an element... of teacher and pupil (and) it made for a very good relationship. I was very much younger than he was... but he looked very young for his age.

'He was a very healthy man. He never had an illness, not even a headache. He was really tough. He used to say that he was built of steel and concrete. Of course beside him I looked very frail, especially in those days because my hair was very black and my skin was very fair and I was very slim, which gave the impression that he was a very strong man.'

Simon and Sonia did not divorce and Maureen returned once more to see her mother when she was taken ill. 'In the end it wasn't very serious,' she recalled, 'and I went back and lived in a flat (in Paris) near the Van den Berghs.' In 1932, when Maureen was 24, she became nominally a 'Companion' or 'Governess' to Simon's daughters. The couple fell into a typical lifestyle for some wealthy families at that time, with a few hours after work allotted to the mistress and the rest of the time to the family. Although in Simon's case, less time was now allotted to Sonia. This did not go down well with Simon's immediate family.

'He was unreliable when it came to dealing with his relationship with Maureen,' said Tamara. 'He would tell us he wouldn't see her again, and then of course he would go ahead and do so.' Showing at least some sensitivity, Simon avoided various family reunions, which would have required him to appear with his wife.

Maureen was practical and began to take over many basic duties. The couple travelled together on lecture tours. Maureen accompanied him to seminars, looking after him, making sure he had all his papers. She would pack his bag, put out his shirts and select his ties and shoes. 'I had to take care of everything he had to carry, as having been brought up with servants, he didn't know where to begin,' she explained. 'I don't know what he had done before, because his wife didn't do it for him. He must have got the maid to do it. He expected me to have everything that he needed and that everything would be ready for him. I would find his notes stuffed into his pockets – and once his passport, which he thought he had lost, tucked away in a shoe.'

Simon may not have been able to pack a bag, or organise what sort of clothes he should wear, but he knew where his responsibilities lay when it came to looking after his daughters and members of his family. 'Father was reliable when it came to mundane things like meeting Aunt Betsy at the Gare de Nord and taking her across Paris to the station to go South or taking her out,' recalled Tamara. 'He always made sure that we had enough money on us and that if we were going on trips that everything had been arranged for us... '

Carol Simpson, the granddaughter of Simon's cousin Albert, remembered Simon's kindness when confronted by disparaging remarks made by her mother, Albert's daughter Enid, about Carol's 'dark' Mediterranean looks. 'I was about seven years old and the whole family were on holiday in Frinton,' she said. 'My mother had insisted on dressing me in pale or white clothes since some child had yelled out two years before "there's a black baby". I looked awful in those clothes but she wanted to try and make me look English.

'The children had been paddling about in the pools. She made me wear a hat to stop me from getting any browner. But it had fallen off and she was very angry with me. Simon came over, leant down and brushed my tears away (and said): "She's a lovely bright little girl, she looks very Parisian and she's coming walking with me." He took me by my hand and went with me to find my hat. I have never forgotten that. Whenever he saw my grandfather he would ask how his little Parisian was.'

Years later they would meet in Ireland. Carol, writing under the name of Carolyn Swift,

Carol Simpson, née Samuel, Simon's 'Little Parisian', who became a successful children's author in Ireland

Lisa enjoyed a good life in England

became one of the country's most successful children's authors. '*The Irish Times* had just done a feature about a radio programme I had written, when I got a phone call from Simon to say that he and his companion Maureen were in Ireland and that he was delighted to see I had been doing so well,' she recalled. 'He said he wasn't surprised as I had been such a bright child and all I had needed to do was to get away from home. He was also glad to see that the paper's photograph showed that I still looked delightfully Parisian.'

Lisa and Tamara spread their wings

Both Lisa and Tamara became very successful academically. Lisa wanted to be a doctor but ran against problems: 'In those days you didn't do it. Not if you were a nice girl,' she explained. 'It is quite extraordinary.' She took her baccalaureate in Paris and, being able to speak very good English, went to Oxford and studied at the Radcliffe hospital to be an almoner, a medical social worker helping to look after patients' problems. She then met Cherry Morris, who was head almoner of St Thomas' Hospital in London, and she offered Lisa a job.

In the early1930s Lisa was invited to stay in London by her great Uncle Henry at his house in Kensington Palace Gardens, then, as now, one of the finest addresses in London. Henry's interest in South American and Egyptian artefacts and antiquities had led to his accumulating one of the finest collections in England, which he displayed in great cases in his magnificent house. Henry was by now a widower and loved the company of young people such as Lisa, who shared his interests in music and art.

Life in England was far better for Lisa than it had been in Paris. 'Henry had a wonderful house, he paid for everything. He had about six servants,' Maureen remembered. 'He wanted her to marry her [second] cousin Bob Sainsbury, who she had met whilst staying with her grandfather Isaac on holiday in the South of France.'

In 1887, Simon's father Isaac had acted as a 'commercial cupid' to his brother Sam and his beloved Betsy, when he had persuaded his brothers to make Sam a director of the company, so Betsy's mother would give them permission to marry. Now it was the turn of Sam and Betsy to provide a beautiful location for Simon's daughter Lisa and Bob (Robert) to begin their romance.

Sam retired in 1929 and he and Betsy, although owners of a large house at Wassenaar, gradually began to spend most of their time in Nice, where they owned the home christened 'Arcadia' by their granddaughter Bep. The house sat in the hills above the city, surrounded by lush green lawns, with ponds, marbled walkways, and views over the blue Mediterranean below. The building seemed to create a magic aura for all who visited it. The house rapidly became a summer retreat for all the Van den Berghs.

Bep, the daughter of Simon's favourite cousin George, spent many holidays with her grandparents. 'It was a beautiful house, it sparkled outside and was cool inside. It was a joyous place, everyone relaxed when they came to it,' she enthused. 'Sam and Betsy always had people staying with them because they were so kind and hospitable. Old friends from The Netherlands and of course all the family, Dutch and English, were invited. They gave lots of

The landscape around Nice, painted by Maud Van den Bergh, the wife of Jacob's eldest son Albert, while staying with Sam and Betsy

parties and always made sure we were never bored. There would be trips along the coast to Italy and visits to other towns.'

According to Bep, the couple were popular with the local community because they were generous and set up various charities to help townspeople who lost jobs when visitors stopped going to the Riviera because of The Great Depression in the 1920s and 1930s. 'Sam also established a seat at the University of Marseilles for a Professor of Dutch Language,' said Bep. 'They both had wonderful humour and would not allow anyone to be sad or depressed. The house seemed to capture their spirits. It was impossible not to love it.'

The help the couple gave to the community was remembered during the Second World War, when the town's Mayor, Jean Médecin, bravely showed his support for the family by insisting on speaking at Sam's funeral at the Jewish cemetery. He would later be instrumental in providing identity cards and ration books for members of the family hiding from the Germans.

Frank Instone married Joan, the daughter of Simon's cousin Henry Van den Bergh, in 1932. The couple spent several months with Sam and Betsy during the Summer of 1934. 'I remember throughout that summer there seemed to be Van den Berghs from England and The Netherlands coming down to Nice. It was the first time that I met most of the Great Uncles,' he explained. 'Joan's grandfather Jacob had recently died, but the others still seemed to be going strong. They were all interested in what each other's children were doing. It was rather like a great tribal meeting, lots of laughter, all very relaxed.

'I can remember Isaac very well. He had his granddaughter Lisa with him and was intent on introducing her to everyone. I remember him peering around the side of a palm tree looking to see who was there. He escorted Lisa about making sure that she was enjoying herself. Robert Sainsbury was down there too... And I remember that Isaac made it apparent that he approved of their relationship – in fact he did his utmost to bring them together.'

A relaxed atmosphere, balmy weather and blue skies and seas proved a perfect backdrop to the romance. Isaac's match-making paid off. Robert Sainsbury was the son of Simon's cousin Mabel, whose father Jacob had established the London side of the business with his brother Henry the previous century. He and Lisa were married quietly in a London Register Office in 1937. Neither Simon nor Sonia attended the wedding as their daughter Tamara was ill in hospital.

Robert and Lisa would have four children and stay together until his death in 2000. Their shared love of art encouraged the couple to accumulate one of the finest collections in England. In his memorial to his father, David Sainsbury pointed out that few other collectors would have had the imagination and perception to buy early works by the then unknown Henry Moore, Francis Bacon and Alberto Giacometti. Robert would also show his humanity and support for his wife's love of medicine by serving as a Governor of St Thomas'

Robert Sainsbury won Isaac's approval

Hospital from 1939 to 1968, and as Honourable Treasurer of the Institute of Medical Social Workers from 1948 to 1971.

Marriage to Robert brought Lisa a close relationship with her mother-in-law Mabel, which would give her the support, love and affection she had rarely received from her own mother. Mabel had inherited the Van den Bergh vitality: she and her sister Rosie had once accidentally disrupted Henley Regatta by blocking one of the locks. No one had told the sisters that, having tied their boat to the side of the lock to wait for the gates to open, they were then expected to release the ropes so that the boat was lowered as the water flowed down and out. The boat was left stranded, tied up to the top of the lock. She had also inherited her grandmother Elisabeth's concern for the less fortunate. Mabel adored Lisa who was after all a member of her own family.

'I got on very well with Mabel,' Lisa recalled. 'She was very nice with a good sense of humour. We were different generations of course.'

Henry Van den Bergh died shortly after the wedding. He had written a book about his collection of Aztec and Inca artefacts, which he left to the British Museum. His house in Kensington Palace Gardens was bombed in the Second World War but would eventually be restored to became the Russian Embassy.

Storm clouds gather

As the Roaring Twenties ended, hopes of peace after the First World War were being eroded. In 1929 the New York stock market on Wall Street crashed, following several boom years based largely on property and commercial speculation. The crash coincided with and contributed to The Great Depression, which had a devastating effect on most industrialised countries. Germany was hit hard as American banks called in their loans. Millions of Germans queued for bread as businesses closed and thousands became homeless. Unemployment rose from 1.6 million in 1929 to over 6 million in 1932, representing 33 per cent of the workforce. Weimar politicians, fearing a return to rampant inflation, introduced new stringent fiscal policies, which led to increases in taxes and cuts in wages and unemployment benefits.

In February 1934, a workers' rising in Austria was brutally suppressed by the right-wing government and military. Some 1,200 people were killed, 5,000 wounded and 10,000 arrested as fighting broke out among the socialist housing projects of Karl Marx-Hof and the Reumannhof in Vienna and wider afield. No European country was unaffected by the crippling aftermath of the First World War and subsequent financial mismanagement. Hungry and dissatisfied people looked for scapegoats.

The leaders of the Weimar Republic tried to keep control of an economy and society struggling to survive. Jews were seen as controllers of the big British and American banks and blamed for the withdrawal of loans and resulting poverty. Sturmabteilung (stormtroopers), also known as 'brown shirts', the Nazi paramilitaries who had previously concentrated on street battles with Communists, now turned their attention to the Jews. In the first of the ethnic murders that would herald a campaign aimed at killing and brutalising Germany's Jewish community, they celebrated New Year's day in 1932, by murdering eight Jews.

The German Parliamentary election of July 1932 produced great gains for the Nazi Party, which became the largest party in the Reichstag (German Parliament), though without an overall majority. On 30 January 1933, after months of political agitation by senior figures from the major parties, the elderly, unwell President Paul von Hindenburg appointed Hitler as Chancellor of a coalition government. On 17 February the Reichstag was burnt down in a fire, purportedly instigated by communists. In response, an emergency decree was introduced, harshly restricting civil liberties and freedom of the press and giving the state powers to imprison opponents of the Nazis. Thousands of communists, trade unionists and socialists were arrested. Newspapers were taken over or shut down.

A few Jewish 'enemies of the state', including the philosopher and literary critic Walter Benjamin, novelist and playwright Lion Feuchtwanger and physicist Albert Einstein, left the country or were already on trips abroad and chose not to return. They would later be joined by leading scientists Edward Teller, Lise Meitner, Otto Frisch and Otto Meyerhof.

A new election was called for 5 March 1933. The Nazi party increased its share of the vote but still had no overall majority. However, with social democrat and communist deputies either in jail or in flight from the stormtroopers, on 23 March 1933 the Nazis managed to gather enough support from Catholic and conservative-nationalist parties to achieve the two-thirds majority needed to pass the Enabling Act, which gave Hitler the power to enact laws without consulting the Reichstag. A series of anti-communist and anti-Semitic measures were introduced. Within four months, Hitler and his cohorts took control of the whole of Germany as political parties were banned.

Hitler's Nazi party took control of Germany, effectively outlawing any internal opposition to his regime

On 1 April 1933, the Nazis' daily national newspaper *Der Allemagne* had published lists of Jewish physicians, dentists and medics who were to be boycotted. The Reich Governor of Baden, Robert Wagner, on 6 April ordered the dismissal of all Jewish civil servants. On 7 April, the Law for the Restoration of the Professional Civil Service was passed, preventing Jews and political opponents from serving as teachers, professors and judges, or in other government positions. Shortly after, a similar law was passed concerning lawyers, doctors, tax consultants and notaries. The civil service, including universities, began to be purged of socialists, democrats and Jews. Later that month, questionnaires were sent to all university professors, asking them about the religious origins of their grandparents. By the end of 1933, some 1,200 Jews holding academic posts had been dismissed.

Also in April 1933, the anti-Semitic National Socialist Student Association called for the burning of 'destructive Jewish writing'. Universities drew up lists of books to be burned. On the night of 10 May, more than 20,000 books were burned in Berlin and thousands more on university campuses in cities throughout Germany. The works of Thomas Mann, Bertolt Brecht, Albert Einstein, Ernst Toller and Vicky Baum were consigned to the flames. So was much of German culture. No list has been kept of books and papers destroyed either nationally or by individual universities. It is highly likely that Simon's book *Die Epitome der Metaphysik Des Averröes* would have been one of those thrown onto the bonfire.

In 1820, the German Jewish poet and philosopher Heinrich Heine, then a student in Bonn, condemned an incident in October 1817 when German students burned several 'sub-

Nazi officials in Hamburg collect books for burning, 1933

versive books'. He wrote: 'Wherever they burn books they will also, in the end, burn human beings.' His books were among those destroyed.

Simon's alma mater, the University of Freiburg, was one of the first to set fire to its collection of books deemed heretic to Nazi philosophy. In April 1933, the University had elected leading German philosopher Martin Heidegger as Rector. He shortly after joined the Nazi Party. Freiburg also became one of the first universities to take action against its Jewish staff. It published a list, provided by the head of psychiatry, of all the Jewish members of its medical faculty. Heidegger was to speak out against what he called the growing 'Verjudung', or Judaisation of the German university system.

In Munich, where Simon had studied philosophy, professors from different fields wrote to the Bavarian Ministry of Education giving their support to Jewish philosopher Richard Hönigswald. The Ministry ignored them and compulsorily retired him in 1933.

Munich, the birthplace of the Nazi party, continued to host protests against Hitler. In 1943, during the university's 470th anniversary celebrations, students demonstrated against a call made by the Nazi Party's Bavarian regional leader or 'Gauleiter', Paul Giesler, for all female students to give Hitler a 'son for every year' at university. The previous year, the White Rose group was formed in Munich to protest against Nazi policies. It was led by brother and sister Hans and Sophie Scholl and their friends Christopher Probst, Willi Graf, Alex Schmorell and George Wittenstein, influenced and supported by Philosophy and Musicology Professor Kurt Huber, who had studied alongside Simon. The group wrote and circulated a series of leaflets criticising the regime. The first, written by Hans Scholl and published in the summer of 1942, called upon all German citizens to take responsibility for the evils committed in their name: 'Nothing is more unworthy of a cultured nation than to allow itself, without opposition to be "governed" by an irresponsible clique subject to dark instincts... If the German people are so corrupted and decayed that they do not raise a hand... if they abandon free will, the freedom of mankind to grasp and turn the wheel of history in line with rational decisions... then, indeed, they deserve their downfall.'

Professor Huber, the Scholls, Probst and members of the group were arrested and executed. Condemned to death in April 1943, Huber was to write from his cell: 'As a German citizen, a German University teacher and a man of political conviction, I regard it not only as a right, but as a moral duty to help shape the destiny of my county, to uncover and to oppose manifest evil.'

On 16 September 1934, the Reichstag was unexpectedly summoned to give legal endorsement to actions already taken to deprive Jews of their German citizenship. *The Times* of

London reported on the 'brilliant success' of the Nazis' strategy in obtaining support for its actions: 'The law relating to the Jews which produced fervent cheers in the Reichstag assembly, is in its essence merely a legislation of a state of affairs already in existence.

'For months past mixed marriages have been made impossible in many parts of the country by reason of judicial rulings supplemented by the arbitrary decrees of Nazi regional and local leaders where "the Law for the protection of German blood and German honour" are of minor significance. The law of German citizenship is a much more important enactment, affecting not only Jews but all those who are *personae ingratae* with the Nazis' regime and depriving them of political rights, presumably including that of suffrage.'

By 1936, pressure increased on Jews studying and teaching at German universities, particularly Jewish doctoral students. Professors were told by the State Education authorities not to accept Jews as students. Deans of several universities publicly supported the party line. On 15 April 1937 universities were ordered not to allow Jewish students studying for doctorates to sit for examinations. Jewish professors and students knew there was no future in Germany. Many joined the armies of refugees fleeing to other countries. Between 1933 and 1939, some 250,000 Jews, approximately half the Jewish population, left.

Simon was horrified at what was happening at his old universities. Herman Marx remembered a conversation between his father Eugen and Simon: 'Both talked about being shocked that people they knew had shown themselves to be anti-Semites. My father less so than Simon as, being German, he had been made more aware of these feelings. But Simon had been treated with more courtesy as he had been a foreign student. Both were dismayed that people they thought of as friends were patently not. Simon couldn't understand what Heidegger was up to in Freiburg. He had thought he would have led the universities in their opposition to the Nazis. Both of them were devastated that Germans were behaving in such a "medieval way".'

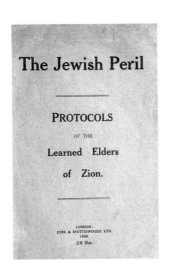

English edition of the long-discredited *Protocols of the Learned Elders of Zion*

Unrest and instability in France

Throughout these years, some of France's most prominent writers, including Louis Ferdinand Céline, Pierre Drieu La Rochelle and Jean Giraudoux, kept up a vitriolic campaign against Jews; later most were to join the Vichy Government and become Nazi collaborators. Protests against the growth of anti-Semitism and fascism in Germany were depicted by these right-wing writers and journalists as being unpatriotic. French Jews were accused of serving their own interests rather than those of their country.

Right-wingers throughout Europe seized on the *Protocols of The Learned Elders of Zion* as indicative of a Jewish conspiracy for world domination. First published in 1903 in the St Petersburg newspaper *Znamya* and in book form two years later, the document purported to be the secret plans of Jewish leaders to rule the world by manipulating the economy, controlling the media and fostering religious conflict. The *Protocols* had been exposed as a forgery in the 1920s, fabricated to whip up anti-Jewish feelings, but this has not stopped their use, even to this day, by anti-Semites. Sam Van den Bergh, having been involved in trying to establish a Jewish State and as a major industrialist, was one of those named as being behind the *Protocols*.

Anti-Semitism seeped into academia in France. Action Française, a royalist movement founded by the ultra nationalistic, proto-Fascist Charles Maurras at the turn of the century, attracted fresh support among a new generation of right-wing intellectuals. Throughout the 1930s, Simon's long-time mentor and friend Professor Alexandre Koyré was not allowed to become a member of the French Academy because he was Jewish, despite strong support from leading academics.

In 1931, the writer and Action Française supporter Georges Bernanos published his treatise *La grande peur des bien-passants (The great fear of the right thinking)*. In it he wrote: 'In this engineer's paradise, naked and smooth like a laboratory, the Jewish imagination is the only one able to produce these monstrous flowers.' According to Bernanos, Christian civilisation values and that of the nation were being threatened by the increasing domination of the Jews. He claimed that the new post-war capitalist economy was controlled by the concentrated financial power of 'les gros', a mythical 'two hundred families', which both the political left and right in France identified as being Jewish. At the beginning of the 20th century, 90,000 Jews lived in France. By 1935 this number had risen to 260,000, with approximately 55,000 more arriving by the beginning of the Second World War as refugees from Eastern Europe, Germany, Austria, Belgium and The Netherlands. Two thirds lived in Paris, which was seen as a reasonably safe place.

Those arriving in Paris included Germans such as the political philosopher Leo Strauss and Professor Richard Walzer, a friend of Simon's from his Berlin days who was married to Sophie Cassirer, daughter of the well-known Jewish art collector Paul Cassirer. Walzer was an expert in Greek and Arabic philosophy. Many of these exiles found it difficult to come to terms with leaving a homeland to which they had contributed so much. The playwright Bertolt Brecht, who fled Berlin on the morning after the Reichstag fire, believed exile would only last a short while. 'Don't go too far away,' he advised his friend the writer, anti-fascist and anti-war activist, Arnold Zweig, 'in five years we will be back.' Brecht's exile was to last 15 years.

The playwright Bertolt Brecht's exile from Germany lasted 15 years

In 1933, the Austrian novelist Joseph Roth observed the desolation of his fellow refugees as they tried to come to terms with their new existence: 'When the bailiff took power and the janitor took over the "state apartments," and the guard dogs broke free, then the German Jew was forced to see that he was even more exposed and more homeless than his cousin in Lodz had been a few years before... In a way the German Jew is even worse off than the Eastern Jew. He has forgotten how to wander, how to suffer, how to pray.

'Émigré German Jews are like a new tribe: Having forgotten how to be Jews, they are learning it all over again. They are unable to forget they are German and they can't lose their Germanness. They are like snails with two shells on their backs.'

Scared about what was going to happen to them in Paris, new refugees gravitated to each other, seeking comfort among their own kind. Dr Friedrich Zimmermann, of the Oriental Institute, Oxford, a friend of Professor Walzer, spoke years later of how exile had strengthened friendships: 'They were a very close-knit group, some of whom ended up sleeping together, marrying each other. Some moved on to America, others to Egypt and Turkey. Their paths would often cross each other. It was in some ways insular. They relied on each other as they tried to keep themselves going.'

The French Jewish establishment became concerned at the numbers of foreign Jews living in France. In 1933, lawyer Jacques Helbronner, President of the Central Consistory, the representative body of French Jews, called on the Government to control Jewish immigration by only allowing intellectual Jews to remain in the country. In 1936 he criticised the previous 1933 liberal French immigration policy.

In 1937 Joseph Roth wrote: 'The only country that so far has issued valid papers to German émigrés is France, although these again do not offer proper freedom of movement for those who hold them. Even these papers, however, were only made available to a limited number of émigrés, who had entered France before a certain date – and even then under only certain conditions. It is difficult, if not impossible, to get even this legal document stamped with the visa of any other country. Italy, Poland, Lithuania, even England, are all reluctant to admit "stateless" travellers.

'In effect only "prominent" refugees are able to travel on them – Jewish journalists, newspaper publishers, film actors, or directors: people who are acquainted with the ambassadors and consuls.'

In 1933, the 'Stavisky affair', in which several prominent radical and republican French politicians were implicated in a series of financial scandals surrounding the Russian-born Jewish financier and embezzler, Serge-Alexandre Stavisky, caused a great outcry and added to anti-Semitism. The discovery of his body in mysterious circumstances in January 1934 led to the resignation of Prime Minister Camille Chautemps of the Radical Socialist Party.

Attempts by his replacement Édouard Daladier, also from the Radical Socialist Party, to purge Government ministries of corruption failed to placate both right and left. Protesters fought on the streets. The city came closer to insurrection than at any time since the rising of 1871, which led to the establishment of the Paris Commune. On 6 February 1934, a riot was quelled in Paris with some 15 protesters killed by the police.

Divisions in French political and social life rose to the surface again with the 1936 election of the left-wing Popular Front government, headed by Leon Blum, the Jewish leader of the French Section of the Workers' International (SFIO), which contained several Jewish Ministers. The Popular Front's social reforms, such as the right to strike and collective bargaining, were actively fought by the right who often resorted to anti-Semitic slurs. The government fell out of power in June 1937, to be replaced by a National Unity Government, led by Édouard Daladier who would be party to the Munich agreement that brought about the dissolution of the Czechoslovakian republic. Daladier, along with Leon Blum, would be tried for treason by the Vichy Government in1942 and imprisoned by the Germans.

Anti-immigration measures, which had seen the expulsion of foreigners without valid papers, culminated in November 1938 with a new law allowing the immediate expulsion of aliens. A number of professional bodies began to lobby for the expulsion of Jews from their jobs. Simon Van den Bergh, a neutral Dutch citizen, began to feel uncomfortable about what fate awaited him and his family. Right-wing newspapers, read by millions of French, launched anti-Jewish campaigns calling for all Jews in France to be put under alien status. Jewish students took to the streets to fight right-wing students.

The aftermath of 'Kristallnacht', a co-ordinated attack on Jewish properties throughout Germany, Austria and parts of recently occupied Sudetenland in Czechoslovakia

Simon's École des hautes études had opened its doors to several German Professors. Now realising their futures in France could not be guaranteed, they made moves to leave. Alexandre Koyré and Richard Walzer were among those who recognised how precarious their positions had become. Koyré left for America and Walzer for England.

Fascism tightens its grip

On 7 November 1938 a young Polish Jewish student Hershl Greenspan (also known as Herschel Grynszpan), protesting at the expulsion from Germany of Jews of Polish birth (which included his parents), assassinated Ernst von Rath, a junior official at the German Embassy in Paris. German retribution was swift. Kristallnacht – crystal night, the night of broken glass – became synonymous with Nazi cruelty towards the Jews. Two days later, nearly 100 Jews were murdered, many thousands were arrested and deported to concentration camps, and synagogues and Jewish property were ransacked or destroyed. A week later Jewish businesses were told they could only open again if controlled by non-Jewish management. Jews were made to pay for the destruction of their property. None of those left in Germany could have had any doubt about the danger they were in.

Kristallnacht ripped away the last shred of innocence from ordinary Germans. A group of professors from Simon's old university in Freiburg, including prominent economists, Walter Eucken, Constantin von Dietze and Adolf Lampe, and the historian Gerhard Ritter, spoke out against the Nazi regime. The group joined the right-wing civilian resistance group lead by Carl Goerdeler, a former mayor of Leipzig. Some Freiburg professors continued to protest throughout the war despite the risk of arrest and torture. Following the failure of the 20 July 1944 assassination plot to kill Hitler, some were executed and others imprisoned in concentrations camps. Goerdeler was executed on 2 February 1945.

In Paris, Simon watched in horror as friends were harassed from their positions first in Germany and later in Austria. Thousands of refugees, Jews and non Jews, many with only the possessions they could carry, poured across the borders looking for safety. Maureen recalled: 'Simon hated war and cruelty. He was a civilised man and couldn't understand why people behaved in this way. He felt powerless because there was no way he could stop what was happening. He would become upset and very depressed when he met his German and Austrian friends and heard their stories of what had happened to them. These were people he admired and they had been treated appallingly. He would sit for hours, smoking non stop, listening to them, trying to help them decide what they were going to do next. Sometimes he would walk around for hours trying to work things out. He always made sure that there was food and lodgings for these people.'

German Jews arrested in Baden-Baden, following the co-ordinated attacks of Kristallnacht

The Netherlands received people bewildered, scared and alone, stripped of their homes, work and self esteem. By the mid-1930s, hundreds of Dutch companies had gone bankrupt, making thousands unemployed. The Netherlands had one of the world's most liberal refugee laws but, fearing the country might be overrun, they gradually restricted the numbers allowed in. By 1936 the Dutch Government had virtually banned all recently arrived German Jewish refugees from legally working in the country. In 1938, following Kristallnacht, the government closed its borders. Any German refugees who managed to cross into The Netherlands after that event were deemed 'undesirable aliens' and detained in special work camps.

Dutch Jews, worried about growing pulic concern at the rising expense of supporting refugees, approached the Government and undertook to meet all costs. Sam and Betsy van den Bergh and other members of prominent families worked hard raising money to feed and help German Jews. The couple's house Wiltzangk in Wassenaar had often been used in the late 1920s and early 1930s as the site for conferences. British politicians, including William Wedgewood Benn, Labour Secretary of State for India, the Liberal Minister Sir Herbert Samuel and Zionist Leader Chaim Weizmann, had all stayed at the house taking part in debates and talks on international affairs. These talks now continued, concentrating on what could be done about the British administration of the Palestine mandate and the increasing threat to German Jews.

A camp at Wieringen to help the refugees was set up by Sam's son, George, along with other leading Jews. Simon donated money to provide food for the refugees, pay for passages to other countries ready to accept them and for training in new trades. Professors and many other professionals would have to become farmers and carpenters if they were going to fulfil the entry requirements for Palestine, or to obtain visas and survive in other countries.

Recalling the efforts the family made to help the refugees, Betsy wrote about Wieringen: 'Here the poor refugees, who in Germany had been in intellectual professions, were learning new ones such as land working and agriculture, which in the future would be more useful to them than their previous ones... Beautiful carpentry and welding work were manufactured there. Agriculture and animal husbandry were also practised. Also girls worked in the kitchen and looked after the groceries.

'Sam went to Wieringen and saw standing in the blazing sun on a bale of hay a learned German who had escaped from Germany. He felt sorry for that unfortunate man who had to work in this way. But Sam was reassured by him; he told him that he preferred the freedom that he was enjoying there, to his earlier work as an intellectual.'

The sculptor and writer Frederic Zeller was born in Berlin. He was 14 years old in 1938. Following the terrors of Kristallnacht, he escaped across the border to The Netherlands, where he was granted temporary asylum in a camp outside Rotterdam for Jewish refugees. He had huge gratitude for the help he had been given. 'The Dutch were doing all they could, and much more than any other nation in Europe or for that matter in the world,' he insisted. 'They had taken us penniless, when no one else would. They looked after us as best they could, even though they had grave unemployment problems and there were many needy Dutchmen.'

The van den Berghs banded together. They held fundraising events to help the refugees, found homes for young children and provided food and clothing for the dispossessed. George van den Bergh's daughter Bep, then a student at the Dutch Royal Academy of Art, joined her cousins in fighting the Dutch Nazi Party's attempts to stir up anti-Semitic feelings. 'They would try to organise demonstrations against us and they would try and intimidate people to stop us helping [the Jewish refugees],' she explained. 'We would push them out of the way, reassure people that we could look after these refugees and that they would not be a burden on anyone. Sometimes it got very physical and that was when the young men would stand in the way of the Nazis. They would do stupid things like changing the signposts we had put up, telling people how to get to the various functions we organised. They tried to send them in the wrong direction but we would send people out to check on what they did.'

One big fundraising party to raise money for the Wieringen refugees was held by Sam and Betsy at Wiltzangk, despite an attempt by the Dutch National Socialist Party (the Dutch Nazis) to disrupt it. 'The party was a great success,' she recalled. 'The Dutch Nazi Party tried to wreck the party by removing the advertising boards, but many friends of the Jewish work village sent double the amount of money than they were originally going to have given. Also non-Jews gave more.'

A final party as war clouds gathered in Europe: Sam and Betsy's Golden Wedding Anniversary

Sam and Betsy's youngest grandchildren were not immune from what was happening and responded irreverently by naming their donkey 'Hitler'. 'In the past the big children had a donkey called 'Chamberlain' so politics via these names became involved in their lives,' wrote Betsy.

As war clouds gathered in Europe, the family was reunited for one of their last celebrations. In late August 1937, Simon travelled to The Netherlands to join his many cousins for Sam and Betsy's Golden Wedding anniversary. The party was held over three days at their house in Wassenaar, in what was one of the most beautiful warm summers of that decade. The family staged one of their celebratory reviews, called *We Made Margarine So That We Could Eat Butter*, which reflected their feelings about their background. Huge marquees had been erected in the gardens, where dinners and theatre performances were given in the evenings. It would be the last time many of the large family would see each other.

Against the background of the celebrations, many compared notes on what they thought would happen in the future. As Simon walked with George in the gardens, admiring the ladies dressed in their latest fashions, or stubbed out a cigarette as he sat talking with Eugen Marx, it would have been impossible not to discuss the likelihood of war. Although they were shocked by what the Germans were doing to fellow Jews, they would have felt assured that as assimilated Dutch citizens in a neutral country, the terrors would pass them by. Few could have imagined that within a few years some would have been murdered by the Nazis, others would be forced into hiding and others, such as Simon Van den Bergh and his family, would themselves become refugees.

Ibrahim Madkour: *The Philosophy and System of Aristotle in the Arab World — its translations, study and applications*

Preface by Simon Van den Bergh (translated from the French)

Left: Illuminated page from a 15th-century Hebrew edition of the *Canon of Medicine* by the Persian physician and philosopher, Avicenna

For the first time, Mr Madkour's work offers us an overview of Aristotelian logic in Arabic, based on the original writings. Mr Madkour has quite rightly drawn his analysis from the oeuvre of Avicenna, who represents Muslim philosophy at its zenith.

The importance of Arab logicians lies not in their originality, but rather in the fact that they have a wonderful grasp of very dull and purely technical subjects, primitively expressed in a language whose nature is totally different from their own. These logicians focus closely on the works of Greek commentators, which they have followed step by step.

In an albeit somewhat arbitrary way, these latter have lent Aristotle's logical writings their definitive order. They have added thereto the *Introduction* by Porphyry and they have discussed issues upon which the Master had not formed any clear opinion – for example, the relation between logic and the other sciences, and its place in the Aristotelian system. Like the Stoics, they busied themselves with linguistic studies and more actively than Aristotle himself, for whom grammatical considerations often influenced logical conceptions. From the Stoics

Marble head of Aristotle from the Kunsthistorisches Museum, Vienna, Austria

17th-century French engraving of
Porphyry

PORPHIRE   SOPHISTE

they also borrowed… the important term possibly best translated as 'signification'. In addition, they adopted the Stoic theory of hypothetical judgement… and the idea of inference, with which Aristotle seems to have been unacquainted.

For all this, in its broad outline, Aristotelian logic was regarded, among Greeks and Arabs alike, as a sure and complete science, some of whose details are, needless to say, open to criticism, but whose principle is steadfast. As far as matters epistemological are concerned, commentators have rarely touched upon them, just as they have only barely examined the serious problem of the relation between thought and reality. Broadly speaking, they have vaguely imagined that there must be a congruence between reality and thought, and that the latter is an image of the former. They have failed to see that this conception contradicts one of the fundamental principles of Aristotelianism, namely that reality is individual and knowledge universal.

It was the Greek Sceptics, whose arguments have at times been reproduced by certain theologians and mystics of Islam (Sohrawardi, for example), who first saw the difficulty: they actually noted the inconsistency of a system claiming that what is known is not real and that what is real is not known. But Aristotle's supporters paid little heed to these objections and certainly observed that the Sceptics

For all this, in its broad outline, Aristotelian logic was regarded, among Greeks and Arabs alike, as a sure and complete science, some of whose details are, needless to say, open to criticism, but whose principle is steadfast

19th-century Spanish lithograph of Avicenna

everything counter to such a notion.

As a loyal Aristotelian, Avicenna made no criticism of his master's basic doctrines; he often appears, however, as a subtle dialectician when it comes to points of detail examined by earlier commentators. Mr Madkour has faithfully followed our author's often extremely complicated thinking. The value of his book resides not only in the fact that he has managed to produce very accurate French translations of difficult writings in Arabic, but also in the fact that he has analysed and discussed them with excellent understanding, offering a constant demonstration of sound knowledge of the philosophical and logical literature.

I think that this book will therefore be a most helpful tool for the historical study of logic.

were only able to arrive at their negative theory on the problem of knowledge on the basis of the selfsame positive judgements whose value they denied. They were attached to Aristotle and as such regarded his logical conceptions as the only possible method of thought, duly neglecting

Chapter 8 The worst of times

By the mid-1930s Europe was spiralling out of control as it entered a new dark era of war and persecution. High ideals were swept aside by new dogmas. Adolf Hitler's Nazism, with its harsh racial doctrine, found an ally in Benito Mussolini's Italy. Freedom of thought gave way to persecution, imprisonment, murder and concentration camps. The lives of the Pokrojskis in Eastern Europe and the Van den Berghs in the West would be tainted by brutality.

In April 1934 Jacob, the eldest of Simon and Elisabeth's sons, died aged 86. Arnold, the family architect and instigator of their move to Rotterdam, had died two years previously at 75; age was beginning to catch up with the brothers. A kindly man, Jacob had devoted most of his life to business, setting up the British operations with his brother Henry and only retiring in the 1920s. He owned several fast cars and his love of speed had twice landed him in trouble with the police. His health had never really recovered from a car accident two years before his death.

In 1933 Hitler withdrew from the Disarmament Conference, set up by the League of Nations after the First World War to promote peace, security and human rights, and began German rearmament. The European powers' resolve was repeatedly tested as Germany stepped up demands for the return of its former territories in the East and the restoration of its old powers. On 7 March 1936 the re-equipped and well-trained German army marched into the demilitarised Rhineland, in breach of both the Treaties of Versailles and Locarno, signed after the First World War. France, Great Britain and the League of Nations protested but did little else.

In France, political scandals led to the fall of one government after another and the economy was struggling. The French were concerned that the civil war raging in Spain, where the fascist dictator General Francisco Franco was ruthlessly securing victory against Republican forces, could spill into their own country. France, divided between left and right, didn't want to get involved.

German troops goose-step down Les Champs Élysées (Nazi propaganda photograph)

Picasso's *Guernica*, exhibited at the World's Fair in 1937, reminded the French public what Hitler's bombers could do

In November 1937 Paris hosted the *Exposition Internationale des Arts et Techniques Appliqués à la Vie Moderne*, also known as the World's Fair, where artist Pablo Picasso's painting *Guernica* was unveiled. The painting's raging protest at the brutal destruction of the Spanish town earlier that year by German bomber planes shocked and reminded the French public of what was happening to their neighbours – whether they wanted to get involved or not.

Simon was a frequent visitor, escorting young members of his family and his students to see the exhibits. Maureen spent several afternoons walking around the various pavilions and remembers that Simon found the whole exhibition fascinating, particularly the Middle Eastern and Indian displays. 'He encouraged his students to go as he thought it was important that they should see as much as possible,' she said. 'He found it difficult to understand why Germany had been invited to take part in the exhibition. He was upset at the totalitarian style of the German pavilion, lamenting that a country which could produce Goethe and Schiller could have descended into such banality. He felt that it showed what the country had become.'

The first country on the list for German expansion was Austria, as Hitler shredded every treaty Germany had signed. The Austrian son of a customs officer, Hitler had since the early 1920s agitated for Austria to adopt his Nazi doctrine and unite with Germany. On 12 March 1938 the German army marched across the border, in what Hitler called the 'Anschluss' ('link-up' or political union). Austria was proclaimed a province of the German Reich. The country's President Kurt Schuschnigg and members of his government were jailed and later thrown into concentration camps for the duration of the Second World War.

Jews were made to scrub the streets. Thousands were imprisoned in anti-Semitic actions, far worse than those perpetrated in Germany. Political opponents and Jews were expelled from both teaching and student bodies in the universities. Vienna University, where Simon studied in 1904, dismissed 45 per cent of its professors and lecturers. Arthur Seyss-Inquart, appointed by Hitler as head of Germany's new Austrian province, would later become Reichskommissar of the Nazi-occupied Netherlands, where he was in charge of civil affairs. His actions would have a direct impact on the lives of those van den Berghs still living in the country.

The newly formed state of Czechoslovakia was next on Hitler's list. One of the new nations created after the First World War, Czechoslovakia comprised lands which included

Germans, Poles and Hungarians. Germans in the Czechoslovakian province of Sudetenland, under Hitler's influence, claimed they were being ill-treated and called for self autonomy and equality. On 29 September 1938, after months of German belligerence and threats of war, the British and French Prime Ministers, Neville Chamberlain and Édouard Daladier, caved into Hitler's demands and agreed to German occupation of Sudetenland, without consulting the Czech government. The new state was sacrificed without a murmur. Chamberlain's announcement of 'peace in our time' was greeted with relief by most members of the British and French public, but with dismay and shame by others.

Within six months, Hitler showed his utter contempt for Chamberlain by invading the remaining part of Czechoslovakia. The capital Prague had offered a place of refuge for Germans and Austrians fleeing Nazi rule. As German troops entered the city, thousands of Czechs joined the growing armies of refugees desperately seeking somewhere to hide from terror.

While Hitler made plans for expansion, the British public were preoccupied with the relationship between their King, Edward VIII, and the twice-divorced American Wallis Simpson, which would lead to his abdication. Finally in 1938, after the horror of Kristalnacht, the British Home Secretary Sir Samuel Hoare met a large delegation representing Jewish and non-Jewish agencies working on behalf of refugees . He agreed to allow child 'victims of Nazi cruelty' to enter Britain. The agencies promised to fund the operation and to ensure that none of the refugees would become a financial burden on the public. The rescue mission, called 'Kindertransport' (also the Refugee Children Movement), took place in the nine months prior to the outbreak of World War II. Britain took in nearly 10,000 predominantly Jewish children from Nazi Germany and occupied territories in Europe. Britain would take in more Jewish refugees than most other countries.

Simon and Sonia's son-in-law Robert Sainsbury and his brother Alan were among the first to respond. They would not only pay towards getting Jewish children out of Nazi-occupied lands but also supported them over the following years. In early 1939, the two brothers and their wives set up a hostel in Putney, south-west London, for some 20 Kindertransport children. Guenter Treitel, later to be knighted and become Emeritus Professor of Law at Oxford University, was one of these children. Speaking in 2000 at the memorial service to Sir Robert Sainsbury, he praised the interest the family had taken in them. 'Alan and Robert Sainsbury and their ladies... kept in close contact, regularly visiting us, taking us around London, showing us the sites,' he recalled, '[they] set up a house on the South Coast where we could go on holiday.'

The flow of refugees increased as Germany stepped up its threats to Poland, with attention focused on the former Free City of Danzig (Gdansk). It was an autonomous Baltic Sea port and city-state, including over 200 surrounding towns, villages and settlements, established under the Treaty of Versailles after the First World War. Danzig was separated from Germany and placed under League of Nations 'protection', with special economic-related rights reserved for Poland. Most residents of the city-state were German. Hitler made numerous demands to reunify Danzig with Germany, which were rejected by Poland. Through 1938 and early 1939, all over Europe, people tuned into their radios to listen to the

Jewish refugee children from Germany after their arrival in England in 1938

latest developments. Simon was no exception. He understood German, so he would sometimes listen to broadcasts of Hitler's speeches, becoming impatient and angry, according to Maureen. 'It would take a long time for him to relax afterwards. I would try and get him to talk about his work as a way of getting him to settle down,' she recalled. 'He couldn't understand how the German people, particularly a few people he had once known, had followed this man.'

Sam van den Bergh was one of the few Dutch who understood the true threat from the Nazis

The home front

As France and Britain stepped up diplomatic efforts, the Dutch slumbered on. The Netherlands was neutral in the First World War and had not been a signatory to the Versailles Treaty, which led to so much belligerence from Germany. The country was one of the founders in 1920 of the League of Nations, intended as a forum to bring peace to Europe and the rest of the world. The Dutch believed their neutrality would continue to be honoured by all the present powers.

The Van den Berghs' manufacturing interests were now represented by Unilever. Its directors had few doubts that a war in Europe was imminent. Like other large multinationals with interests in Germany, it had already faced the reality of dealing with the Nazi Government. On 1 July 1934, Hitler's Economics Minister Hjalmar Schacht stopped all international German debt payments. All future profits made by foreign companies from their German subsidiaries had to be spent on goods manufactured in that country. Van den Berghs had been founded on the bartering of goods for butter; now Unilever bartered profits in exchange for other goods and concessions.

Top of the list was a ship, Unitas, to be constructed in Hamburg shipyard in 1938. The ship survived the war in Hamburg docks and would trigger a dispute when the British Government tried to seize it as part of reparations. The Dutch Government was swift to point out that it was owned by a Dutch company and therefore could not be forfeited. The row escalated and led to a major diplomatic breakdown. Unitas was eventually restored to the Dutch. Sir Patrick McRory, later company secretary of Unilever, was to say that the Dutch Government had even threatened 'to go to war' with the British unless the ship was returned to them.

While the Dutch and British public ignored the rattles of war, Unilever's management prepared for the worst and from 1938 quietly began to reorganise their enterprise. Unilever's German operation was now autonomous but arrangements were made to offer German

Jewish workers jobs in other countries. This enabled the families of many of their German Jewish workers to escape persecution with their money and belongings. Later Unilever was able to help others, such as the family of the Chief Rabbi of Berlin.

Van den Berghs living in The Netherlands, who had helped rescue Jews from Germany, might have been expected to be suspicious of German intentions. Yet, like their fellow Dutch nationals, they believed they would be safe and ignored Hitler's proven failure to honour other claims of neutrality. They continued with their everyday lives. Only a few, like Sam Van den Bergh who had carefully read Nazi publications, had suspicions about what might happen. His wife Betsy noted in her book: 'Sam always said that once you had read *Mein Kampf* you would know what the Dutch Jews would face. His advice was that every Jew in Germany had to get out, even though it might mean that they lost everything, that freedom was much more important than the material losses.'

Living in Paris, Simon remembered that German troops had been stopped from entering the city in the First World War and felt safe. Surely, even if there was to be another war, the French and their British allies would stop the Germans invading France. He was more concerned about what would happen to relatives in The Netherlands, whom he believed might be in danger. Many people feared the Germans would not treat Holland as neutral, especially as they had taken in so many Jewish refugees. Simon, along with a few other members of the family, started to transfer money from The Netherlands to Switzerland or America. Simon advised his father, by now living permanently in the South of France where he had been joined by his brother Zadok and wife Charlotte, to invest his money abroad.

On 20 May 1939 there was great excitement among travellers when Pan American Airways introduced its first scheduled commercial transatlantic service. The Yankee Clipper, a four-engined flying boat which flew from Long Island near New York to Lisbon in Portugal, would provide another safety route for refugees fleeing to America.

The Van den Bergh family spent the long hot Summer of 1939 in the South of France. It was the last time they would be together. The mood was subdued as reports came in of new German army manoeuvres near the Polish border. Sam shared Simon's belief that Hitler would ignore The Netherlands' past neutrality. He and Betsy rented another house near their own in the hills above Nice and tried to persuade their sons George and Sidney and their families to remain with them. At the end of August, despite their parents' pleas, George and Sidney returned to The Netherlands.

A fast and comfortable way out for those who could afford it: Pan Am's Boeing 314 'Clipper' service began in May 1939

Betsy wrote: 'Neither of us had any doubts as to what Hitler would do next and also what he intended to do to the Jews of Holland. We had desperately tried to persuade George and his family not to return.' George's son Hans recalled the arguments. 'I was only a small boy but I remember the tension,' he said. 'Looking back I can't understand why he decided to go back [to Amsterdam]. He must have been aware of the risk. I think that he wanted to share the dangers that his countrymen might face.'

Abrasha (right) and his father, Naftali (Alter) Glikson, in Poland just before the war. Abrasha made several trips to try to persuade his family to leave the country

Although Sidney Van den Bergh also returned to Holland, he made arrangements to get his family out of the country. Having watched Nazi storm-troopers marching in Berlin, he had no doubts about what the future held in store: 'It was chilling, terrifying. Flames held high, flags and standards, waving. Pure brutality. Looking at those people and having read *Mein Kampf*, I was scared about what would happen to us.'

Simon had been made aware of the dangers threatening Sonia's family in Poland by her nephew Abrasha, who stayed with them in Paris. Worried about rising anti-Semitism in Germany and Poland, Abrasha made several trips home from Argentina to Europe to try to persuade his mother Pauline, his sister Mina, her husband Romen Wajnstein and their little daughter Ariela to join him in Argentina. He became increasingly frustrated and desperate as his family refused to leave their homes, believing – as did other Polish Jews – that Hitler would not seek to annihilate them.

On 23 August 1939 Hitler and Soviet leader Josef Stalin signed the Nazi-Soviet Pact agreeing not to go to war with each other and (secretly) to the division of Poland. The Polish Ambassador to France held what was to be his last grand summer party. The next day the lights were switched off and many of the staff returned to Poland.

Outbreak of war

Friday 1 September 1939 was a grey day. A little light rain was falling on the Polish plains. At 5.20am, without warning, a German plane dropped bombs on Puck, a small Polish fishing village, and on a nearby airbase in the Hel Peninsula. Twenty five minutes later, the German training ship Schleswig-Holstein, lying off the disputed port of Danzig, fired its first shells at the Polish base and ammunition depot at Westerplatte. Fifty three German army divisions crossed the Polish frontier. Without any formal declaration of war, Germany began its invasion of Poland.

The word 'Blitzkrieg' entered the English language as German soldiers on motor bikes and in tanks poured across the border. Polish soldiers mounted on horseback charged German tanks in wave upon wave of suicidal attacks. German guns shelled the small villages of the plains and German fighter planes strafed the crowds of terrified refugees fleeing the invading armies. Every strategic town and city was bombed. The lessons learned by the German air force in the destruction of the Spanish town of Guernica had been perfected. The Unilever factory in Warsaw was severely damaged in the bombing.

Britain and France issued an ultimatum, calling upon Hitler to withdraw his forces from Poland and return to negotiations. On Sunday 3 September, as the deadline approached, British Prime Minister Neville Chamberlain took to the airwaves to tell the people of Britain that war had been declared. Later that afternoon, and before the ultimatum expired, the French President followed suit.

On 6 October the last significant units of the Polish army surrendered. Some 700,000 Polish soldiers were taken prisoner by the Germans and another 200,000 by the Russians; the countries had swept into Poland in a joint pincer movement. A ghetto for Jews was set up in the Lublin region of central Poland.

During the latter part of the Polish defence, Suwalki, its railway repeatedly bombed, came briefly under the control of the Russian army. On 12 October, in accordance with the Nazi-Soviet pact, it was transferred to German control. Suwalki was incorporated into the province of East Prussia and its name changed to Sudauen. Tensions had been increasing in the border area near Suwalki for some weeks as Russia and Germany built troop numbers. Some of the wealthier Jews, aware that hostilities were building, had already fled to other parts of the country or over the border into Lithuania. Later others were to escape to Russia.

As war broke out, Abrasha was in London on his way home after one last attempt to persuade his family to leave Poland. Now it was too late. His son Carlos said the news of the invasion had a devastating effect on Abrasha: 'My father ... was frantic with worry. His family had refused to leave their homes. His sister did not want to separate from the rest of the family. Some family members said nothing was going to happen.'

Two of Sonia's sisters, Rosa Raiza and Anna, now aged 57 and 52, had remained in Suwalki. Anna, also known as Jenny, the hat-maker who stayed with Sonia in The Netherlands on her way to live in America, had returned home in the 1920s. Now she faced German brutality as Jews in Suwalki, young and old, healthy and sick, were subjected to mental and physical abuse. Many were forced to do menial labour. Jewish stores were looted and synagogues were desecrated. Shootings and torture became the order of the day.

On 9 December 1939, the last 3,000 Jews remaining in Suwalki (out of a Jewish population of about 9,000 before the war) were ordered to remain in their homes. They were picked up by heavily armed German soldiers, put in sealed trains and transported to several villages and towns in Lublin. They were later moved to Biala Podlaska, Lukow, Miedzyrzec-Podalski and Kock, and would share the fate of the local communities: most were shot in a forest near Lomazy; others died in concentration camps and others in shootings and hangings elsewhere.

By the end of 1941, over 500,000 Jews in Poland and Russia had been killed by the SS, the Nazis' 'Shield Squadron', which was responsible for the worst of the crimes against humanity perpetrated during the Second World War. Their intention to murder all European Jews was made clear. By 1945, 90 per cent of Poland's 3.3 million Jews had been murdered and Poland's total war dead totalled over 6 million.

What actually happened to Anna and Rosa Raiza is uncertain. Rosa Raiza is last noted as being alive in 1941 but there is no mention of Anna. The Jewish Holocaust memorial Yad Vashem reports the death of Rosa Raiza as having taken place in Suwalki. Perhaps they died together. They probably shared the fate of many of their brethren. The two women, trau-matised after months of brutalisation, would have been marched along with their fellow Jews, further and further into the woods. They would have clung to each other, trying not to fall as they were bludgeoned by the Germans. They would have been forced to undress and stand in a line in front of large pits as dogs tore and snapped at them. These two gentle women would have felt shame as they tried to cover their nakedness with their hands. As the Germans looked on laughing and drinking, they waited in terror for their deaths. Their actual murders would be unrecorded, just two among millions.

Other members of the Pokrojski family are mentioned as having been killed at Auschwitz and other concentration camps. Sonia's eldest sister Pauline realised that she had more to fear from the Germans than the Russians and escaped to Sarny in the western Ukraine along with other Jews. She was able to get messages through to Abrasha to let him know she was safe. On 15 December 1939 he sent her some money. Transfer receipts record that the money was sent via Moscow to an address at 37 Trzeciegomaia, Sarny, Ukraine. This is Pauline's last-known residence.

She was still in Sarny when Germany invaded Russia and occupied the town on 5 July 1941. Actions against the Jews began straight away with indiscriminate murder, seizure of able bodied people for forced labour and extortion of large sums of money. Jews were rounded up on 1 October, the Jewish day of Atonement that year, when they were ordered to wear a yellow badge and take part in a census. A ghetto was established in April 1942 and in late August the Germans began to 'liquidate' the community. Some 14,000 Jews were mur-dered during that time.

Pauline's daughter Mina, her engineer husband Romen Wajnstein and their daughter Ariela, had remained in Romen's home town of Bendzin in Upper Silesia (in present-day south-west Poland). In 1946 Abrasha would receive a letter from his cousin Stella in Poland. A survivor of the Holocaust, Stella gave evidence to Yad Vashem and described how Pauline told her husband Naftali (also known as Alter) Glikson that she wanted to find and stay with Mina and Ariela, who had been evicted from their apartment and sent to live in a ghetto. She was never able to fulfil that wish. Stella later tried to find Mina but was unsuccessful. Most of the Jews in her town did not survive.

Evidence from Helena Zygielman and Lusia Kaplan to Yad Vashem in 1999 reveals that their friend Mina Wajnstein was aged 42 when she died. The testimony goes on to record her deportation; her place of death is unknown. Mina's husband and their six-year-old daugh-ter Ariela are reported as having died in Bendzin, at an earlier time than Mina. Pauline is reported as dying with other Jews from Suwalki at Sarny .

Pauline's last years and months were tragic. Her son had pleaded with her and her fam-ily to leave the country. The last tenuous contact with him, when he sent money to her at Sarny, might have given her reason to feel they could get out. Instead, she and her family were herded into ghettoes. Her granddaughter Ariela would have had little chance; moth-ers and children were the first to succumb. The fact that Mina was deported without her daughter indicates Ariela probably died beforehand from starvation. The men would have been worked to death or shot.

Abrasha (right) with Romen Wajnstein, Mina and a family friend in Warsaw, 1939, during an unsuccessful attempt to persuade them to leave

The sparse reports at Yad Vashem are the only records of the family's fate.

As Poland was dismembered by Germany and the Soviet Union, and thousands were murdered, Britain and France spent eight months locked in what became known as the 'phoney war'. War had been declared but the Allies did nothing to aid Poland and learnt nothing from studying the new 'Blitzkrieg' German tactics of invasion. As German and French troops eyed each other uneasily over the supposedly infallible 'Maginot' line, ladies of High Society raised money to plant roses on the line in an attempt to lighten the lives of the French soldiers and stop them getting bored.

While life for most French citizens went on as normal, the future of some 3.5 million aliens living in the country became more hazardous. Leftists, gypsies and other 'undesirables' were rounded up with Jewish refugees and confined in prison camps, which were comparable to concentration camps in Germany. The writer Arthur Koestler was among those arrested in October 1939 and sent to Le Vernet internment camp near the Pyrenees, where he joined other former comrades of the International Brigade who had fought alongside him in Spain.

In his book *Scum of the Earth*, Koestler described the despair of refugees like himself: '[The Nazis] had hunted me all across the Continent, and whenever I had paused and stopped thinking there was safety, they had come after me... They had come after me all the way from Berlin to Paris, via Vienna and Prague, and down the Atlantic coast, until in this outermost corner of France they had at last caught up with me.'

As France and Britain rearmed, Hitler continued with his plans to invade The Netherlands and Belgium, predicting that this would lead to the defeat of Allied forces as they rushed to aid those countries. One of the captured documents used as evidence at the

Nuremburg Trials after the Second World War revealed that Hitler plotted for the subjugation of Belgium and The Netherlands before the war began. In a memorandum dated 23 May 1939, Hitler outlined his intent: 'England is our enemy. Dutch and Belgian air bases must be occupied by armed force. Declarations of neutrality must be ignored. If England intends to intervene in the Polish war, we must occupy Holland with lightning speed. We must aim at securing a new defence line on Dutch soil up to the Zuider Zee.'

German troops land near Rotterdam

Nazis invade The Netherlands

At 9pm on 9 May 1940 German signallers tapped out the word 'Danzig' to the thousands of German forces hidden along the country's western borders. On 10 May 1940, with some 3 million soldiers, Germany invaded The Netherlands and Belgium. Five hours beforehand, the Dutch Prime Minister Dirk Jan de Geer had taken to the airwaves in an evening radio broadcast to calm the fears of his citizens. Germany, he reassured his listeners, had honoured The Netherlands' neutrality during the last war; he had full confidence that they would do so again.

The Dutch woke as German parachute troops landed near Rotterdam, seizing control of the roads and canals linking the country. The Germans warned the Dutch that they would be executed if they tried to sabotage the occupation. The shocked Dutch people, unused to war, huddled under tables and in their cellars as bombs fell and their own army tried to fight back against a well-organised invading force, which included German soldiers dressed in Dutch uniforms.

On 13 May Queen Wilhelmina, once a visitor to the Van den Bergh factory in Rotterdam, her daughter Juliana and her granddaughters escaped to England. She was outraged that Hitler had broken assurances made personally to her that Dutch neutrality would be honoured. Queen Wilhelmina, later to be described by British Prime Minister Winston Churchill, as 'the only man' in the governments in exile, remained in Great Britain for most of the war and acted as a rallying point for Dutch resistance.

Dutch forces, no match for crack German troops, held out for four days. On 14 May 1940 The Netherlands capitulated as its government fled to London. At the very hour of Dutch surrender, the German Air Force launched one of the heaviest bombing raids of the war on Rotterdam, flattening the port area, which included the old synagogue at Boompjes, where Simon had received his Bar Mitzvah and his family had attended so many services. The Unilever factories survived the worst of the bombing. Three days later the Gestapo raided the Unilever office, trying to trace the company's Jewish connections.

One of the first acts by the Dutch Government-in-Exile – now led by a new Prime Minister, Pieter Sjoerds Gerbrandy, a Professor of Law at Amsterdam and an old friend of both Simon and George Van den Bergh, was to pass decrees taking control of all Unilever and other Dutch multinational companies' assets outside The Netherlands. This was aimed at preventing the Germans incorporating Unilever into any German companies, as they had done with other businesses and would later do in France, to organisations such as tyre-maker Michelin. However, the Germans proceeded to fill half the Board of Directors with their own representatives, even while investigations went on to prove that the Dutch Company was under British control. A new German Reichskommissar was appointed in July 1941 to oversee Unilever's continental business.

Unilever operated throughout the war in all the countries invaded by the Germans. Despite German interference, it would at times act as a base for members of the resistance, enabling them to move around Europe under the guise of working for the company. Members of German military intelligence (the Abwehr, headed by Admiral Wilhelm Franz Canaris) would often turn a blind eye to the resistance activities and use them as a conduit for their own men to plot against Hitler.

Unilever company directors. Back row, from left: Paul Hendriks, Jacques Polak, Roelof Maathuis, Paul Rijkens. Front row: Donald, Albert, Sam, Leo and Sidney Van den Bergh.

Paul Hendriks, brought in by Sam to run the company and a close friend of the family, had returned from England to The Netherlands in August 1939 to take care of the Dutch side of the business. He was eventually arrested with several of his staff and deported to Germany. He had tried but failed to stop the Nazis deporting Unilever staff, including Arnold's grandson Frank Kleerekoper and Zadok's son Simon. Directors and managers of local Unilever factories throughout Europe tried to protect the lives of van den Bergh family members and their Jewish staff but many of the Jewish workers were sent to concentration camps and killed.

While Rotterdam burned and the border between The Netherlands and Belgium was sealed by German troops, Jewish and Dutch refugees besieged ports trying to get out of the country. German-born Eugen Marx, the husband of Simon's cousin Bertha, had been involved with George van den Bergh in helping rescue Jews from Germany. He had little doubt about what the Germans would do if they caught him. Eugen and Bertha joined the thousands of hysterical refugees milling around the ports, being strafed by gunfire from German planes while trying to get onto one of the few remaining boats that had not been sunk. Unable to get away, the couple returned to their home where, on 15 May 1940, they became two of the 200 Dutch citizens who that night committed suicide. They left a note to say they were not prepared to live under or work for the Germans as slaves. They would have undoubtedly been deported and killed. Eugen and Bertha's son Herman Marx escaped with friends in a lifeboat. Drifting in the sea, he was picked up by a British ship and landed in England.

Herman was one of many who blamed the Dutch Government for failing to recognise the danger the country faced. 'We left it until the last moment to try and escape. We believed what the Government said to us,' he explained. 'They gave no impression of being worried about being attacked and they carried out a great propaganda exercise to convince us all that nothing was going to happen... We had been neutral in the First World War and the Dutch didn't realise that these Germans had no intention of honouring any sort of agreement.'

Herman was surprised that his cousin Frank Kleerekoper had stayed to look after his sick father. Like his own parents, he had no doubt of the danger he would face if he remained in The Netherlands: 'I couldn't have stayed, even for my parents. I would have definitely been sent to a concentration camp and killed. I knew exactly what they would have done, my parents had no doubt.'

In an inquiry held after the war into the Dutch Government's failure to enlighten the country to the dangers they faced from the Germans, representatives stated they had been aware of the threats to their neutrality. They had naively hoped to convince the Germans that no strategic advantage would be gained by invading the country.

In an Erasmus Lecture given at Harvard University in 1988, Louis de Jong, the first Director of the Netherlands' State Institute for War Documentation and close friend of Simon Van den Bergh, described his own escape: 'We decided to try to escape to Britain by boat. So did tens of thousands of Dutchmen among them many Jews; but nothing had been organised, it was difficult to approach the harbours and there were hardly any ships. Near the coast, where perhaps 30,000 desperate people were milling about, my wife and I became separated from my relatives. Like most people they returned home. We stayed. We found a boat. We were among the very few who succeeded in crossing the sea and reaching Britain.'

De Jong spent most of the war working, alongside Herman Marx, for Radio Oranje, the radio service of the Dutch Government-in-Exile in London. He also contributed, with Simon (when he had escaped from France), to various publications dropped by allied planes on the Dutch. His family left behind in The Netherlands were deported and killed.

The Germans had accumulated lists of those to be arrested when they invaded a country. A 'Black Book' was produced of those, such as directors of major organisations, to be detained and interned when the Nazis invaded Great Britain. These included Sam's son Sidney, Jacob's sons Albert and Sidney and his grandson Clive, plus other members of the Van den Bergh family.

Sam's son Sidney escaped to England on one of the last ships from Rotterdam, having pushed his favourite car into the sea so that the Germans wouldn't be able to use it. He had already sent his family to safety in England, America and Canada. One of his sons, Sidney, was to become Professor of Astrophysics at Vancouver University and another, Maarten, became head of Shell and then of Lloyds Bank

Called up the previous August by the Dutch army as a Reserve Captain, Sidney was now put in charge of outfitting the remnants of the Dutch army who had escaped to England. Sidney was later appointed Aide de Camp to Queen Wilhelmina's son-in-law Prince Bernhard and would eventually become the first Jewish General in the Dutch

Sidney photographed after the war, along with his and some of the other van den Bergh entries in the Nazis' 'Black Book'

Sidney in uniform as Aide de Camp
to Prince Bernhard

Army. Herman Marx was appalled that Sidney did not do more to help his parents, Bertha and Eugen, escape while he was sending his own family to safety. He would never forgive him.

A controversial character, Sidney married five times. On 29 April 1959 he was appointed to be Minister of Defence in the Dutch government headed by Jan De Quay. Three months later he was cited in a divorce action brought in San Diego, California by a retired business-man Frederick Lek. The case featured in French and German as well as Dutch newspapers. He resigned from the government but his experience as a Director of Unilever – to which he returned – allowed him to continue to play an active part in Dutch politics, particularly in international affairs.

Sidney and Simon met up in London and were to keep in contact for the rest of their lives, although Simon didn't like Sidney because he thought he was only interested in mak-ing money and enjoying the trappings that went with it, according to Maureen. 'Simon used to be embarrassed about all his money, but Sidney seemed to flaunt it,' she said. '[Simon] didn't share any interest with him intellectually and found it difficult to talk with him. The last time we saw him was at a party held in The Netherlands in the late 1960s to celebrate the anniversary of Van den Berghs. This was the last time that Simon went there and he did-n't really want to talk to him. I rather liked him, but he could be difficult.'

Persecution and death

On 7 October 1940 at 6.45am the Nazi secret police, the Gestapo, arrested Sam's eldest son George van den Bergh, who was a socialist Member of Parliament and Professor of Law at Amsterdam University. He captured his feeling of shock in a chapter he wrote for a Dutch book about wartime: 'Two men came to my door... I was detained at my house. A young German in civilian clothes and a German soldier holding his rifle stood before me. When I asked why they were arresting me, and under whose authority, the young man in civilian clothes showed me a piece of paper and read it out to me.'

The document was 'Installation 1; Of the Reichskommissar of the Occupied Netherlands Region; The Hague, September 9th 1940'. It said Germans taken prisoner at the beginning of hostilities by the Dutch in the East Indies 'were mostly interned by the Dutch authorities in undignified and unhealthy conditions. This treatment by the Dutch authorities is in stark contrast to the considerate and swift treatment applied by the occupying Power on the Dutch people. To my regret I am therefore obliged to have to take into custody a number of Dutch nationals, including you, until this unbearable state of affairs has been ended for the sake of German honour.' It was signed by Dr Arthur Seyss-Inquart, the Reichskommissar to the Occupied Netherlands Region.

'The document... had come out of nowhere,' George recalled. 'I had half an hour to get things ready. Furthermore I could also take one suitcase with enough clothes to keep me warm in winter. Why then had I been chosen to lose my freedom in retaliation for the Dutch Indies! I couldn't think why. I had never been to the East Indies, neither did I have any par-ticular link or association with the Indies. So why of all people had they chosen me? Later on, in numerous discussions with my fellow sufferers, we tried to answer these questions but we couldn't understand.' In his last hurried words to his wife Nelly, George was able to alert her to a code that he would use in any letters or cards that he might be allowed to write, to let her know what was really happening to him.

George was taken with other leading Dutch Professors, lawyers and politicians to Buchenwald, to be held as hostages. He was eventually set free after the Red Cross, who were overseeing the interests of both German and Dutch hostages, protested at the numbers of Dutch hostages dying in Buchenwald. They responded to an alert by George's wife who reported that one of his codes indicated he was ill. After the war George was honoured for maintaining morale among his fellow Dutch prisoners by making sure they stuck together and celebrated their various Dutch holy days and organising discussion groups.

George had been married twice and had children from both marriages. The different treatments meted out by the Germans to the two families reflected the convoluted logic used to define who was of 'the race' and who was not. George's first wife, the poet Jeanette van Dantzig, was Jewish as were his four children from that marriage; three – Robbert, Bep and Joost – remained in The Netherlands, the fourth, Ada, had stayed with George's parents in France. His children by his second, non-Jewish wife Nelly, categorised as being 'half Jews', remained safe throughout the war. Jews married to non-Jews were also exempted. George, released from Buchenwald, protected by his Red Cross status and married to a non-Jew, remained untouched for the rest of the war and was able to use his influence to help protect his children and some of his former students.

On 12 March 1941 the Jews of The Netherlands were left in no doubt about Germany's plans for their future; nor were the Dutch left in any doubt about what would happen to them if they tried to help the Jews. Reichskommissar Seyss-Inquart declared: 'The Jews are the enemy with whom no armistice or peace can be made. We will smite the Jews where we meet them and whoever goes along with them must take the consequences.' Within months Dutch Jews were forced to wear the yellow star. Deportations would shortly follow.

The yellow star issued to Dutch Jews

Various lists offering protective status, such as one for Portuguese Sephardic Jews, were set up by the Dutch Permanent Secretary for Interior Affairs, K. J. Fredericks, and other civil servants trying to save the lives of some of their compatriots. Others were set up by the Germans to be used as bargaining tools with other countries.

George's first wife, Jeanette, and their three children who stayed in The Netherlands were included on one of these lists. Along with some 600 prominent Jews who were regarded as being beneficial to the nation, they were imprisoned in 1942 in St Michelgracht castle near the town of Barneveld, instead of being deported to concentration camps with the rest of The Netherlands' 100,000 Jews. The castle prison had been set up by Fredericks and the Secretary General for Education, Science and Culture, who were friends of George. In 1943 most of the 'Barneveld Hostages' – which included one future Prime Minister Willem Schermer-

Dutch Jews being marched to
Amersfort camp

'Warning!': German occupying
forces' poster setting out the
consequences of any Dutch acts of
sabotage

horn – were sent to Westerbork, the transit camp for deportation to the East. Others were to follow after the Allies' invasion of France in June 1944.

In October 1944, Jeanette, Robbert and Robbert's new wife Lotte were sent on the last train to the Theresienstadt ghetto, in what is now the Czech Republic, where they survived the war, being repatriated to Switzerland in April 1945. Bep and Joost remained at Westerbork, where their Uncle Sidney, now Aide de Camp to Prince Bernhard, found them when the Allies finally took control of all of The Netherlands in May 1945.

George's sister Elisabeth Andriesse and her family, using her husband's previous contacts with German politicians and bankers, were able to bribe their way out of the country. They were escorted by the SS down to the border between France and neutral Spain.

However, the influential Van den Bergh and Unilever contacts failed to help most of the family in The Netherlands. Only one of Zadok's children was to survive, his daughter Lucie and her husband Leo Polak. Murdered by the Germans were his son Max and daughter-in-law Jeanette. His youngest son Simon, known as Sies – one of the little boys who had an accident during the show for his grandparents' Golden wedding anniversary who became a lawyer working for Unilever – and his wife Elly died in Auschwitz in 1943. Their two baby daughters, Lily and Annie, were safely hidden in convents in Belgium and found by Dutch authorities after the war who gave them to a family who had lost their own daughters. Later, one of the girls, Lily, would run away to find the van den Berghs and be brought up by George. Eric, Sies's son, survived, as did Lucie's son and daughter.

Arnold's grandson Frank Kleerekoper (a visitor to Simon in Paris) who worked for Unilever, was deported despite an appeal to the Gestapo from one of the German Economic Commissioners for The Netherlands. In the letter, the Commissioner referred to Frank Kleerekoper's 'influential relatives' and the fact that the 'foreign parts' of Unilever might be useful to Germany at the end of the war, but to no avail. Frank, the half-brother of Rosalida Polak, died on 30 January 1945 from starvation, dysentery and ill-treatment at the beginning of a death march from Neuengamme concentration camp in Germany. His wife Miep de Jong survived deportation.

None of Maurits' children were to survive. Simon's brilliant cousin Jacobus had finally been confined to a psychiatric institution in The Hague. On 5 March 1943 he was gassed at Sobibor. His sister Louise (Loutie), a well-known artist, had gone into hiding but had been betrayed to the Germans. Captured and having little doubt as to what would happen to her, she tried unsuccessfully to commit suicide. The Nazis waited until she had recovered, then deported her to the East where she died in Auschwitz on 7 December 1943.

Arnold's daughter Lydia (Beebs) Van Raalte had divorced her husband Frits in the 1930s. Her son Frans tried to escape from The Netherlands but was caught by the Nazis and executed in Breda on 21 June 1942. Beebs was herself deported to Sobibor where she died on 2

July 1943. Arnold's granddaughter Lucie Juliette Tels (daughter of Annie) and her two children escaped to America. Her husband Harry Tels was murdered by the Germans at Mauthausen concentration camp on 10 July 1941.

The training camp for Jewish refugees, to which Simon had contributed funds, was taken over by the Germans and became a concentration camp and assembly point for sending Jews to the East. Some 200 young men from the camp were transferred to Amsterdam and were among the first to be rounded up and sent to Mauthaussen concentration camp in Austria. None would return.

Fear in France

As Dutch relatives faced the terrors of German invasion, Simon and his family living in France realised the danger they, too, faced. Isaac, who was becoming increasingly infirm and needed constant nursing, had remained in Nice where he lived with Sam and Betsy. Simon's wife Sonia and daughter Tamara also stayed in the South of France with Ada, one of George's daughters, in a villa at La Baule, rented by Sam and Betsy. 'It had been decided that if the Germans came close to Paris we would all, including my grandfather, go to Bayonne and from there to Portugal and America,' Tamara explained.

Within days of the fall of Belgium and The Netherlands in May 1940, the French and British armies, led by politicians and generals still locked into First World War tactics, were cut in two as the German armies swung towards the Channel Ports. While the French and British armies fought rearguard actions to evacuate their soldiers from Dunkirk, some 9 million French and Belgian civilians and soldiers, harassed by German dive-bombers, took to the roads fleeing south away from the approaching German armies.

In the French documentary *Le Chagrin et La Pitie* (*The Sorrow and the Pity*), made in 1969, Pierre Mendes France, a member of the French Government who was arrested by the Germans but later escaped to join the resistance, described the fear and chaos: 'The Germans didn't hesitate to shoot refugees. This wave of people moved south. Confused, lost; they jammed up the roads and made it impossible for quick movement of our own troops. It was all confusion.' Also appearing in the programme, another refugee Georges Adrey recalled how families became separated. 'In this mass of people, nobody could find anybody else. Nobody knew where they were going. People just moved on; that was it,' he said. 'Towards the south, far from the "others", they fled. They fled from real or unexpected horrors. People who took to the roads, crossed others who were going in totally the opposite direction.'

Simon remained for the moment in Paris, where Maureen, having suddenly collapsed in pain, had been taken to the American Hospital. Doctors were having difficulty locating the cause of the illness. On 10 June 1940 Italy declared war on France and Great Britain; the French Government, led by Prime Minister Paul Reynaud, was already fleeing Paris. As news came of the German victories, Maureen, terrified of being caught, was taken in an ambulance to Bordeaux. 'It was a nightmare, people yelling and crying. German planes kept coming down and shooting us,' she recalled. 'I was in an ambulance and they had given me something to help the pain and I kept hearing all this noise. The journey to Bordeaux took

Retreat from Dunkirk, May 1940.
British troops wait to be evacuated
from the northern French coast

hours. Everyone was worried about whether we would find a boat. My major memory is of panic and noise and not feeling well.'

Maureen parted company with Simon, who was to travel south to join his wife and daughter, and sailed on the last boat to leave France – a P&O liner – to Plymouth. Tired and still unwell, she arrived safely in England, where she was met at the dockside by women with blankets, food and cups of tea. 'We were all scared and cold. It was the first time that I had ever eaten a Cornish pasty,' she remembered. 'But I wasn't feeling at all well and I was taken straight away to a hospital where they found out that I had appendicitis. It was in the centre of my body and not in the usual place. That was why I had been ill and why they hadn't found out what was wrong with me.'

On 14 June 1940 Paris was declared an open city. The few Parisians who watched the German soldiers goose-step along Les Champs Élysées cried. Two days later Prime Minister Reynaud resigned, when the cabinet rejected his plans to refuse to sign the armistice with Germany and to continue the war from Algeria. As Germany took control of the north, the former First World War hero, the elderly Marshall Philippe Pétain, was brought in to lead the French Government as it sought terms for peace. On 22 June the French and Germans signed an armistice in the very train carriage where the Germans had signed the peace treaty at the end of the First World War. At midnight on 24 June the armistice came into force, cutting France in two. Petain's Government, based in Vichy, would rule south and central France.

Now the French themselves became refugees, as thousands poured into towns along the Mediterranean coast. Jews had lived in Nice for centuries; some 1,000 were living there before the war broke out. They had, like Sam and Betsy, become members of the community, taking part in local politics, establishing their own schools and even their own graveyard on the Chateau Hill. Their numbers swelled as some 5,000 Jewish refugees from Paris and elsewhere in France, and from Germany, Austria and Eastern Europe, haunted the cafes, restaurants and parks, desperately trying to find hiding places and to get visas to safety. The wealthier found rooms in hotels on the Promenade des Anglais, the poorer faced hardship in miserable hostels in the backstreets. The one thing they all shared was the knowledge that if caught, they would be deported to German concentration camps.

On 2 July 1940 Vichy Ministers estimated the number of refugees in the country at more than 8 million, of which the vast majority, 6.2 million, were French. A further 1.8 million were Belgian and 150,000 were Dutch. Some of the finest artists, writers and philosophers in Europe found themselves counted no better than the poorest refugee from Poland or Germany. Artists Max Ernst, Andre Breton and Marc Chagall would eventually escape, helped by American committees set up to rescue intellectuals. But for now they sat in their little hotel rooms, smoking cigarettes and counting their few remaining Francs. For most there was little respite. Some 190,000 refugees flocked to Marseilles, the biggest port in the south. Here there might be a last chance for a passage to safety. But ships were few and visas impossible to obtain.

Most of the French would return to their homes as would the Belgians and Dutch, as they gradually realised there was nowhere to go and they would probably be safer in their own countries.

Flight from danger

During the First World War, Italy had been an ally of Great Britain and France. Italy was now Germany's staunchest ally and seemed poised to take over southern France. In the summer of 1940, Sam and Betsy, fearful of an imminent invasion, put their escape plan into action and bundled their relatives and friends into cars and drove to Bayonne. The port, like all those on the west coast of France, was besieged by refugees, many of them Jewish from Belgium and Luxemburg, desperate to leave. The last British ships had departed, leaving thousands to try and find space on any of the small boats still operating. Sam and Betsy were worried about whether the older members of the family, which included Isaac now aged 87, 81-year-old Zadok and his wife Charlotte, would survive what was likely to be a dangerous, uncomfortable voyage. Believing that they would have no trouble crossing the Spanish border, Sam and Betsy decided to drive across the Pyrenees to Spain.

The party divided as Simon and his family, understanding that the French Government would do little to protect them, decided that the priority was to leave French soil as soon as possible. 'It was clear in my mind. I had no doubt what would happen to me as a Jewess in France,' said Tamara. 'As far as I was concerned there was no choice. So we all gathered in Bayonne. I did not believe in waiting and, with other Dutch people, father, mother and Ada, we rented a fishing boat that had brought sardines to Bayonne and sailed to Porto [in Portugal]. We were crammed aboard the sardine boat, in terrible conditions. But we had to go in the boat. It would have been far too dangerous to stay. We would have been sent to the concentration camps.'

This was the last time Simon would see his father. As he and his family endured the boat trip, the older members began their slow journey to Spain. At the border they, like many others, were to have their hopes of safety crushed when it became clear they could not barter their large cars for visas. The Spanish Government, concerned at the numbers seeking to

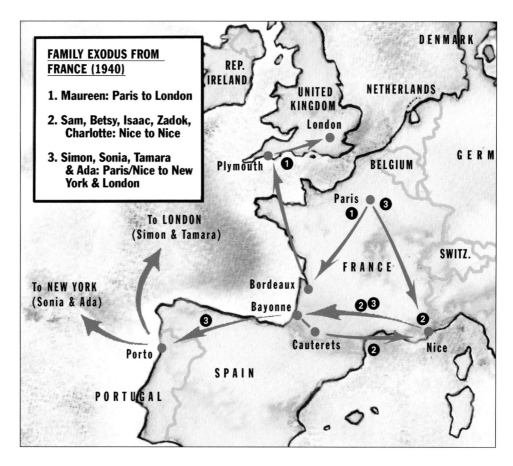

enter their country and still trying to recover from civil war, closed their frontier. For some it was the final straw; literary critic Walter Benjamin committed suicide on the border clutching a last manuscript.

Sam and Betsy were forced to return to Nice. Describing their escape attempt Betsy wrote in her book: 'We left the cars in Cauterets and Sam hired a coach instead in which the whole family could travel. It was a sort of emigration: Sam, Betsy, Isaac with his nurse, Zadok and Charlotte, [our staff] Margeurite, Jeanne "the kitchen princess" and her sister, and finally, [family friends] Vliet with his wife and children. One and a half days later we were safely back in Nice.'

On 4 February 1941, Sam died aged 77. He had been heartbroken at hearing that his son George had been taken hostage by the Germans and sent to Buchenwald. Zadok died in Nice on 13 June 1942 at the age of 83. His son Simon (Sies) was to announce his father's death in the Jewish newspaper *Het Joodsche Weekblad*, published in The Netherlands on 19 June. There would be no notice of Simon's own death a year later in Auschwitz. Betsy, armed with visas from the American Government, finally escaped with Zadok's widow Charlotte to America, where she remained until after the war.

Isaac was too old and ill to travel. He remained in Nice, moving with his nurse into a small flat where he remained for the rest of the war, thanks to help from Unilever's local office. Simon had made a request to Unilever in London, where his cousin Albert was in the process of retiring as Vice-chairman. Albert arranged for the Dutch-speaking Monsieur Olivier, a friend of the family and head of Unilever's Marseilles operation, to look after Isaac.

Monsieur Olivier travelled to Nice every month to see him. Simon promised to repay Unilever all expenditure incurred in looking after his father – a debt he honoured after the war.

According to Maureen, Simon would remain grateful to Monsieur Olivier for the rest of his life. 'He collected potatoes and all kinds of food; he would take them, as well as some money, over to Nice. He would spend time with Isaac,' she explained. 'Isaac lived there peacefully and quietly, nobody ever molesting him. Simon wrote Red Cross letters from England to him. Isaac received very few of them.' Isaac remained secreted away in his small flat throughout the war. Protected by the Mayor of Nice, Jean Médicin, and provided with food and money from the Unilever office, he had no need to appear on any register or to receive help from the local authorities. He simply fell through the net. After the war, Monsieur Olivier revealed that the local authorities had been told that the Jurgens were Jewish and that Isaac was a Catholic! Landing in France in September 1944, Tamara, a Second Lieutenant in the Free French Forces, was able to travel to Nice and became the last member of the family to see her fragile grandfather, just six months before he died.

Arcadia, Simon and Betsy's house and the scene of many family parties and holidays, became the home of successive Italian and German commanders, who were also informed by the Mayor of Nice that the owners of the property were not Jewish. Unlike other Jewish-owned properties in the South of France, the house was not stripped of its paintings and books.

While Isaac hid in Nice, his first wife Clara's family in The Netherlands came to the rescue of many Jews who faced financial hardship. Clara's brother, Bernard van Leer, set up a foundation in Amsterdam on 26 August 1941, making available the sum of 150,000 Guilders for the 'advancement of art and science among Dutch Jews'; a further 600,000 Guilders was added after the enforced liquidation of the van Leers' company by the Nazis. The foundation, originally administered by their cousin Lodewijk Ernst Visser, was taken over by Albert Spanjaard after Visser's death in 1940. Spanjaard was a relative of the late Henriette Van den Bergh. Most of the van Leers would be deported.

A defining moment

Simon, Sonia, Tamara and Ada arrived safely in Porto, in neutral Portugal, mingling among refugees, all vying to get visas allowing them to stay in the country or to leave for safe destinations. It was here that Simon and Sonia were given a choice that would define whether they would remain together; Simon was offered a teaching position at the University of North Carolina, matched with a much-prized visa for the United States. He and Sonia could have gone together and started a new life in America. The position would have established him with a professional academic role, giving him the recognition he wanted.

Tamara wanted to go to England to join the Free French. Instead of going to America with Sonia, Simon turned down the job offer and travelled with Tamara and joined Maureen in England. He took his decision knowing that Maureen would not have been allowed to join him in America. Although Maureen was Irish she was deemed a British citizen, hav-

Tamara, as an active member of the
Free French forces

ing been born before the foundation of the Irish Free State in 1922, which meant she had to apply to the British Government for permission to go to the United States. They turned her down. Simon's decision not to accept the invitation from the University of North Carolina and instead to join his mistress in London caused the final split in a marriage that had been deteriorating for many years.

Sonia had little doubt that the Nazis had rounded up her family in Poland. Living in Paris she had heard stories from Jewish refugees fleeing persecution and seen how terrified they were. By the time the family escaped to Portugal, the BBC was broadcasting news about what was happening to Jews in Poland. Although she was married to a Dutchman and had a Dutch passport, Sonia may well have thought the Germans would have still looked on her as a Pole. The Nazis had, after all, deported all German Jews born in Poland. Sonia was scared and had no intention of remaining in Europe to be hunted down. America offered safety. Armed with a visa, obtained for her by her brothers in the United States, Sonia sailed with Sam's granddaughter Ada to New York.

More surprisingly, while in Portugal, Sonia converted to Catholicism. Arnold's granddaughter, Rosalida Polak, said the family believed Sonia converted to protect herself. 'She was obviously scared,' she explained. 'Although the Catholic Church had done little during the 1930s to protest about what the Nazis had been doing to the Jews, most people thought the Church would protect Jews who converted to it. I don't know whether she had much contact with the church later.'

According to Maureen, Simon didn't take the conversion seriously: 'Simon just wrote it off as being a wild idea of hers and that it was one she had taken just to help her out of a jam. Neither of them was religious so it wasn't a shock about her leaving the Jewish faith. She had got interested in odd spiritual movements before, she always seemed to be looking for something to get involved in.'

Nowadays the Catholic Church is rather more circumspect about who it takes into its congregations. Conversions can take a great deal of time with the priest working alongside the applicant for many months. At that time it actively sought to recruit Jews and had few reservations about converting a scared Jew like Sonia. Throughout the Second World War, many priests accepted Jews hoping that a change to another religion would save them. However, the Germans did not recognise conversion to all branches of Christianity equally: in The Netherlands, Jewish converts to Catholicism were deported; those who had converted to the Dutch Church or to Protestantism were not.

Tamara was less surprised and more sympathetic, believing that Sonia's reason for conversion was more profound. 'She wanted to believe in a religion. She had looked at other beliefs. She had gone to other churches,' Tamara explained. 'It was part of her need to find something.'

Sonia was right to be scared. The percentage of the Dutch Jewish population who died in the Holocaust was far higher than in other western European countries. Having been brought up in a fair, civilised society, Dutch Jews underestimated the Nazis' brutality and accepted German lies in good faith. Over 100,000 out of 140,000 died. The only country that lost a greater percentage of its Jews was Poland, where 80 per cent of Jews were killed.

Records of a meeting held on 20 January 1942 at a villa on Lake Wannsee, near Berlin, chaired by Reinhard Heydrich and including Adolf Eichmann, detail the 'final solution' in which the Nazis intended to wipe out all Jews in Europe. Over lunch, delegates representing industry, various parts of German government and the occupied Eastern territories, formulated plans to eliminate 11 million of Europe's Jewry. Figures included not only those in countries already under German rule but also 330,000 of those in Britain, 3,000 in Portugal, 6,000 in Spain and 4,000 in Ireland.

Sonia's brother Eddie Hollander had few doubts about the danger his sister and her family faced. He was determined to bring them to safety in America and worked non-stop to get them visas. 'He was terrified that something might happen to them,' remembered his daughter Leonore. 'He had heard the reports of what was going on in Poland and was determined to try and do something to help Sonia and Simon. He went everywhere trying to make sure they could get visas.' Eddie was also worried about stories of food shortages in Great Britain, where rationing had begun on 1 December 1941. So he sent over food packages. Simon was never to forget his brother-in-law's efforts and remained in contact with his family for the rest of his life.

When Sonia arrived in America she moved into an apartment hotel on New York's Upper East Side near Central Park and was reunited with her brothers. They had all changed their names to Hollander and had carved out new successful lives for themselves. Two of the brothers, Max and Archie, had become cinema projectionists. Never to marry, Max lived in a hotel and wrote articles about film. Sam, a veteran of the Spanish-American war, had also found success in the USA, owning a liquor store in Brooklyn as well as a summer camp. Sam and his wife Rose, born in Poland in 1885, had been instrumental in organising the Temple Bethel in Rockaway Park, New York. They had two children: twins Helen and Bertram born in 1908. On 1 January 1918, Eddie, owner of a successful fish restaurant, married Mildred Richter, originally from Leeds in England. They also had two children: Billy born in 1918 and Leonore in 1922. Billy joined the American army and fought in Europe during the war. The youngest brother, Archie, became active in the trade union movement. In 1946 he married a Catholic girl called Mary Zoll who would become a close friend of Sonia's.

Sonia was not the only member of Simon's family to go to North America. His eldest daughter Lisa sent her daughter Elizabeth, who had been born in 1938, to safety there. Lisa's son David was born in Canada in 1940. The children remained there for the rest of the war, while Lisa returned to her husband Robert in England. Sonia and her daughter were seldom

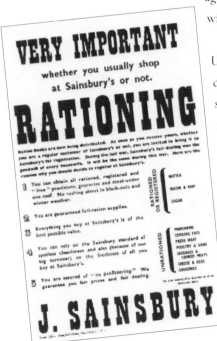

Some of Sainsbury's wartime rationing methods would be taken up by the government and used across Britain by other companies

to meet. Robert Sainsbury and his brother Alan were Directors of the Sainsbury's food retailing business, working night and day (as his grandfather Jacob and his brothers had done for Van den Berghs in the First World War) to ensure the company would be able to supply the British people with food. The systems he set up would be adopted by other companies.

Despite work pressures, Robert and Alan found time to care for the 20 Kinderstransport children they had rescued. 'A few days before the war began we were evacuated to new billets in Reading,' recalled Professor Sir Guenter Treitel, who was one of them. 'All the Sainsbury children were called together by the headmaster of the school who told us that it had occurred to the Sainsburys that, as we had no parents living in this country, we hadn't got any pocket money and that he had been given the money for us to each have six pence a week. In the midst of all the problems that they had, they had time to think of 20 refugee children they had rescued. Our main debt is that they saved our lives.'

Having escaped the Nazi occupation of Paris, Smon and Maureen faced regular bombing raids, food shortages and other problems in London

Exiled in London

When Simon reached London he found a delicate Maureen who was still recovering from the appendicitis that had nearly killed her. For the first time, the couple began openly to live together, staying in a hotel for a short while before moving to lodgings near Hampstead Heath. They were short of clothes, most having been left behind in France as they fled to safety. With little money, they had to accept charity from friends and family. Life was bleak. Simon and Maureen lived with other refugees, all pooling their food coupons to eke out their rations. With the sound of bombs falling night after night, tensions among the lodgers ran high, as they were thrown together with little in common, all worried about what was going to happen to them.

Herman Marx had visited Simon frequently in Paris and now gravitated to him in London. 'I was working at the BBC and lived in Hampstead near them. I would see them at least once a week,' he remembered. 'We would have dinner together. It was all very sad, as we were worried about what was happening to everyone in The Netherlands. They didn't have much money and things were rather rough for them. The place they were living in was like an old-fashioned boarding house, very basic, very dark and uncomfortable. Simon was used to never being short of anything and he found it difficult to adjust; he was also very worried about Maureen's health and how Sonia was. He was very concerned about how she would get on in America.'

Anti-Semitism was still present in England. Some leading English Jews reminded, perhaps of their own vulnerability as recent immigrants, were far from happy at welcoming new refugees to their country. English Jews had been among those who had spoken against

Great Britain offering homes to German and Austrian refugees before the war. Some of the English Van den Berghs even turned their backs on their Dutch relatives.

Arnold's granddaughter, Rosalida (the daughter of Simon's cousin Constance Polak), remembered how hesitant some of Jacob and Henry's descendants had been about helping or welcoming these Dutch family members into their homes. 'My father [Jacques] faced anti-Semitism within Unilever when he first moved over here during the 1930s. The 'English' families were friendly when their cousins came over on holidays but some of them, often the wealthiest, weren't so kind when they arrived as refugees,' she said. 'It was a very lonely life for people like Herman and Simon. The Dutch families were left alone to look after themselves and this continued after the war when the Dutch desperately needed help, having lost our cousins and homes, some were terribly ill. Little was done to help them.'

'Unacceptable behaviour'

Further tension was caused by Simon and Maureen living together. 'Maureen was very unhappy as she was unable to go out much with Simon. They still had to be fairly discreet about their relationship as they weren't sure how friends and relations would respond to them going out openly together,' recalled Herman. 'Simon told me that he was worried about how unhappy Sonia would be if she heard that Maureen was visiting the family. He knew how fragile Sonia was.'

Some of the Van den Bergh family, who had become part of the English establishment with their daughters becoming debutantes and their sons joining the best clubs, tried to distance themselves from Simon and Maureen. Instead of feeling compassion for these two refugees, they were shocked by what they considered 'unacceptable behaviour'. Couples didn't live together 'in sin'. One of those who disapproved was Henry's daughter, Elisabeth Roskill, the wife of an Admiral and no stranger to controversy herself, having married out of the faith and being cut out of her furious father's will. 'We were totally frozen out by Elsie Roskill, who looked on me as a "terrible woman",' said Maureen. 'She was very snobbish and wouldn't have anything to do with us. She was very rude to us.'

Maureen was still recovering from her illness when she was summoned by the authorities. She was given permission to go back to Ireland but was told that if she stayed in England she would have to take a job. 'I was called up before the Board of the Ministry of Labour. I was told I wasn't fit for work and they told me to come back in two weeks time, and they would find a job for me,' she said. 'So I got a job in a crèche and I worked in it throughout the war, because they thought I was too frail to do anything else.'

Tamara arrived in England with her father and moved into the Hampstead house of Constance Polak, where she shared a room with Rosalida. Both girls enlisted. Although born in The Netherlands, Tamara had lived nearly all her life in France. She joined the Free French forces and became a Second Lieutenant. She arrived in France a few weeks after D Day in 1944 and eventually worked in camps for displaced people. Her newly-bought flat in Paris was requisitioned by the Germans in June 1941, when they seized the property of Jews who had fled. She was particularly upset when she returned after the war to find that the Germans had taken her skiing kit. Rosalida, also born in The Netherlands, joined the Dutch army.

In London, Simon was reunited with some of his fellow students of Arabic philosophy. One was Richard Walzer. In 1927 he had become Assistant Professor and from 1933, Privat-dozent at the Institut für Altertumskunde (Institute for Antiquities) at Berlin University. In 1933 he was one of the first professors to realise that he and his family had no future in Germany and left with his wife Sophie Casirer, a leading authority on art, to become a lecturer at Rome University in Italy. Fluent in English, French, Italian and Hebrew, he specialised in Greek, Classical and Semitic Philosophy. He arrived in England just as war broke out, taking up a position at Oxford University. He died in 1975.

Ralph Pinder Wilson, then a student at Oxford and later head of Oriental Antiquities at the British Museum, got to know Simon through Professor Walzer who taught him Arabic Philosophy. 'In those days Arabic was taught like a dead language and you also had to know Greek,' explained Pinder Wilson. 'I had come out of the army and I had to be away from Oxford for a term, as I had had a duodenal ulcer. It was suggested to me by Walzer that I should go and read some Arabic with Simon Van den Bergh. He was working on his *Incoherence of the Incoherence*. He was very intense about his work.'

Simon taught Pinder Wilson at his parents' home where they would have tea. They knew Simon had a partner so they suggested he bring her too, which was the beginning of a friendship between the two couples. 'My parents used to see a lot of Simon and Maureen,' Pinder Wilson recalled. 'It seemed a pity that she wasn't always able to go to things with him. They were living in a miserable place.'

Simon's old friend Alexandre Koyré, now safely in the United States, wrote trying to encourage him to move there. In 1940 he had given his first lecture at the University of Chicago and discovered how little the students knew about Philosophy when, reading one of his student's papers, he came across a reference to a 'Mr Aristotle'. He tried to persuade Simon to join him in teaching 'old cultures' to 'new ones' but Simon declined and remained in London, where he continued to teach students referred to him throughout the war.

Simon also helped the Dutch Resistance. In 1943, he joined three other Dutch academics in producing a booklet *Voices of Freedom*. The booklet, the size of a large matchbox, was a 93-page anthology of quotations on freedom, culled from philosophers, writers and politicians from all ages. It was produced by the publishers of the Dutch Government-in-Exile's paper *The Whirlwind*, and was dropped in canisters to resistance groups in The Netherlands throughout the war for circulation among the population. It was also dropped in September 1944, just before the Battle for Arnhem. Read avidly by the Dutch who risked execution for doing so, the booklet was looked upon as a vital part of the propaganda war.

Chapter 9 Life together; Lives apart

Saturday 5 May 1945 marked the end of war in Europe. Up to 60 million people had been killed (the total number of deaths globally has never been confirmed), including nearly 6 million Jews. The last months of the war had caused devastation in The Netherlands, where over 16,000 people died from malnutrition during the coldest winter on record. There were 210,000 direct Dutch war casualties, nearly half of them Jews, and a further 70,000 died from disease or hunger; 30,000 Dutch children had been left orphaned.

Millions of displaced people returned home and were reunited with surviving family members or began the task of tracing friends and family who had remained in occupied Europe. Tamara, Rosalida and Sidney Van den Bergh, returning before the end of the war, were among the first to go back to France and The Netherlands: Sidney in 1944 as an Aide de Camp to Prince Bernhard; Rosalida with the Dutch army; and Tamara with the Free French Armed Forces. Others would not return until peace had come.

France suffered post-war tensions. Approximately half a million French men and women had died, including some 200,000 military and 79,000 Jews. In the last year of the war alone, some 500,000 dwellings had been destroyed. Survivors turned against each other as old scores were settled. Retribution by vigilantes led to anarchy. In the South of France, small civil wars broke out as Communists and de Gaullists broke their uneasy peacetime truce to try to secure control of the big cities.

Simon wrote repeatedly to the authorities asking for permission to visit his father. Each request was turned down. He was finally granted permission to travel to Nice towards the end of 1945, but before he could do so Isaac died. Aged 92, Isaac was the last survivor of Simon and Elisabeth van den Bergh's seven sons. Simon was devastated. 'He had desperately wanted to see his father. Simon had written to him through the Red Cross in Switzerland and he didn't know whether his father had got his letters,' Maureen explained. 'He was so worried about him because he was so old. He was desperately unhappy when he heard the news. It was so cruel, all those years apart and just when it looked as though he would see him again,

Across Europe, people returned to bombed-out homes and began rebuilding shattered lives

The garden at Wassenaar. The house had been commandeered and desecrated by the occupying German High Command

Isaac died.' Simon inherited his father's money, which had been banked in Switzerland. Also monies held in France throughout the war were made available, so at least Simon and Maureen were able to live more comfortably.

Between 1942 and 1945, a total of 18 million people were sent to concentration camps, of these some 11 million were killed, according to the Red Cross. Oss, which had been liberated during the autumn of 1944, had become 'Jew Free'. Simon's relatives died at Sobibor, Auschwitz, Belsen and Neuengamme. The Dutch, having kept meticulous lists of their Jewish citizens, now kept those of the deported.

Returning with the Dutch Forces, Arnold's granddaughter Rosalida was given the chance to visit and work in the concentration camps but refused. She had no illusions about what nightmares would be waiting. 'I couldn't face going to them,' she said. 'I knew that my own brother and other members of the family had died in the camps and I couldn't deal with seeing these places. It was too painful and terrible. I worked in the camps set up for refugees in Belgium and The Netherlands. I still see these stick-like people at night.' Later Rosalida would move to Israel and marry. Her stepson is the internationally respected author Amos Oz.

All Simon and Tamara's books were stolen from their apartments in Paris by the Germans. Members of the family who returned to The Netherlands found their houses stripped, paintings taken, papers and books destroyed. Although Sam and Betsy's house in Nice had been left intact, their house in Wassenaar had been commandeered by the German High Command. Many of their Jewish books and artefacts were destroyed. Their son Sidney found pages from the Judica presented to Sam and Betsy on their 50th wedding anniversary thrown around the garden. Arnold Van den Bergh's paintings had been looted and sent to German collectors and galleries. Eventually his grandson Herman was to reclaim some after recognising them in a book.

Lisa and Robert with their four children (from left); Celia, Anabel, Elizabeth and David

Slowly, members of the Van den Bergh family began to rebuild their lives. Lisa returned to America to collect her daughter Elizabeth and son David. In 1945 she gave birth to Celia; three years later she had another daughter, Annabel. Simon and Sonia were never reunited. Sonia stayed in America, to be near her brothers.

The worst fears of Sonia's family in the USA were confirmed as the number of deaths of Polish Jews in the Holocaust was published. Approximately 6 million Poles died during the war, of which at least 5 million were civilians and 3 million were Jews. The largest population of Jews in Europe had been decimated. Sonia's nephew Billy, a serving soldier in the American army, had fought in Europe. He searched vainly through lists of survivors and the dead, travelling from camp to camp looking unsuccessfully for any trace of his relatives. There are special monuments to Holocaust victims at Suwalki's Jewish cemetery. Pauline's son Abrasha, having failed to convince his mother and sister to join him in the States, suffered from depression and 'survivor guilt' for years after learning of the deaths of his family. After the war, Abrasha's relationship with Simon and Sonia and his American uncles became closer, with them taking the place of his own immediate family.

On 18 March 1955, 10 years after the war had ended and when someone could legally be judged to be dead, a New York lawyer wrote to the surviving family members to inform them that 'Enna Pokrojska', also known as Anna or Jenny Hollander/Pokrojski, had passed away at an 'unmentioned' date. She had deposited money, earned when she had worked in the USA, in various American banks to go to her relatives. Her brothers Sam, Eddie and Archie, sister Sonia and nephew Abrasha were all named as beneficiaries.

Sonia in New York

Trans-Atlantic relations

Sonia moved to Florida for a short while but returned to New York, and lived in an apartment on the Upper East Side, just off Central Park, where she was able to see her nephews and nieces. She became close to her brother Eddie's daughter Leonore and his daughter-in-law Annette. Leonore, whose mother had died when she was very young, frequently saw her aunt and was impressed by her kindness. 'She spoke with a delightful French accent. She was very artistic,' she recalled. 'There were special occasions when we met up. My mother had died when I was very young and she was very concerned for me. I remember her taking me to this expensive dress shop and buying me a beautiful black evening gown, my first one... I must have been 19 or 20 and so she was a fascinating person to me. She was so very elegant, very refined and charming. She didn't go out much; she seemed to keep to herself.'

Health worries may have been why Sonia preferred to stay at home, where she would sometimes invite family members to lunch or dinner. Unfortunately she had a rather haphazard approach to entertaining. At one dinner she forgot to serve the soup, only remembering that it was still boiling away as the meal was finished.

Annette Bendett who had married Sonia's nephew, Billy Hollander, remembered how very smart she was: 'Sonia's dress was conservative and tasteful. I don't think she was interested in the latest fashions. She always appeared well groomed. Her apartment was very elegant. She had a marvellous taste in choosing beautiful colours, paintings and lamps. I have a beautiful iron candlestick holder that she brought back from Portugal. I can picture her picking it up in the shop, examining it carefully and saying I'll take this.'

Sonia's family were aware that Simon and Sonia had separated. They were told that Simon had become involved with someone who worked for the family. According to Leonore, Sonia didn't talk much about what had happened but Simon always made sure she knew he was thinking of her by sending flowers every few months, on an anniversary or other celebration. That continued for the rest of her life.

Abrasha and Luba's visit to New York in 1960. Back row (from left): Archie Hollander, Jack Ferguson (Tamara's husband), Abrasha Glikson, Bernie Gorman (Leonore's husband).
Front: Tamara Van den Bergh Ferguson, Luba Alperevich Glikson, Mary Zoll (Archie's wife), Leonore Hollander Gorman

Abrasha's wife Luba met Sonia for the first time when the couple visited New York in 1960 from Argentina. Sonia was sad when Luba and Abrasha left to return home. She told Luba how much she would miss her phone calls and visits. Later, when Luba made a trip on her own to New York, Sonia invited her to visit. They continued to write to each other until the end of Sonia's life.

Sonia had always been interested in dancing and music. Living alone in New York, unhampered by other people's opinions, she now found the freedom to study. She wrote to Luba to ask her to find a book with Latin American children's songs for her. She wanted to translate the lyrics and set them to music for her grandchildren and the children of her American nephews and nieces. Annette recalled Sonia taking singing lessons and having recordings made of her voice, although none of them survive. 'I believe she sang to the children in a hospital,' she said. 'The important thing is that she enjoyed it. She was interested in so many things and when you think about it, she acted on many of her interests. She wanted to sing. It was a way of expressing herself. I think it was admirable and also very brave of her.'

Her grandchildren met Sonia rarely. Elizabeth and David saw her when they studied in America. Celia kept up a correspondence with her and remembered that she had numerous umbrellas: 'She had to buy a new one every time she went out, as she had forgotten to take an umbrella with her.'

Although she welcomed her brothers and their families to her home, Sonia took a different attitude toward her own family. They took tea with her in New York restaurants but were never invited to her apartment. Sonia had very strong views on who she would see. 'She refused to see my parents because she said that the atmosphere in the apartment was too humid,' said Celia. 'She would put them off visiting her.'

In 1955 Tamara, who had been asked by Simon to 'keep an eye on' her mother, moved to the United States. Three years later, on 12 September 1958, she married John (Jack) D A Ferguson, a Canadian of Scottish origin. Both her parents went to the wedding. Simon flew over; it was the first time he and Sonia had met for 12 years.

Tamara was to become a leading Clinical Sociologist, gaining a Masters in Sociology at Columbia University in 1962 and her Doctorate in 1970. She was Assistant Professor at the University of Detroit until 1971, when she became Associate Professor at the University of Windsor, Ontario in Canada. In 1978 she became Associate Professor of Sociology at Wayne State University Medical School, Detroit, a post she still holds. From 1982 to 1999 she was an associate of the Psychiatry Department of Harper Hospital Medical School in Detroit. She has written and contributed to many major publications on clinical sociology and achieved something her father never did, by becoming a tenured Professor.

Lisa remained in London where she and her husband Robert put together one of the world's finest collections of modern art. Her relationship with her father, never a particularly easy one, often ran into problems because of their different attitude towards contemporary art. One disagreement was after the end of the Second World War when Simon gave Lisa and Robert some money to take to Paris. 'We spent it on a painting,' she confessed. 'He had wanted us to have a good time. We went to see a friend of ours who was a dealer. My father didn't care less about [modern] paintings or collecting them and was horrified at what we spent. He thought we should have spent it on ourselves.' Her attempts to get him interested in contemporary art failed and exposed an anomaly in his character: 'I can remember taking him to see the Giacomettis and other modern art. He didn't think that we should have bought those sort of things. Although he thought in an abstract way, he didn't like abstracts.'

Simon and Maureen had moved into a flat in Lowndes Terrace, Chelsea, but their relationship was uneasy. Before the war, Simon had fallen in love with a very beautiful Polish woman called Elizabeth. Herman Marx confessed to having fallen in love with her himself: 'She was very beautiful, very charming, I adored her. She was very intelligent. I can remember her, as opposed to Maureen, from the time in Paris.'

Now she appeared in London where she was reunited with Simon. Maureen left him and moved to New York. Both Rosalida Polak and Ralph Pinder Wilson remember Simon and Elizabeth living together at a house in Lawrence Street, Chelsea, for a few years after the

Jack Ferguson in 1964

war. She had two sons from a previous relationship, whom Simon helped support. Said Rosalida: 'She was much more intelligent than the other women he knew: she played musical instruments and could talk about all the things that he was interested in and on the same level. Maureen was much more of an aide than a friend, which Elizabeth was.'

Ralph concured: 'Elizabeth was attractive and she was able to speak about philosophy with him. Simon was very gallant of course and he paid to keep up the flat for Maureen. Then Maureen went off to New York. He bought this house for Elizabeth. then she died [of cancer]. Maureen contacted the family and he asked her to come back, and she did.'

Simon in pensive mood

According to Maureen, Simon wrote to Sonia over and again, asking for a divorce. 'His cousin Connie and her husband Jacques Polak approached Sonia on their first visit to America after the war and asked why she wouldn't give him a divorce,' said Maureen. 'She said "no not under any condition". She had changed her mind, originally she had said yes.' But Rosalida, Connie and Jacques' daughter, painted a different picture. 'My parents saw Sonia but never pressed her on the marriage,' she insisted. 'Simon never put any pressure on Sonia to give him a divorce despite what he said to Maureen. Maureen kept threatening that she would leave him or would even threaten to commit suicide. I don't think that he would ever have got married again if she hadn't been so forceful.'

Tamara agreed that Simon hadn't wanted a divorce. Despite all the problems and the many years of separation, Simon still felt a strong connection with Sonia. 'He had asked my mother to come back from America but when she refused he asked Maureen to,' she said. 'He rather put my mother on a pedestal saying that she had moral principles, she wouldn't hurt anyone. He was worried that she hadn't much sense of money. He didn't want a divorce, he couldn't make hard decisions. She was the mother of his children and that was important.'

It was still unusual for couples to live together without being married and Maureen felt Simon was embarrassed. 'He always felt it when people said, "your husband is over there", and I would say "Mr Van den Bergh is not my husband". He didn't like that,' she explained. 'I went to Ireland and changed my name by deed poll [to Van den Bergh] and then everything I had had to be put into that name. Sonia knew all about it. But she still refused to give him a divorce.'

In 1966 Luba Glikson visited London for a week and saw Simon almost daily at his and Maureen's new home at 26 Lowndes Street in Chelsea. Maureen was ill at the time and Simon took over the arrangements for Luba's trip. They lunched together, visiting museums and galleries. Old habits of introducing young people to art came to the fore; he would pull Luba away from looking at some work of art to look at another he thought she should see.

Worried about hurting Sonia's feelings and knowing that Luba was going to visit Sonia in New York, he asked her not to tell Sonia that she had met Maureen. During conversations over lunch or dinner, Simon admitted he was dissatisfied with the way he had lived his life. He revealed he was not totally comfortable about being rich, as he had never had to work for money. Luba told her son Carlos that she had been 'puzzled by his attitude', as she did not consider all that he had achieved in his studies and teaching, plus his ability to understand several Arabic dialects, could be deemed as him not having worked!

Simon remained in contact with Abrasha and Luba, sending letters and presents to them and their three sons. Those letters and presents meant a great deal to the boys, in particular to the middle son, Carlos Glikson, even though he never met Simon. 'My father loved him very much and my mother Luba, too,' he said. 'I keep books in my library today that he handpicked and sent when we were children. Beautiful books he chose according to our ages, timing the heavy packages to arrive by ship precisely for the holiday season. And now years later, I still can see myself opening the packages. I also remember his letters with the tiniest handwriting! I was a boy. I didn't write much but my mother used to write to Uncle Simon as well as to Sonia and they had a very nice correspondence. He would write to us too and ask about us. I felt he was very kind and caring, and it meant a great deal to feel that he had dedicated special time to me.'

Sonia's niece Leonore and her brother Billy's children were also to receive presents of books from Simon, as were Sam Hollander's grandchildren. 'They were sent in beautifully wrapped parcels from Harrods,' remembered Leonore. 'The books were selected with each child in mind and were always deeply appreciated. A great deal of thought had gone into each present and it meant a great deal to us.'

Simon's translation of Averroës *Tahāfut Al-Tahāfut* – finally published in 1954

Recognition at last

Simon remained in London where he continued to tutor students interested in the work of Averroës and became an examiner for the Oxford and Cambridge Board. He was also hard at work on his translation and interpretation of *Averroës' Tahāfut Al-Tahāfut* (*The Incoherence of the Incoherence*). He had spent nearly 30 years working methodically on the book. The length of time it was taking caused some amusement within the family, according to Rosalida: 'He had laughingly given it the name of *The Whatness of the Whatness* to explain how esoteric the whole venture was.'

Simon was a perfectionist who could never bring himself to finish something because he thought it could still be improved. Yet academic friends were urging him to complete the book. Tamara recalled how Professor Alexandre Koyré, now returned from America and finally receiving the overdue honours from French academics, was becoming concerned. 'He told him that he had to finish

Professor Erwin Rosenthal, an authority on the work of Averroës, insisted that Simon's work was appreciated

Professor Richard Walzer recommended Simon's book to his students as 'an outstanding classic'

it sometime and that the more he went over things the more difficult and complicated he was making it for himself to finish it,' she said.

Simon listened to his old friend and mentor. In 1954, the E J W Gibb Memorial New Series published Simon's translation of *Averroës' Tahāfut Al-Tahāfut* (*The Incoherence of the Incoherence*). Reproduced again in 1987, in the Unesco Collection of Great Works, Arabic Studies, the book with its introduction and notes is still widely used in Arabic Philosophy courses.

In the early 1950s Simon met Erwin Rosenthal, Professor of Oriental Studies at Cambridge University, who was himself an authority on the work of Averroës. He and his wife had emigrated from Germany in 1933 within weeks of Hitler coming to power. The two men became close friends; that friendship was extended to Professor Rosenthal's daughter Miriam. At the time of its first publication, Simon admitted to Erwin that he was disappointed that few people took notice of his *Tahāfut*. He thought that he had never been taken seriously because he had not held an academic appointment at a university.

Miriam remembered her father being worried that Simon felt his work was not appreciated but he insisted that wasn't the case. 'Like any academic discipline, there was so much rivalry you were either in or out,' she explained. 'Some of them were very difficult. Unlike my father, [Simon] had never needed to work for money. He had travelled around Europe and hadn't needed to get a job, and this had acted against him in that he felt he was treated as an "amateur" academic.'

Other academics also emphasised that Simon was respected. They were aware of Simon's wealth but they also understood the quality of his research. Professor Jan Just Witkam of Leiden University recounted how his teacher, Professor G W J Drewes, a friend of Simon's, told his students that he admired his attitude: 'He always told us, his students, that [Simon] was of independent means,' said Witkam, 'and that he therefore had no material necessity to participate in academic life. He did it because he loved it. His work did much to illuminate that of Averroës.'

In his introduction to the book, Simon acknowledged the help he had received from Professor Richard Walzer. Dr Friedrich Zimmermann, University Lecturer in Islamic Philosophy at the Oriental Institute, Oxford University, Fellow of St Cross College and a close friend and student of Walzer, remembered him recommending the book to his students and referring to Simon all the time. 'When I went to study under Walzer I bought the book. I hadn't known anything about Islamic philosophy and I learned about it from Walzer,' he said. 'He certainly impressed upon us that this was one of the few outstanding classics. And as far as I am concerned I still pass on the message to my students. It hasn't lost its value.'

Both Walzer and Rosenthal were to refer to Simon's book in their own publications. *Averroës' Tahāfut Al-Tahāfut* (*The Incoherence of the Incoherence*) is still widely used by students and is seen as being an important explanation of Averroës' work. Dr Oliver Leaman of The University of Kentucky frequently uses the book in his courses because Simon was an important scholar of Averroës. 'His translation was a very significant contribution. It is about 50 years old and has not been repeated and that is something!' he pointed out. 'The commentary is flawed by his determination to see Greek philosophy everywhere in Islamic philosophy, but despite that it is an excellent work. I use it all the time, as does everyone interested in Averroës. It's the notes that mean much and they could make another book.'

Praise for Simon's work also came from Professor George Wickens, formerly of the University of Toronto's Department of Near and Middle Eastern Civilizations, who said Simon's work is highly regarded by qualified colleagues: 'He was of that generation of European scholars who were deeply dedicated, solidly grounded in what I would call "real disciplines" and equipped with a formidable arsenal of linguistic and other skills.' Wickens believed Simon Van den Bergh represented the essence of what an academician should be. 'Alas, they are all gone, as are nearly all of his immediate successors,' he lamented. 'There have been catastrophic changes in academic attitudes over the last 30 years or so. As far as the Humanities/Liberal Arts are concerned, these are now at best moribund. Rapidly passing intellectual fads, commercialism and corporate administrative structures have reduced them to a sort of shallow status... We now have "historians, philosophers and literary theorists" with little or no knowledge of languages, or even accurate facts, and no depths or breadth of general knowledge, culture and ideas.'

Simon and Maureen enjoyed walks in the hills around Monte Carlo

According to Zimmerman, Simon's work reflects the different attitudes towards philosophy in the United Kingdom and Germany, with the latter looking for a more rounded approach, not one based on strict disciplines. 'I had an ancient professor, years ago in Germany, who would tell us that philosophy *is* the history of philosophy. It was only when I came to the English-speaking world that I discovered that history and philosophy are treated as totally different departments in the academic system here...' he explained. 'For me, Simon Van den Bergh was a typical exponent of the continental tradition in being a historian and a philologist at the same time as being a philosopher. There is no contradiction in this. Anyone working on anything on the history of philosophy needs to combine the three subjects. And so I have no problems with seeing him as a philosopher.'

The respect is echoed in Germany, where Simon studied. Professor Dr Hans Daiber, of the Oriental Department of Johann Wolfgang Goethe-Universität, Frankfurt am Main wrote: 'Simon Van den Bergh mainly remains known to us as the specialist of Averroës. His English translation of *Tahāfut Al-Tahāfut* is a standard book and remains valuable as a tool of historians of Islamic philosophy.'

By the 1950s, Simon, now nearing his eighties, found it difficult to refuse any work he was asked to do. He was tired and Maureen worried about him. 'He was always being asked to look after things... would you look at this, would you check this, will you look after this pupil, will you take this pupil?' she said. 'He was doing a lot of examining for the Oxford and Cambridge Board, and he never said no. He said to me: "you know as long as I am here, I will be unable to relax".'

In July 1970, Simon and Maureen travelled to Kashmir where Simon climbed in the foothills of the Himalayas

Wexford Opera House, now the home of the Wexford Music and Arts Festival, an annual event that Simon and Maureen supported in its early days

The twilight years

Simon still enjoyed walking in the mountains; Maureen and he would often go on trips to the South of France and Switzerland, so he could hike among the hills he so loved. Simon's idea of a walk was a 20-mile trip. Fortunately for Maureen, he regarded her as being delicate and insisted that she rested.

In the late 1950s the couple moved to Monte Carlo, where Simon could combine walking with meeting their numerous friends who lived there. 'We used to go down there for holidays and then he said would I be prepared to go and live there? And I said yes, it's going to mean a lot for you,' recalled Maureen.

Simon had spent years studying and teaching Arabic philosophy but had never travelled to Persia and the East. Maureen encouraged him to take longer journeys. In July 1970, Simon and Maureen travelled to Kashmir. Simon wrote to Luba describing how, despite his age, he had done some climbing in the foothills of the Himalayas; it was an 'unforgettable experience'. The couple made several trips to Ireland, where Maureen's arrival, exquisitely dressed in furs, made quite an impact on her family, as her second cousin Richard Byrne remembered: 'There was little money around at that time in Ireland. Maureen, who was called Aunt Maureen by us all because of her age, used to arrive dressed in minks. And with little fox stoles draped around her shoulders. Simon terribly impressed me as he wanted to learn Gaelic.' Simon and Maureen became early supporters and visitors to the Wexford Music and Arts Festival, after it was founded in 1951.

The deaths of his closest relatives and friends meant trips back to The Netherlands became fewer. Simon disliked the country and its people and, according to Maureen, disliked the language even more. Once when George's son Robbert went to stay in Monte Carlo, Maureen and his wife Annie left the men alone but when they went back into the room, Robbie was speaking in Dutch and Simon was talking back to him in English. 'He

George van den Bergh (above), whom Simon (above right, in London) often teased about his left-wing views

remained a Dutch citizen. He didn't give that up but he never cared for Holland,' Maureen said: 'He was bored with the language and the country.'

On one of the few trips back to The Netherlands, Simon was to see his cousin and great friend George Van den Bergh, then an eminent Professor, inventor, socialist and humanitarian. Simon often teased George about his left-wing views. 'George had been worried about the influence of multinationals in the global economy. He thought they wielded too much power,' Maureen explained. 'He had put a proposal to the Dutch Government that they should call on the United Nations to take control of organisations such as Unilever. Simon claimed that George wanted to see his ancestors rise from their graves! He [claimed] that George came up with ideas like that to get money out of the company.' George made a similar proposal before the Second World War, when he suggested that the League of Nations should take over Unilever. 'Simon said that Sam had given him money to keep him quiet. George used the money to help set up the Dutch Labour Party!'

Life in Monte Carlo was one of leisurely days in the sunshine, long walks, swimming, going to concerts and entertaining. Jacob Van den Bergh's eldest son Albert always saw the couple when he visited the Riviera. 'His wife Maudie had just died and he came down to Monte Carlo so that he could go to the casino,' Maureen recalled. 'He would arrive about 4 o'clock in the afternoon and would sit and have a drink with Simon. They would talk about old times and the family. Simon found him a bit boring because he couldn't talk about the intellectual things that he was interested in. Bertie would have his drink and then head off to the casino.'

Young people were always welcomed. Professor Rosenthal's daughter Miriam visited Simon and Maureen at their flats in London and Monte Carlo. She introduced her future husband Julian to them and remembered their 'exquisite taste' and very 'deep conversation'. 'They lent me their flat in Monte Carlo in the early 1960s; I remember this beautiful view over the sea from their balcony,' she said. 'I also saw them in London. They had the most beautiful paintings and I remember being given tea on a wonderful delicate tea set. They had a marvellous Buddha. Simon had no small talk. His whole conversation was talking about philosophy; Julian's first meeting with him was spent listening to him talking in great depth about... the nature of existence and all the philosophers' questions. Dinner parties would be spent with Simon discussing philosophy and Maureen talking about cats.'

Miriam's husband, Julian Hodges, remembered his first meeting with Simon – and their wedding present: '[It was] delicate antique pottery, from him and Maureen. It was chosen with great care and was exquisite.'

On 29 June 1969 Sonia died in her New York apartment at 166 East 63rd Street of a heart attack. She was 77. Her niece Leonore recalled that the death came suddenly and unexpectedly: 'No-one knew she had died. Eddie and Archie kept ringing her apartment but there was no reply. They went round and found her dead.' Annette, the wife of Sonia's nephew

Archie, Eddie and Max Hollander in New York: Eddie was touched by the way he found Sonia's room

Billy, said Sonia's death had a profound effect on her father-in-law. 'The night she died she had prepared to eat her evening meal by setting the table beautifully,' Annette recalled. 'Eddie was so touched by the way he found the room. I imagine that is how she always did everything even in private. It affected us all.'

When Leonore cleared Sonia's apartment she discovered that, despite living in America, she still felt vulnerable. 'She had all these purses with money in them. It was as though she was expecting something to happen and that she would have to move on,' said Leonore. 'It was as though she was scared, it was very sad.'

Simon was immediately informed that Sonia had passed away. She was still a Catholic when she died. Her death certificate reports that Simon, her husband and living at Sonia's address, had officially notified the authorities of his wife's death. She was cremated on 1 July 1969 at Ferncliff Crematorium in Hartsdale, New York. 'It was a wet day,' Leonore recalled. 'There were very few people present. It was the first time that I met Lisa and her husband Robert, I remember having a coffee with them. Simon was very quiet and sad, obviously thinking about their lives, it was all very sad and poignant.'

Now there was no longer any excuse for Simon not to marry Maureen. On 24 November 1969 Simon, who was then 87, and Maureen, 61, were married at Chelsea Register Office. Maureen felt people who had previously been shocked at their relationship would now accept her: 'Only our most intimate friends knew that we had got married. Once that happened Lisa was quite happy to invite us to their house. Other people seemed to find it easier too.' The wedding was small and private, with only a few very close friends attending. Celia was disappointed not to be told about her grandfather's marriage. 'We were not allowed to know that they had got married. We weren't able to give them presents. They probably didn't want us to know that they weren't married before,' she suggested.

At that time Simon and Maureen were living in the Palais Albany, at 26 Boulevard Des Moulins, Monte Carlo, where his daughters and their husbands would visit them. Tamara and Jack travelled from America to tour the South of France. In the past, Sam and Betsy's home, Arcadia, in Nice had attracted members of the family. Now Simon and Maureen's home acted as the magnet for new generations. These included Sonia's great nephew Martin Gorman, the grandson of her brother Eddie and recipient of some of those books sent at Christmas. He took his fiancée to meet Simon in the summer of 1976 and joined the long list of those to appreciate Simon and Maureen's hospitality and good taste.

Herman Marx made several visits to Simon in Monte Carlo. 'It was always marvellous to see him. He always wanted to know what was going on,' Herman said. 'He would take me out for long walks up into the hills. George Van den Bergh had died by that time. His son Robbert was there at the same time. He had been criticised for selling Arcadia but I remember that Simon said he understood as he found it difficult to go to some of the places we had all been to [before the war].'

Simon took great interest in the lives of his grandchildren, sending photographs of them to Luba in Argentina. Simon was generous to everyone, even if his 'other wordliness' led to problems, despite his good intentions. His granddaughter Celia recalled that when she and her future husband Conrad Blakey were asked what they wanted for a wedding present,

Simon and Maureen at home

they requested cutlery from Jensen. 'Simon took us around the shop ordering eight of every-thing. The only thing was that he had forgotten to order anything to put them in,' she laughed.

His grandson, David Sainsbury, also recalled how absent-minded his grandfather was, once putting on shaving cream instead of sun cream. David remembered a trip he and his eldest sister Elizabeth took with Simon to The Netherlands when they were 13 and 15. He was most impressed when Simon went into a bank, took out a lot of cash, stuffed it into his pocket and ran across the road with his two grandchildren, scattering banknotes in his wake. Both David and Simon were keen runners and he remembered running along the beach with the old man, as well as holding philosophical discussions on topics such as whether God was both omniscient and omnipotent. As the grandchildren grew up and began rela-tionships of their own, it became normal for them to take their new partners to meet their grandfather. David took his future wife Susie to visit; his sister Celia and her husband Con-rad visited Simon on their honeymoon.

Celia was impressed by his talent for the piano. 'He could play beautifully, without music in front of him; he had an ear for music and could play a tune after listening to it,' she recalled. 'He and Maureen loved going to the Wexford Festival. We would often see them on their way back.' His love of walking continued well into old age and Celia remembered the distinct way he held himself as he walked: 'He used to walk along, head down, concen-trating on the pavement and what he was talking about, but not looking where he was going. He used to get annoyed when the Monte Carlo Rally was taking place and all these obstacles had been put up.'

Simon and Maureen made frequent trips back to England to see Lisa and her family. In 1978, Dr Freidrich Zimmermann and his wife were invited to dinner by Lisa Sainsbury to meet her father. Zimmermann was delighted to accept the invitation to meet someone whose work he knew so well and admired. Unfortunately, it turned out to be a rather

Simon with his great-grandchildren in 1975

embarrassing evening. 'I had been specifically asked as someone who knew his work, to tell him how much I thought about it,' said Zimmerman. 'We were collected by car and taken to the house. Unfortunately Simon was not wearing his hearing aid. I talked away to him about his work. Lisa sat opposite yelling at him to tell him what I had said. I can remember Lisa getting frustrated and berating him for not putting in his hearing aid. He blithely sat there not being able to hear a word I said to him.'

Old age began to affect Simon. For the last six months of his life, he was wheelchair-bound. He began to have problems with his memory. 'Opa', as Celia's sons knew him, grew frustrated. 'He was no longer able to remember all the languages that he had worked in,' she recalled. 'He was very frustrated that he could no longer read German. His books had been published in German and he was annoyed that he could no longer read them.'

Herman Marx, on holiday with a friend, visited Simon in Monte Carlo during those last months. 'It was the last time I was to see him. Simon was delighted to see us but grew tired after a while,' said Herman, who was concerned that Maureen was bossing Simon around and talking about what she eventually wanted to do with the apartment after he died. 'She seemed to want to return to London where there were good doctors to look after her. I was rather disappointed but it was so good to see him and he was happy to see us and talk about my parents.' Simon reflected on his life, talking about the people who had died and who he missed. 'He began to talk about Sonia, saying how much she had been in his thoughts, about how strange and sad their relationship had been,' recalled Herman. 'He admitted that he should have been more patient and kinder to her. I think that he had a lot of regrets. Maureen wasn't too happy with him talking about Sonia.'

Simon always got his way when he wanted something and that didn't change with old age. Simon's son-in-law Robert Sainsbury had told Maureen that he thought he knew the reason why Simon had always got what he wanted – it was because he had kissed the blarney stone. Maureen agreed: 'If I wasn't very keen on something, he would say "darling won't you do it to please me?". So you found yourself saying yes, and then you would find yourself doing something that you didn't want to do. "It would make me so unhappy if you won't do it"- this was all the blarney. But it worked.'

Tamara felt Simon's most redeeming feature was his sense of humour, of being able to see things in context. 'It was a rather Jewish self-deprecating way of looking at life,' she said. 'He had a great deal of charm. I can remember how he looked, his hand near his face describing how something meant one way or another.'

Simon's death came on Sunday 25 November 1979 at 3pm. He was 97 years old and died gently in his sleep at his apartment in Monte Carlo. His second wife and long-time companion Maureen was alone at his side and had rejected offers from Tamara and Lisa to fly down. 'I wanted to be alone with him. I thought he would prefer me to be with him alone,' she explained. 'He had suffered two cardiac arrests and when he died, it was his heart. I had two nurses from England looking after him and he had full medical care. He just closed his eyes. He died quietly in his own room, just passing his life away.'

There were no obituaries in either the Dutch or English newspapers. Simon, a man of letters, much honoured by academics for translating and teaching the works of the great Arabic philosopher Averroës, passed away without comment. He had led a charmed, vibrant, sometimes controversial life, a life of privilege. Yet he had dedicated that life to 'intellectual rigour'.

His book has become a universal piece of literature, opening minds to Arabic philosophy. 'He studied Arabic. He didn't speak it fluently but he could write about it. How important his knowledge would be today,' said Lisa. Simon's *Averroës' Tahāfut Al-Tahāfut* (*The Incoherence of the Incoherence*), the book he spent some 30 years working on and published for the first time in 1954, the work he thought had not received proper recognition, now features in encyclopaedias, is used in universities and praised by academics.

A man who was a perfectionist, who his daughter Tamara said wanted to 'write the best book ever', would have been delighted.

Extracts from Simon's introduction and notes to *Averroës' Tahāfut Al-Tahāfut (The Incoherence of the Incoherence)*

Introduction

WHEN WE HAVE read the long discussions between the philosophers and theologians we may come to the conclusion that it is sometimes more the formula than the essence of things which divides them. Both philosophers and theologians affirm that God creates or has created the world. For the philosophers, since the world is eternal, this creation is eternal. Is there, however, any sense in calling created what has been eternally? For the theologians God is the creator of everything including time, but does not the term 'creation' assume already the concept of time? Both the philosophers and theologians apply to God the theory that His will and knowledge differ from human will and knowledge in that they are creative principles and essentially beyond understanding; both admit that the Divine cannot be measured by the standards of man. But this, in fact, implies an avowal of our complete ignorance in the face of the Mystery of God. Still, for both parties God is the supreme Artifex who in His wisdom has chosen the best of all possible worlds; for although the philosophers affirm also that God acts only by natural necessity, their system, like that of their predecessors, the

Platonists, Peripatetics, and Stoics, is essentially teleological. As to the problem of possibility, both parties commit the same inconsistencies and hold sometimes that the world could, sometimes that it could not, have been different from what it is. Finally, both parties believe in God's ultimate Unity.

And if one studies the other works of Ghazali the resemblance between him and the philosophers becomes still greater. For instance, he too believes in the spirituality of the soul, notwithstanding the arguments he gives against it in this book; he too sometimes regards religious concepts as the symbols of a higher philosophical or mystical truth, although he admits here only a literal interpretation. He too sometimes teaches the fundamental theory of the philosophers which he tries to refute so insistently in our book, the theory that from the one supreme Agent as the ultimate source through intermediaries all things derive; and he himself expresses this idea (in his *Alchemy of Happiness* and slightly differently in his *Vivification of Theology*) by the charming simile of an ant which seeing black tracings on a sheet of paper thinks that their cause is the pen, while it is the hand that moves the pen by the power of the will which derives from the heart, itself inspired by the spiritual agent,

It is not so much after abstract truth that Ghazali strives; his search is for God, for the Pity behind the clouds

Haruniyeh dome, in the ancient city of Tus, in the north-eastern Iranian province of Khorasan, is believed to be the burial place of Al-Ghazali.

the cause of causes. The resemblances between Ghazali and Averroës, men belonging to the same culture, indeed, the greatest men in this culture, seem sometimes greater than their differences.

Emotionally the difference goes deep. Averroës is a philosopher and a proud believer in the possibility of reason to achieve a knowledge of 'was das Innere der Welt zusammenhält' [the world together in its innermost]. He was not always too sure, he knew too much, and there is much wavering and hesitation in his ideas. Still, his faith in reason remains unshaken. Although he does not subscribe to the lofty words of his master that man because of the power of his intellect is a mortal God, he reproaches the theologians for having made God an immortal man. God, for him, is a dehumanized principle. But if God has to respond to the needs of man's heart, can He be exempt from humanity? Ghazali is a *mu'min*, that is a believer, he is a Muslim, that is he accepts: his heart submits to a truth his reason cannot establish, for his heart has reasons his reason does not know. His theology is the philosophy of the heart in which there is expressed man's fear and loneliness and his feeling of dependence on an understanding and loving Being to whom he can cry out from the depths of his despair, and whose mercy is infinite. It is not so much after abstract truth that Ghazali strives; his search is for God, for the Pity behind the clouds.

Notes

THE LOGIC OF facts forces the Aristotelians to establish distinctions which – since in their system there is no subject, no 'ego' and they identify the things known with the knowledge of things – they are not entitled to make – ie the distinctions between (1) self-knowledge, (2) the knowledge the individual 'self' possesses, (3) the things known. By 'unity of knowledge' is here meant the unity of experience and knowledge in each of us through the unity and identity of his 'self'. Unity of knowledge... is affirmed by Aristotle in another sense, when he declares that the study of all species of being *qua* being belongs to a science which is generically one, whereas the study of the several species of being belongs to the specific parts of this science. But it is not true that knowledge, although the knower is a unity, need not possess plurality, when the things known form a plurality, for knowledge is dependent on the things known and has to conform to their nature. What is true, and seems to me a primary truth, although it is denied both by the idealist and by the relativist, is that the object of knowledge is not affected by the fact of being known. A cat may look at a king, and the king is not affected by the cat's awareness of him. All knowledge implies being, implies facts that can be known and that are independent of this knowledge. Being is prior to knowledge (and even the possibility of being which enables us to act through knowledge is prior to knowledge). If the object of knowledge were affected by its being known, nobody could twice perceive an identical thing, nor could the same object be perceived by many or the same thought be common to many; and however inexplicable it may be, we are aware of living in one unique common universe and of communicating our thoughts, and even the relativist and the idealist are forced to admit that at least their theories would be true, ie correspond to the facts, even if no one ever held them. God, therefore, is not affected by our loving Him or our knowing Him, but as to His knowledge, either God's knowledge is dependent on our decisions and acts in so far as it follows them; or God knows them from eternity, and then the human drama is but a puppet-show; or the eternal sequence of becoming and passing away is eternally beyond His ken.

Appendix I: Family trees

SIMON VAN DEN BERGH'S FATHER Isaac was the fourth of Simon van den Bergh (Senior) and his wife Elisabeth van der Wielen's seven sons. Simon's mother Clara suffered poor health after the birth of her children and devoted her time to Simon's elder sister Liesje, who was disabled. Isaac was the most technically-minded of Simon and Elisabeth's sons.

Simon adored his grandparents, Simon and Elisabeth, and was particularly close to his uncle Sam, his wife Betsy and their son George. Sam was a leading strategist for van den Berghs, a Liberal member of the Municipal Council of Rotterdam and became a Senator in the Dutch Parliament.

The other brothers had varied careers: Jacob and Henry set up Van den Berghs' British operations; Maurits became Receiver of Registration at Eindhoven; Zadok became a Conservative member of the Municipal Council of Amsterdam and a Senator in the National Assembly. Simon's great friend was Eugen Marx, who married Simon's cousin Bertha (the daughter of his avid art-collecting uncle Arnold and his wife Julie).

The family tree also shows Simon's marriages, plus his daughters and their families.

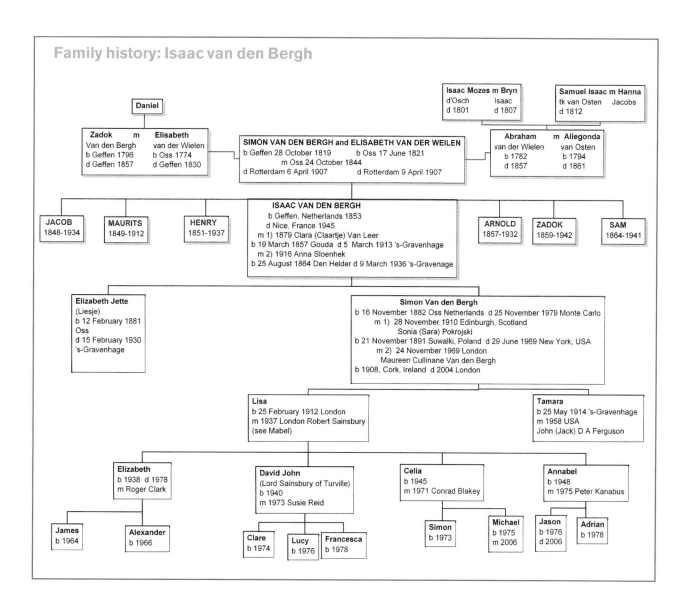

MABEL SAINSBURY, NÉE *Van den Bergh*, was the second-eldest daughter of Jacob Van den Bergh and his first wife, the Englishwoman Lydia Isaacson, who hosted Simon on many of his visits to London. Mabel had great vitality in her youth. She and her younger sister Rosie once inadvertently disrupted Henley Regatta by blocking one of the locks with their boat when the lock gates opened. She was also known for her charitable works.

In 1896, Mabel married John Benjamin Sainsbury, of the prominent British grocery chain Sainsburys. Mabel and John had four children; the youngest, Robert, fell in love with and in 1937 married his second cousin Lisa, Simon's eldest daughter (after her grandfather Isaac played unofficial cupid). Lisa was by this time living in England and had established herself as a medical social worker.

Lisa and Robert, who was later knighted, went on to have four children of their own, to continue the family tradition of charitable work and to establish one of Britain's foremost collections of modern art.

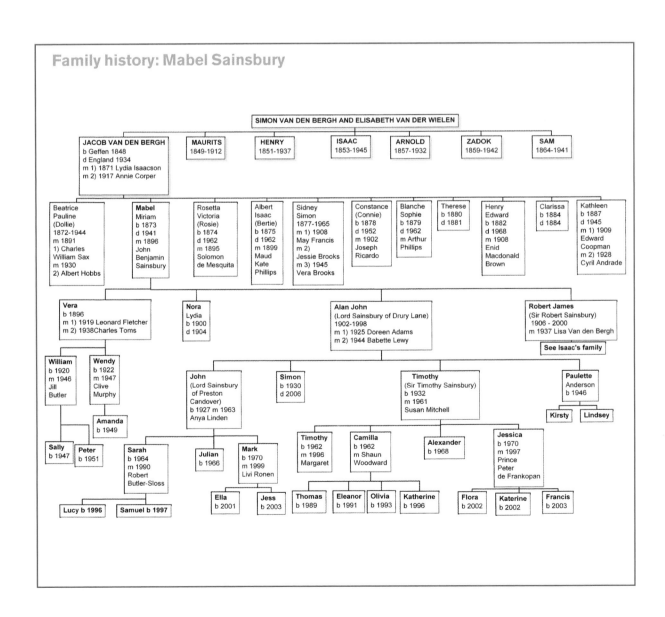

SIMON VAN DEN BERGH'S FIRST wife Sonia Pokrojski was born in the town of Suwalki, which is in present-day Poland but was then in Russia. The youngest of Chonel and Leah's daughters, she was named Sara but adopted the more western-sounding Sonia when she moved to Germany in 1908 to study. Instead she met Simon and would never again see Suwalki.

Her five surviving brothers – Max, Sam, Billy, Eddie and Archie – emigrated to the USA, away from anti-Semitism and Russian persecution. They took the surname Hollander on arrival, derived from their mother's maiden name of Gollandersky. Sonia joined her brothers in New York when she fled France during the Second World War, maintaining regular contact with them and their families, particularly Eddie's daughter Leonore, his son Billy and his wife Annette.

Sonia's nephew Abrasha, the son of her eldest sister Pauline, stayed with Simon and Sonia on his way to Argentina and he and his wife Luba kept in close contact with both of them for the rest of their lives. Their son Carlos was a grateful recipient of Christmas gifts from Simon.

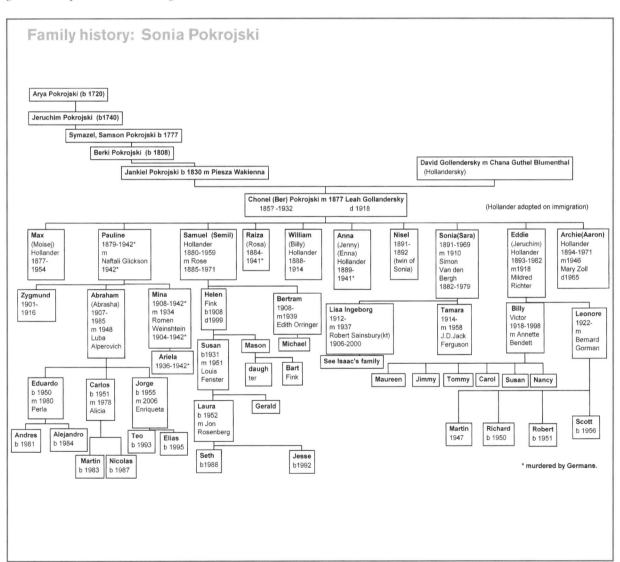

Appendix II: Family exodus from Poland and The Netherlands

MANY POKROJSKIS AND Van den Berghs were exiles from their homelands.

Sam Pokrojski was the first to leave Suwalki at the age of just 15, under threat of conscription into the Russian army. He escaped without official papers by wading across rivers, hiding from police and sneaking over the border into Germany, from where he sailed to America. Brothers Max, Billy, Eddie and Archie followed. Their sister Anna left in 1911, staying with Simon and Sonia in Scheveningen on the way. She returned to Suwalki in the 1920s but is thought to have been murdered, with her sister Rosa Raiza, by the Nazis. Her eldest sister Pauline fled to Sarny in the Ukraine at the start of the Second World War but there is no trace of her after 1941 when Germany invaded.

Herman Marx (whose mother, Bertha, was a cousin of Simon's) and Sidney van den Bergh escaped by boat from the Nazi invasion of The Netherlands, unlike many of their relatives who were either murdered or captured, or committed suicide rather than tolerate Nazi atrocities.

This map shows journeys from northern Europe; see page 147 for the flight of Van den Bergh family members from France.

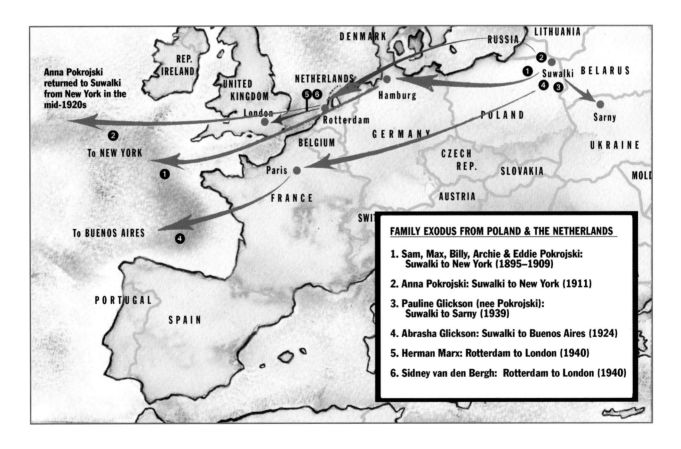

FAMILY EXODUS FROM POLAND & THE NETHERLANDS

1. **Sam, Max, Billy, Archie & Eddie Pokrojski:**
   Suwalki to New York (1895–1909)

2. **Anna Pokrojski:** Suwalki to New York (1911)

3. **Pauline Glickson (nee Pokrojski):**
   Suwalki to Sarny (1939)

4. **Abrasha Glickson:** Suwalki to Buenos Aires (1924)

5. **Herman Marx:** Rotterdam to London (1940)

6. **Sidney van den Bergh:** Rotterdam to London (1940)

Acknowledgements

There are various people I must thank for all their kindness and help in the preparation of this book: these include my friend Jenny Fitzgerald Bond who sat up with me night after night after the death of my husband, helping me to read through the book and offering her suggestions on how to make this intricate story clear to the non family member; to Reinhild Weiss for the German translations, glasses of wine and marvelous dinners; my dearest cousin Maureen Simpson for all her support and memories of life with her great-grandparents and for giving me permission to use Maud Van den Bergh's painting of the French Riviera, and also for presenting me with Maud's gun shrapnel-damaged painting! My thanks also go to Christopher Stone, the original 'godfather' of this project whose sensitivity and kindness has meant much; to Joe Burns who inherited the role and spoke a lot of sense; Denise Searle, a dear friend, and the best editor a writer could have; and to Nick Pearson who embraced the concept of designing this book with a fervour that has left me in awe.

I would like to thank the following for all their help in providing information, photographs and help. In particular I must thank the Van den Bergh family members and the descendants of the Pokrojski family for allowing me to delve into their histories and in providing photographs: Tamara and Jack Ferguson; Lady Lisa Sainsbury; Celia Blakey, with whom I spent a very enjoyable day; Carlos Glikson, for whom the word thanks doesn't go nearly far enough; Leonora Hollander Gorman; Marty & JoAnn Gorman; Annette Hollander; Bep Sturm Van den Bergh, who provided me with so much information about the family and gave me so much help in understanding what they were like; Dr Hans Van den Bergh; Rosalida Klausner; Peter Van den Bergh; Lily Van den Bergh; David Ricardo, a dear friend as well as a cousin; Dr Dick Van Zuylan; and also to Judith Portrait. Sadly since beginning this book not only family members have died, but also friends of the family such as Miriam Hodges and Ralph Pinder Wilson, both of whom generously provided their memories of Simon.

The following organisations and individuals also provided information, help and photographs: Ton Bannink and Rene Tromoline, Unilever Historical Archives, Rotterdam;

Jeanette Strickland and Phaedra Casey, Unilever Historical Archives, Great Britain; Eleanor Bowden, Unilever; The Imperial War Museum; Elizabeth Rose-Bourne and Patrick Redmond (photographer) Wexford Festival Opera; Ros Kavanagh, photo of Wexford Opera House; Annick Ghersin, Bibliotheque National France; Monaco Town Hall; Dr Ludmilla Hanisch, Germany; Hanne Schönig, Germany; Pierre Lory, Religious Sciences, Ecole Pratique des Hautes Etudes; Maarten Tromp, Beheerder Centrale Archiefbewaarplaats Archief & Registratie, University of Utrecht; Mr Jolzmaar, archivist, Haarlem; Dr Henk Buijks, Streekarchief, Archief Brabant-Noordoost Archives's-Hertogenbosch; Sjoujke Atema, Haags Gemeentearchie, Den Haag; Anneke Landheer-Roelants, author of book about 'Van Stolkpark'; Agnes Dunselman, Genealogical Correspondent Archives, Haarlem; Netherlands Institute for War Documentation; Suvalki Lomsa Association; The Rottedagblad; Lea Zeppenfield, The Wiener Library; The Warburg Institute; Central Bureau of Geneology, The Netherlands; Henrie Wolf, President of the Jewish Community, Oss-Veghel; Jelka Kroger, Jewish Historical Museum; Rotterdam Municipal Archives; Amsterdam Municipal Archives; Oxana Korol, Yad Vashem; Doreen J G Arnoldus MA; Karen Franklin, Leo Beck Institute; Dr E van Donzel; Dr Harfkamp, Head of Dutch collection at the British Library; Rabbi Martin Van den Bergh; The University of Freiburg; Leo van Vliet, Leiden University; Winfried Schultze, Head of Archives, Humbolt University, Berlin; Dr Karl Lueger, University of Vienna; University of Utrecht; The Jewish Museum, Berlin; Bella Kirshner, Information Services, Yad Vashem; University of Heidelberg; London University; Freiburg City Hall Archives; Heidelberg City Archives; Berlin City Archives; Munich City Archives; Christine Burns, The Edinburgh Synagogue; Newington (Edinburgh) Register Office; Brill Academic Publishers.

PETA VAN DEN BERGH-STEEL, *November 2009*

Picture credits

CHAPTER 1

akg-images: *xii, 10.* Ancient Art & Architecture Collection: *7, 12 (bottom).* The Bridgeman Art Library: (Private Collection/Photo © Lefevre Fine Art) *3 (bottom),* (Musee de la Dynastie, Brussels/Patrick Lorette/Giraudon) *6,* (Israel Museum, Jerusalem/The Stieglitz Collection/ donated with contribution from Erica & Ludwig Jesselson) *11,* (Museo Correr, Venice/Giraudon) *14.* La Collection FRAB/Patrimonie des Biblioteques d'Aquitain: *8.* Mary Evans Picture Library: *12* (top), *13.* Nick Pearson: *2, 3 (top), 15.* Sam van den Bergh's book on his parents: *4 (top and bottom), 9 (top, bottom and top right).*

CHAPTER 2

akg-images: *28.* Peta Van den Bergh-Steel: *21.* The Bridgeman Art Library: (Private Collection/ ©Bonhams, London) *16.* Collection Museum Jan Cunen, Oss: *27 (top),* (Photography Peter Cox, Eindhoven): *27 (bottom).* Mary Evans Picture Library: *22.* Oss Council: *17, 19.* Sam van den Bergh's book on his parents: *24, 29.*

CHAPTER 3

akg-images: *43, 44, 45.* American Library of Congress: *34.* The Bridgeman Art Library: (Bibliotheque-Musee Forney, Paris/Archives Charmet) *42.* Haarlem City Council: *40 (top and bottom).* Mary Evans Picture Library: *39.* Rotterdam City Council: *35.* Sam van den Bergh's book on his parents: *30, 32, 33, 36, 41.*

CHAPTER 4

akg-images: *51 (bottom), 52, 58, 59, 61, 62.* Ancient Art & Architecture Collection: *63.* LP Pics: *54.* Mary Evans Picture Library: *57.* Sainsbury's Archives *51.* Sam van den Bergh's book on his parents: *46, 47, 48, 50.* tillwe/Till Westermayer/Creative Commons/www.flickr.com /photos/tillwe: *55.* Werner Forman Archive: *60.*

CHAPTER 5

akg-images: *75, 77 (top)*. The Bridgeman Art Library: (Private Collection/Photo © Bonhams, London) *69 (top)*, (Bibliotheque des Arts Decoratifs, Paris/Archives Charmet) *74*. David Sainsbury: *66, 72*. Carlos Glikson: *67, 69, 70 (top and bottom), 71*. Mary Evans Picture Library: *76*. Nick Pearson: *67 (top)*. Private Collection: *68, 79*. ROTI Archive: *77 (bottom)*. Suwalki Council: *78*. Tamara Ferguson: *64*.

CHAPTER 6

akg-images: *80, 86, 89, 90*. Carlos Glikson: *83*. Den Haag City Council: *85, 92*. kate_d/ www.flickr.com-photos-kate_d: *96*. Lady Lisa Sainsbury *84, 93 (top and bottom), 95*. Mary Evans Picture Library: *91, 97*. Sparkpics: *98*. Reproduced with the kind permission of Unilever: *87, 99, 100, 101 (top), 101 (bottom), 102, 103 (top), 103 (bottom)*.

CHAPTER 7

akg-images: *117, 121*. Bep Sturm Van den Bergh: *110, 123*. Bep Sturm Van den Bergh/Peta Van den Bergh-Steel: *109*. The Bridgeman Art Library: (Kunsthistorisches Museum, Vienna) *125*, (Museo Real Academia de Medicina, Madrid/Index) *127*. Carlos Glikson: *108*. Eyre & Spottiswode Ltd: *118*. Lady Lisa Sainsbury: *113, 114*. LP Pics: *104, 122, 124*. Maureen Simpson: *112, 114*. ROTI Archive: *116, 119, 126*. Tamara Ferguson: *107*.

CHAPTER 8

akg-images: *138*, akg-images/© Succession Picasso/DACS 2009: *130*. Carlos Glikson: *134, 137*. Imperial War Museum: *140, 143 (top)*. LP Pics: *128, 133,145, 151*. Mary Evans Picture Library: *131*. Netherlands War Museum: *143 (bottom)*. Nick Pearson: *147*. van den Bergh: *132*. Sidney Van den Bergh: *140, 141*. Sainsbury's Archives: *150*. Tamara Ferguson: *149*. Reproduced with the kind permission of Unilever: *139*.

CHAPTER 9

akg-images: *154*. Ancient Art & Architecture Collection: *172*. Annette Hollander: *157, 165 (bottom)*. Bep Sturm Van den Bergh: *156 (top)*. Carlos Glikson: *156 (bottom), 159, 165 (top right)*. Celia Blakey: *167, 168*. Lady Lisa Sainsbury: *160*. LP Pics: *161*. Ludmilla Hanisch, Hanne Schönig: *162*. Martin Gorman: *158*. Maureen Van den Bergh: *170*. Miriam Hodges: *162 (top)*. ROTI Archive: *171*. Sidney Van den Bergh: *165 (top left)*. Tony George/Creative Commons/www.flickr .com/people/drtonygeorge/: *164* (top). Wexford Festival Opera/Patrick Redmond Photographer: *163* (bottom). 松林L/Creative Commons/www.flickr.com/people/axio: *163*.

APPENDICES: FAMILY HISTORY

Peta Van den Bergh-Steel: *175, 176, 177*. Nick Pearson: *178*.

Every effort has been made to contact copyright holders for all material used in this publication. The publishers apologise for any accidental omissions and will be pleased to incorporate missing acknowledgements in future editions.

Bibliography

. . . And The Policeman Smiled: Barry Turner, Bloomsbury, 1991

Anne Frank in The World: Anne Frank Stitching (Foundation), 1985

Ashes in The Wind, The Destruction of Dutch Jewry: Dr J Presser, Souvenir Press, 1968

Atlas of the Jewish World: Nicholas de Lange, Facts on File, 1995

The Best Butter in the World, A History of Sainsbury's: Bridget Williams, Ebury Press, 1994

Birds Eye, The Early Years: W J Reader. Birds Eye Foods Ltd, Walton-on-Thames, 1963

Blind Eye to Murder: Tom Bower, Warner Books, 1995

Berlin, A Modern History: David Clay Large, Allen Lane, London, 2001

Berlin Metropolis, Jews and The New Culture 1890–1918: Emily D Bilski, University of California Press, 2000

The Bohemians: Dan Franck, Phoenix, 2001

Chronicle of 20th Century History: editor John S Bowman, Bison Books, 1989

Chronicle of the World: Longmans

The Coming of The Third Reich: Richard J Evans, Allen Lane, 2003

Coming Clean: Andrew M Knox, Heinemann (Unilever), 1976

Countdown to Victory: Barry Turner, Hodder and Stoughton, 2004

Countdown to War: Geoffrey Cox, William Kimber, 1988

De Noord Nederlandse Natie: Dr G J Renier, N V A Oosthoek's Uitgevers MIJ, Utrecht, 1948

The Dutch Under German Occupation: Werner Warmbrunn, Stanford University Press, 1963

The Enemy at His Pleasure: S Ansky, Metropolitan Books, New York, 2002

Family, Family Firm and Strategy - six Dutch family firms in the food industry 1880-1970: Doreen Arnoldus, Askant, Amsterdam, 2002

Faust's Metropolis, A History of Berlin: Alexandra Richie, Harper Collins, 1998

A Field of Buttercups: Joseph Hyams, Frederick Muller, 1969.

The First Industrial Nation: Peter Mathias, Methuan and Co, 1969

The First World War: Hew Strachan, Simon and Schuster, 2003

The Fontana History of Germany 1780-1918: David Blackbourn, Fontana, 1997

Food in History: Reay Tannahill, Penguin, 1988

From a Ruined Garden: The Memorial Books of Polish Jewry: Jack Kugelmass & Jonathan Boyarin, Schocken Books, 1983

Grand Tours and Cook's Tours: Lynne Withey, Aurum, 1998

Hitler's War Aims: Norman Rich, Andre Deutsch, 1973

A History of Food: Margaret Leeming, BBC Books, 1991

History of the First World War: Liddell Hart, Papermac, London, 1997

History of the Second World War: Liddell Hart, Papermac, London, 1997

The History of Unilever; three volumes: Professor Charles Wilson, Cassell, 1970

Holland at War Against Hitler – Anglo-Dutch Relations 1940-1945: edited by

M R D Foot, Frank Cass, 1990

Holocaust: A History: Deborah Dwork & Robert Jan van Pelt, John Murray, 2002

Holocaust Journey: Martin Gilbert, Columbia, 1997

Honderd Jaar Nassaukade: de geschiedenis van Van den Bergh en Jurgens, 1991

In The Name of the Volk, Political Justice in Hitler's Germany: H W Koch, I B Tauris Publishers, New York, 1997

The Jewish Community in Poland: Isaac Lewin, New York, 1985

Jewish History Atlas: Martin Gilbert, Weidenfeld and Nicolson, 1992

The Jews in Polish Culture: Aleksander Hertz, Northwestern University Press, 1988

The Jews in Poland: ed Chimen Abramsky, Maciej Jachimczyk, Antony Polonsky, Blackwell, 1988.

The Jews of Poland: A Social and Economic History of the Jewish Community in Poland from 1100 to 1800: Bernard D Weinryb, Philadelphia, 1973

The Judgement of Nuremberg 1946: Her Majesty's Stationery Office, 1999

Konin, A Quest: Theo Richmond, Jonathan Cape, 1995

Kroonprins van Mandelstein: S van den Bergh, Loeb & Van der Velden, 1979

Life in the Third Reich: edited Richard Bessel, Oxford, 1987

Lord Leverhulme's Unknown Venture: Myles Wright, Hutchinson Benham, 1982

Margarine, An economic, social and scientific history, 1869-1969: edited by J H van Stuyvenberg, Liverpool University Press, 1969

The Memorbook: The History of Jews in The Netherlands, 1960

The Modern Netherlands: Frank E Huggett, Praeger, 1971

A Moveable Feast: Ernest Hemingway

Nazi Germany: Klaus P Fischer, Constable, London, 1995

Nazi Germany and The Jews, the Years of Persecution 1933-39: Sam Friedländer, Phoenix, 1997

The Netherlands: Peter King and Michael Wintle, World Bibliographical Series, 1998

The Netherlands and Nazi Germany: Louis de Jong, Harvard University Press, 1990

Never Again: A History of the Holocaust: Martin Gilbert, Harper Collins Illustrated, 2000

Nineteenth Century European Civilization 1815-1914: Oxford University Press, 1958

One Step Ahead A Jewish Fugitive in Hitler's Europe: Alfred Feldman, Southern Illinois University Press, 2001

The Oxford Companion to World War II: Oxford University Press, 2005

The Origins of the Final Solution: Christopher R Browning, Heinemann, London, 2004

Patriots and Liberators, Revolution in the Netherlands: Simon Scharma, Fontana Press 1992.

People's Witness: Fred Inglis, Yale University Press, 2002

The Polish Way: A Thousand Year History of the Poles and Their Culture: Adam Zamoyski, Frankin Watts, 1988

Porträts vertriebener Orientalisten und Orientalistinnen 1933-1945: eine Hommage anläßlich des XXVIII. Deutschen Orientalistentags Bamber 26-30.März 2001: Ludmilla Hanisch/Hanne Schönig, Orient-wissenschaftliches Zentrum der Martin Luther Universität Halle-Wittenburg

The Proud Tower, A portrait of the world before 1890-1914: Barbara Tuchman, Macmillan Press, 1983

Rotterdam, The Gateway to Europe: edited by J Shraver, A D Donker, Rotterdam, 1948

Shtell: The History of a Small Town and an Extinguished World: Eva Hoffman, Vintage Books, 1999

Some Liked it Hot, the British on Holiday at Home and Abroad: Miriam Akhtar/Steve Humphries, Virgin, 2000

The Story of Port Sunlight: published by Lever Bros, 1953

Strange Victory, Hitler's Conquest of France: Ernest R May, Hill and Wang, 2000

Total War: Peter Calvocoressi & Guy Wint, Pelican Books, 1974

Trading With The Enemy: Charles Higham, Robert Hale, 1983

Twice in a Lifetime, from soap to skyscrapers: Charles Luckman, Norton, 1988

The Wandering Jews: Joseph Roth, W W Norton & Company, 2001

The Weimar Republic: Torsten Palmer & Hendrik Neubauer, Konemann, 2000

What I Saw: Joseph Roth, Grant Books, 2003

Index